VALLEY
EGYPT

Kristin Hetzer

This is a provocative story of financial elder abuse and the demise of a sixty-year family farm.

Printed in the United States of America

ISBN:
Softcover: 978-1-969367-00-7
Hardback: 978-1-969367-01-4
eBook: 978-1-969367-05-2

For permission requests, visit and write to the publisher at:

Kristin Hetzer Publishing
655 Deep Valley Drive Suite 260 Rolling Hills Estates, CA 90274
kristinhetzer-valleyegypt.com

CONTENTS

PREFACE

Valley Egypt is a case study that affords readers the opportunity to better understand the serious consequences of financial elder abuse and provides readers with an increased awareness of how to mitigate this escalating problem. Using a personal family story as a vehicle for learning, the author presents readers with a preparatory tool kit, which includes educational components concerning trusts, estate planning process, petitions, mediation, mental capacity, and fiduciary duty while presenting a legal case, calling attention to the mental capacity of an aged parent, undue influence by children, and breach of fiduciary duty by the trustees.

Illustrative of how unethical business practices may impact untold generations to follow, this case study also highlights how financial elder abuse, perpetrated by a family member, was aided by a lawyer employed by a prestigious law firm within the state. The law firm appeared to sanction past actions by its vigorous defense of legal documents changed over the last years of the elderly parent's life (see "Petitions and Mediation" and "Solidarity").

If you are a parent or a child of an aging parent, an investment advisor, or legal estate professional, you will find this narrative to be an important resource. Explanations of various pitfalls of the legal system are given to help understand the workings of a system where an estate and/or heirs may suffer financial harm. As an extreme example, *Valley Egypt* provides you with valuable information, from what to be aware of to how to prevent fraud and financial elder abuse of those you care about.

For those in college and university courses in business and finance, *Valley Egypt* will help you better understand why you should be interested in this increasingly important topic. Financial industry experts will find this book a valuable resource for professional educational compliance requirements and for its eye-opening case study on fiduciary duty, undue influence, and financial elder abuse. As a caveat, this book may also upset those in the legal profession confronted with plain outright corruption and wrongdoing by professionals who take advantage of a mentally incompetent client. It is imperative that the ethical standards of legal professionals are held accountable for their wrongdoing against any aging individual.

Presented in two parts, the intent of this book is for it to be used as supplementary reading by legal students and financial professionals. Wrongful actions of legal and financial professionals can inflict tremendous amounts of emotional turmoil and pain on elderly persons during the last years of their life. The goal of this author is to better educate industry professionals and protect the elderly from those who prey on what are considered to be protected assets.

Part 1 presents the story of the family farm and its demise after sixty years following the death of both parents. Readers may not be able to relate to the extreme, complicated, and layered dealings of the family members and their story; however, there is something for each person in this work. Each reader will come away with a deeply thought-provoking endeavor that will improve understanding of the growing financial elder abuse problem. Part 2 serves as a family financial planning resource through illustrative examples of how the destructive and tragic events of financial elder abuse can be prevented.

Background: Financial Elder Abuse

The increased aging of our population, social changes, and technological advances are leading to a dramatic increase in the opportunity for financial elder abuse. Approximately ten thousand individuals are retiring daily with the number of Americans aged sixty-five and older expected to more than double, from roughly forty million today to ninety million by 2050.[1] The surge in our aging population has important consequences for family, caregivers, and financial and legal professionals for their care and advice. The perpetrators of financial elder abuse are typically not strangers, and most are people who have gained the trust of the older individual, including service professionals and family members.[2]

In most situations, family members nobly assume a caregiving role; but in others, family members take advantage of the elders' dependencies and become perpetrators of financial abuse. Approximately 60 percent of substantiated Adult Protective Services cases of financial abuse involve an adult child.[3]

Family perpetrators often misuse their powers of attorney to steal money from bank accounts, obtain credit cards to make unauthorized purchases, and to make coercive changes in the elder's legal documents[4] (see "Amendments," "The Investigation," "Betrayal," and "Petitions and Mediation").

It is unknown what factors contribute to the likelihood of family members financially exploiting their elderly relatives. However, scholars and practitioners speculate that family members who exploit their elders are dependent upon them for their own survival. And their actions may be influenced by problems with alcohol, drug abuse, and gambling; and they may themselves suffer from psychological and behavior disorders. Additionally, tensions and inequalities between the elder and family member, perhaps stemming from the relative's dependence and mental

---

1   US Department of Health and Human Services, Administration for Community Living. *Administration on Aging: Aging Statistic.*

2   MetLife Mature Market Institute, National Committee for the Prevention of Elder Abuse, and Virginia Polytechnic Institute and State University, Center for Gerontology. *Broken Trust: Elders, Family, and Finances.* March 2009.

3   The National Center on Elder Abuse. *The National Elder Abuse Incidence Study* (1998). Retrieved on August 4, 2008, from http://www.aoa.gov/eldfam/Elder Rights/Elder Abuse/ Abuse Report Full.pdf. See note 2 above.

4   Sklar, J. B., "Elder and Dependent Adult Fraud: A Sampler of Actual Cases to Profile the Offenders and the Crimes They Perpetrate," *Journal of Elder Abuse and Neglect* 12, no. 2 (2000): 19–32. See note 2 above.

health issues, enhance the likelihood of financial abuse. Some family members also feel a sense of entitlement and believe that they have a right to the money and material goods their parents have accumulated.

They often start with small crimes, such as stealing blank checks before moving on to coercing elders to sign over the deeds to their homes, changing their wills, or liquidating their assets. They feel justified in taking "advance" control over assets that they perceive to be "almost" or "rightfully" theirs. Relatives may believe they are entitled to "reimbursement" for providing care for the elder and/or may even take preemptive steps to secure assets to prevent their presumed inheritance from being exhausted to pay for the elder's care and medical bills[5] (see "The Investigation"). One trait perpetrators of financial elder abuse have in common is that they exhibit excellent persuasion skills. They are very good at cultivating relationships and convincing older adults that they are worthy of their trust and money. In general, perpetrators are not bound by conventional norms or business ethics and rationalize their criminal and abusive behavior (see "Polo Chuck"). Individuals involved in exploiting older adults may use "undue influence"—the substitution of one person's will for the true desires of another. In these cases, the perpetrator uses his or her role and power to exploit the trust, dependency, or fear to gain psychological control over the older adult's decision-making, usually for financial gain. Financial abuse can range from misuse of funds to embezzlement. Examples include forging signatures and cashing checks without authorization. Some signs of potential financial elder abuse are drastic shifts in investment style and abrupt changes in wills, trusts, and beneficiaries[6] (see "Amendments," "The Investigation," "Betrayal," and "Exponential").

The Senior Safe Act, signed into US law in May 2018, empowers financial institutions to report suspected fraud to law enforcement without fear of being sued. This important new law calls attention to

---

5 Dessin, C. L., "Financial Abuse of the Elderly," *Idaho Law Review* 36, no. 2 (2000): 203–226. See note 2 above.

6 Quinn, M. J., "Undoing Undue Influence," *Journal of Elder Abuse and Neglect* 12, no. 2 (2000): 9–17. See note 2 above.

the growing problem of financial elder abuse. Members of the older population are targeted not only because they have accumulated eighteen trillion dollars in assets (67 percent of all US bank deposits), according to American Association of Retired Persons (AARP) but also as they are more likely to suffer from problems with memory and judgment, making them vulnerable to fraud. Many of the losses have gone unreported. "Elder abuse is an often-hidden phenomenon that affects seniors, and financial exploitation is the most prevalent form of elder abuse" (Joyce Rogers, AARP senior vice president of government affairs)[7] (see "Petitions and Mediation").

The phrase "financial elder abuse" often means taking advantage of a wealthy elderly person. The process of aging may result in a decline in mental and physical abilities, and this loss of mental agility creates an opportunity for wealthy individuals to be victims of financial abuse. When family members are involved, it can be difficult to immediately recognize. A few examples of cognitive decline may be memory loss, disorientation, difficulty performing simple tasks, poor judgment, and drastic mood swings.[8]

Diminished capacity is a mental or cognitive condition that affects a person's ability to understand his own acts or decisions. One of the most common forms of diminished capacity in aging adults is dementia, now commonly referred to as a major neurocognitive disorder. Dementia describes a set of symptoms that may include memory loss and difficulties with thinking, problem solving, or language. A person afflicted with dementia often experiences memory loss, confusion, and emotional disturbances. Often, brain damage caused by strokes or illnesses, such as Alzheimer's disease, cause dementia (see "Polo Chuck"). Ninety percent of elder abusers are family members; less than 5 percent of cases get reported to any agency[9] (see "Petitions and Mediation").

Elder abuse is an intentional act or failure to act by a person in a

---

7   American Association of Retired Persons. May 24, 2016.
8   *Webster's Dictionary*. Summarized from definitions of "cognitive decline."
9   National Adult Protective Services Resource Center. *Elder Abuse Is Common, Lethal, and Expensive.*

position of trust, who creates a risk of harm to an aging adult. From a financial perspective, exploitation occurs when there is unauthorized, illegal, or improper use of an aging adult's resources by a person in a position of trust. Unfortunately, as aging adults' cognitive functions start to decline, there exists a greater likelihood they may be taken advantage of more easily. Common signs of elder abuse and exploitation include physical or emotional abuse and neglect. Typically, coupled with this, the aging adult changes his regular habits, and the aging adult becomes isolated from family or professional advisors. The aging adult exhibits erratic behaviors, such as unexplained change in professional advisors and unexplained asset transfers and atypical cash withdrawals[10] (see "Amendments," "Polo Chuck," "Betrayal," and "Exponential").

A significant reason for the underestimation of the occurrence of financial elder abuse is that the victims themselves do not report financial elder abuse for a number of reasons which may include fear of being placed in an unknown facility, fear that no one will really help them even if the abuse is exposed, and worry that the perpetrator might harm them even more. A few notable behaviors exhibited by family members engaged in elder abuse frequently are as follows: exerting influence over the older person's decisions, demonstrating excessive control of the older person, controlling phone use and preventing others from accessing the older person, and having reluctance to leave the side of the older person during appointments[11] (see "Petitions and Mediation" and "Solidarity").

Financial elder abuse is often an unspoken part of family life planning before death. Additionally, this is a story that examines complicated family relationships between a parent and children as well as sibling rivalry, which often explains the physical care of the parent during their aging years. My professional goal is for you, the reader, to learn and prepare your financial estate with knowledge and insight that will honor your legacy and protect your loved ones.

---

10   Alzheimer's Society. *What Is Dementia?* 2016.

11   Deem, D. L., "Notes from the Field: Observations in Working with Forgotten Victims of Personal Financial Crimes," *Journal of Elder Abuse and Neglect* 12, no. 23 (2000): 33-48.
See notes 2 and 10 above.

CAST OF CHARACTERS AND OTHERS

Bertrand — father

Gloriette — mother

Kate — protagonist and second born, successor trustee, and twenty-three-year financial advisor to Bertrand and Gloriette

Chuck — firstborn son, eldest brother, trustee, and antagonist

Ann — third child and antagonist

Cybil — fourth child

Bert or Bertrand II — fifth child, second son, hobby farmer, musician, and wood craftsman

Phillip — sixth child, youngest son, and farm operation partner

Valley Egypt — a country road

Cheetham, Steele and Morse LLP — law firm used by Chuck during the last ten years of Bertrand's life

Ken Powler — twenty-five-year family estate attorney of Bertrand and Gloriette who carefully advised estate documents following Gloriette's passing and who helped Bertrand and Gloriette

	develop their estate plan when they were healthy and of sound mind
Gordon	Kate's husband, twelve-year financial advisor, and stockbroker for Bertrand and Gloriette's trust accounts
Mr. Morse	attorney for Cheetham, Steele and Morse LLP and criminal defense attorney for Chuck who took over the case from Chuck's estate attorney, Mabel Snatt
Finn Nash	Chuck's attorney who changed legal trust documents and replaced Ken Powler, the twenty-five-year estate attorney of Bertrand and Gloriette
12200 Valley Egypt	the house owned by Gloriette's trust
12100 Valley Egypt	the historical stone house and original farm
Mildred	Chuck's wife of forty-plus years and business partner
Cain County	the county where the farm is located
Joseph Stone	principal of Wright, Coolidge and Stone PC and senior partner who was hired by Kate to represent Gloriette's trust
Jack Napp	attorney from Wright, Coolidge and Stone PC specializing in trust fraud cases who was hired by Kate
Richard Charles Sr.	Bertrand's grandfather
Richard Charles II	Bertrand's father and Chuck's grandfather
Aunt Irma	ninety-eight-year-old aunt who was the first sister of Bertrand
Aunt Faye	sister of Gloriette

Lloyd's Bank	Bertrand's checking account with Chuck listed as joint account holder
Dan Canfield	Kate's cousin, minister, favorite nephew, and confidante of Bertrand
Leonard	Ann's husband and antagonist
Gwen or Gwendolyn	Bertrand's female friend after Gloriette's death
Aunt Etta	Bertrand's second sister
Nurse Foe	Bertrand's friend and practicing nurse
Fred Schafte	Chuck's bond broker and social friend during the last ten years of Bertrand's life
Mabel Snatt	Chuck's estate attorney who replaced Chuck's attorney, Finn Nash, after Finn Nash recused himself
Jacob Broader	mediator for mediation 1 and 2
Aunt Janelle	Gloriette's youngest sister
Lydia	Kate's cousin, Bertrand's favorite niece, and sister of Dan Canfield
Dr. and Mrs. Wilders	neighbors to the family farm
Clyde Pettis	Chuck's neighbor and foe
Eudora	the town where the family farm is located
Dick Crumbly	Bertrand's accountant for thirty-plus years
Brenda, Flo, and Bart	Chuck and Mildred's children
Sunny Smart	Kate's friend and confidante

INTRODUCTION

Valley Egypt is a poignant story about elder abuse and the demise of a sixty-year family farm, written from the personal perspective of Kate, the author, the daughter of the abused elderly parent, and a respected professional with over thirty-five years of experience in the financial services industry.

Named successor trustee of her parents' trusts twenty-four years prior, Kate, who is one of six children, realizes upon her father's death in 2016 that she must unravel the complicated financial history of her parents' trusts. After her father's death, Kate becomes aware of the extreme manipulation of the family estate undertaken on the directive of her older brother and younger sister. The estate plan, carefully established by Kate's parents, had been altered before her father's death through her brother's lawyer. The estate manipulations encompassed years of questionable and numerous withdrawals by her brother and father from the mother's irrevocable and father's trusts. These manipulations resulted in the decline in the father's financial assets, which foremost affected the quality of care he received during his final years and subsequently impacted the final allocation of a rightful inheritance equally to all six siblings (see "The Investigation," "Polo Chuck," and "Solidarity").

Unfortunately, variations of this family story are far too common, and they are becoming increasingly more common as the generation of baby boomers ages. In this particular case study, financial elder abuse was perpetrated by two siblings who took physical and financial control of their aging father and his monetary assets. The two younger brothers and Kate assumed their two siblings, responsible for their father's care, had honorable intentions and would act in the father's and family's best interest. As the story unfolds, the reader may determine the sibling team operated primarily for their own financial benefit and that healthcare directives for their aging shut-in father became an ancillary concern (see "Petitions and Mediation" and "Que Será, Será"). Further into the author's investigation revealed deliberate and devious actions of the two caregiving siblings that contributed to the mysterious demise of Kate's relationship with her father and their increased ability to manipulate the family estate.

PART 1

THE STORY

VALLEY EGYPT

The stone house, barn, and eighty acres of land were purchased in the summer of 1958 by Bertrand and Gloriette when Kate was three years old. Before their family moved to the country, they lived on Prince Street in Indian Falls, Minnesota. Their city home had been across the street from an expansive park complete with swimming pools and tennis courts. Kate's memories included watching her parents practice volleys on the local tennis courts and the large public swimming pool full of noisy children playing together. Once the family moved to the country, her days were consumed caring for farm animals, exploring the local woods, and walking through their pastureland. Their family easily transitioned from city dwellers to countryfolk. The gravel road where the newly purchased farm was located was named Valley Egypt; the name described the location perfectly—out in the boondocks.

Bertrand and Gloriette were a young couple with three children: Chuck, Kate, and Ann. Chuck was the first son; Kate followed, and Ann was very young when the family moved from the city to the country. Bertrand worked as medical doctor, completing his residency at the prestigious Catholic hospital in Indian Falls and advancing toward the medical specialty designation of general surgeon. Gloriette remained a homemaker and was delighted to move to the country farm located over twenty miles from the city of Indian Falls.

The picturesque fieldstone house was built during the early twenties. It had a large basement, one bedroom on the first floor next to the kitchen, and a dining and living room. The original farmhouse had no indoor bathroom, and approximately one hundred feet west of the house sat an outhouse. A large black cast-iron woodburning stove took up approximately one-half of the kitchen area, heated the house, and was used for cooking. The floors were solid maple hardwood. Craftsman-style glass-paneled cabinets lined the walls in both the dining and living room. Before moving into their country farmhouse, a bathroom was constructed on the main floor, and the large kitchen stove was removed with central heating installed. This stone house had replaced an old farmhouse that the previous owners occupied during the latter 1880s until the stone house was constructed. Bertrand and Gloriette purchased their new home furnished with antique pieces from the 1800s which had been acquired by the previous homeowner over the decades they owned the property.

A large red barn was located south of the house, and both structures could be seen at the valley of the large hill south of Crest Street Road. At one time, the property was used as a ski resort. A ski tower was built at the top of the hill west of the barn. An old car at the bottom of the hill was used to generate energy for a cable rope tow which stretched to the top of the ski hill. The original builders of the stone farmhouse welcomed family and locals to use of their small ski resort; however, the size of the hill and timing of the venture resulted in an unprofitable operation, and the ski resort was eventually abandoned.

Just before Bertrand and Gloriette moved into their newly renovated home, the cable rope was stolen along with most of the antique furniture that had been purchased with the house. They were originally from a rural farm area in Iowa, prior to moving to the city of Indian Falls, and were unaccustomed to locking their doors. Robberies and criminal activity were rare occurrences even in this area during the fifties. They later learned that a local antique dealer from Indian Falls looted their valuable antiques from their newly purchased farmhouse. Eventually, they discovered the thief's identity; however, they did not ever confront or accuse him. They lamented the lost antiques over the following years. Kate once asked why they never filed a report, and their reply was that the effort would be futile because it was impossible to recover their stolen property. Their response to this incident should give insight into their personalities of being passive complainers.

Three more children were born after Bertrand and Gloriette moved to the country farm: Cybil, Bert, and Phillip. Cybil was two years younger than Ann; Bert followed a year later, and Phillip was the youngest, twelve years younger than Chuck.

The original stone house was built without a garage. During the mid-to-late 1880s, horse and carriage was the primary method of transportation, and widespread ownership of family automobiles was uncommon prior to the twenties. The stone house was eventually expanded by Bertrand and Gloriette to include a two-car garage, with a family room built above the garage during the early sixties, just before the birth of Phillip.

All the children slept on the second floor of the stone house. Chuck and Kate occupied separate large bedrooms. Ann and Cybil shared a bedroom while Bert and Phillip shared the corner bedroom above the kitchen. A large open attic was used as a third floor. The basement was partitioned to accommodate a laundry area, furnace, and chest freezer. The freezer was used for storage of beef and pork, blueberries, garden vegetables, and two-gallon containers of local creameries' ice cream. Chuck and Bert kept spoons in the basement rafters for their shared frequent taste tests of butter pecan and heath candy bar ice cream. Adjacent to the laundry room were shelves which stored Gloriette's canned peaches, pears, plums, cherries, and tomatoes. During the sixties, a bathroom was added to the second floor where the four large bedrooms were located, and a basement bathroom was constructed during the seventies because of the increased foot traffic between the barn and house as the farm expanded its operation.

Not long after the family moved to the Valley Egypt farm, Kate's dad purchased his first calves. The back seat of the small family car was removed to haul the calves from the local cattle auction to their red barn. Thereafter, the car stunk of cow manure and could no longer be used for family transportation. Eventually, beef cattle became the primary product of their farm. Pigs, sheep, and rabbits were also raised at times to find another productive niche to financially support the farm venture. The final years of the family farm included a productive dairy operation which had replaced raising beef cattle when a local stripped dairy facility became available after a neighbor farmer's death. Bertrand, Gloriette, Chuck, and Phillip agreed to set up the dairy venture and outfitted the rented facility with milking equipment, bought dairy cows, and committed to milk twice a day, seven days a week. The dairy operation began during the eighties, over twenty years following the initial purchase of the farm.

Gloriette raised chickens over the thirty years the farm existed, providing fresh eggs and chicken. The chickens were butchered by Gloriette and Kate who fed and cared for the fowl during all the years Kate lived on the farm. Kate gathered eggs from the cackling hens and filled their water containers. Every day, she walked to the chicken coop to scatter chicken feed for the hens and chicks. She enjoyed watching the furry yellow chicks mature up to the point when they began to peck at her legs while eagerly anticipating their meal.

There was a stand of lilac trees between the stone house and barn. The pungent smell of fresh lilacs still reminds Kate of breaking off the bush branches and stuffing a pail full of deep purple fragrant flowers as a young girl. Kate cranked cold pump water over the flowers, making her own sweet-smelling lilac perfume as her gray-and-white farm cat, Mary Poppins, and a litter of kittens circled her while enjoying the afternoon sun. South of the red barn, a pond was dug and stocked with blue gills and sunfish by Kate's parents. Her parents had enjoyed fishing lakes and streams before they were married, periodically reminiscing over these pleasant memories to their children. Later, the amount of farmwork left little time for recreation; however, the family ice-skated on the pond during the winters and used chopped pond ice along with rock salt to make homemade ice cream for birthdays celebrated during the cold winter months.

Over the course of many years, the family raised three English shepherd dogs. The shepherd dogs were chosen for their herding abilities, for six children and the cattle roaming the hills. They were all named Shep: Shep I, Shep II, and Shep III. Shep II was nicknamed Skip. Skip was Kate's favorite dog and close companion during her adolescent years. Kate also took care of her farm cats. She strolled through the woods with the dogs; her fondest memories were hikes and playing games with her dogs and cats. The farm property was surrounded by trees, and sounds of leaves rustling in the wind was constant. The dry, crisp leaves crackled beneath Kate's feet during her walks on cold fall days. She enjoyed deep inhalations of the cold, fresh, and invigorating air.

Their herd of cattle roamed the rolling hills behind the house and barn. Deciduous and pine trees lined the acreage. Many summer Sunday afternoons, the entire family walked through the hills and enjoyed a picnic lunch among the pine trees Kate had planted with her parents not long after moving to Valley Egypt. Walking among the pines reminded her of Christmas season no matter the time of the year. A stand of black cherry trees grew along the top of the hill, and another stand of sour cherry tree lined the lower slope. Kate and her mother picked cherries for preserves, pie, and black cherry jam. There was a sassafras tree at the top of the hill. During Sunday afternoon walks, her father dug a root of the tree to make a favorite and memorable tea for Kate and her mother. The sassafras had a strong aroma, and the combination resulted in a taste of homemade root beer with citrus and clove. Kate noted the distinct fragrance and flavor which stimulated her taste and smell sensations. Black and red raspberry bushes were found at the end of the property not far from a sandy plot where Kate grew pumpkins, potatoes, watermelon, and cantaloupe. Warm Sunday afternoons were often spent walking through the woods picking raspberries and blackberries. Kate had a collection of sweet memories as a child growing up on the Valley Egypt family farm.

During Kate's childhood, the ski hill and ski tower was used for church toboggan parties and sledding outings. Since the ski rope tow had been stolen shortly after her parents' purchase of the property, it was a strenuous exercise to trudge up the hill with their sleds and toboggans. At the bottom of the hill was a creek, and ice-covered snow caused the children to slide into the cold creek when they could not stop the fast sleds and toboggans. Her family hosted winter hayrides, followed by Kate's mother's hot chocolate. Kate could still imagine her mother in the stone house, heating milk and Dutch chocolate in a big pot on the stove. It was often so hot that Kate had to be careful not to burn her tongue.

Gloriette was raised in a Christian home. She often spoke to Kate of her happy childhood and how she loved spending her time outdoors with her father, helping him with his daily farm chores. She was the oldest of identical triplets. She enjoyed farm life and sports, such as softball and basketball. Her childhood friends and family said she was a tomboy. Her sisters cheered for their high school basketball team while she was the star player. She had a beautiful contralto vocal range and sang harmony with her sisters, musically performing for relatives, church, and social functions. Her mother came from a large family of brothers and stepsisters. Gloriette spoke with love and fondness regarding her sisters, brother, mother, father, and many aunts and uncles. The biblical teachings she studied as a young girl and took to heart included instruction that a Christian wife was subservient to her husband. She was taught that the man was the head of the household and was meant to make the important decisions regarding the raising of children and major household decisions. Kate witnessed her mother receiving habitual criticism and harsh treatment from her father throughout her lifetime. Kate's mother had a passive and submissive personality compared to the dictatorial and tyrannical behavior of her husband and father of her children. Kate sensed her mother was bewildered and depressed at times by her father's behavior toward his family; however, she never heard her contradict his demands or harsh criticisms. Gloriette kept her emotional pain to herself.

Her father caused her mother much unhappiness during her life. Gloriette often said, "We had our good times." Bertrand openly flirted with other women in her presence. As a young girl, Kate inwardly cringed as she recalled the deep hurt in her mother's eyes when she witnessed his flirtatious behavior. Kate was often told by her younger brothers and other family friends that her father continued his bad behavior over the remaining decades of his marriage. Kate had an inner sadness that she had been unaware of the extent and duration of her mother's humiliation and had not been able to help soften her mother's emotional hurt.

Bertrand lacked affection for his small children. He often complained about their presence. He would say, "Children are not to be seen or heard." He repeatedly said, "I wish I did not have children." He was typically angry and unhappy and loudly complained at the dinner table. Kate believed he was rarely happy at home. One Sunday afternoon, when their family walked the hills of their farm, Bertrand began to rant about not wanting a family and said that he planned to move away from their family and farm. He angrily complained as they walked up the hill with Chuck, Kate, and her mother following him. He said directly to them, "I am sick and tired of living with you." Kate cried as they walked the pastureland around the ski jump, close to Kate's favorite sassafras tree. After some time, emotionally exhausted from his complaining, Kate and her mother walked down the hill, returning to the big red barn.

Coincidentally, an automobile full of Bertrand's cousins stopped at the barn as he walked down the hill, and they were standing on the barn driveway. The relatives' automobile was not operating properly, and they asked whether Bertrand could repair it. He immediately retrieved a can of gas from the farm gas tank and said to the driver, "Whatever you do, do not start the engine." He poured gas in the carburetor as they started the engine, ignoring his instructions. Immediately, he was engulfed in flames; his skin was on fire and burning. A horse blanket was retrieved from the barn and thrown on him. Kate witnessed the scene from a distance through her tear-stained eyes as her father rolled in the dirt, eventually putting out the burning fire. His right arm was badly burned, and he realized he needed emergency medical care. By this time, her father had received his specialty training as a general surgeon, and his medical practice consisted primarily of surgical operations which could only be done with his medical specialization. Before leaving for the hospital, her father said goodbye to her. As Kate looked directly at him, she believed God was sending him a message to be the Christian father and husband he was meant to be. She hoped the tragic and dramatic event would change her dad. After being admitted to the hospital, his medical doctors told her mother and his surgical partner that they were afraid he had extensive nerve damage and would not be able to operate as a general surgeon. It was a scary time for her mother because she was a homemaker and was not confident that she had work skills to financially support their family. Kate was afraid for her family's future because she sensed her mother's worries. After reflecting on this incident, Kate realized her father had an ongoing internal war within himself, a war of good versus evil. Kate never understood what was behind her father's torment.

After many years, the ski tower platform deteriorated to cement blocks. The children were grown and had moved away from the family home. The platform was eventually torn down and removed at Chuck's request. The old car at the base of the hill remained until it was a rusted pile of rubble. Kate left for college after the summer of 1974. Ann left one year later. Eventually, Cybil, Bert, and Phillip moved out of the farmhouse.

For a brief year and half, from 1972 to 1973, Chuck left the family home to attend an out-of-state college. However, Chuck decided to drop out of school after his first year and returned to the family farm.

Bertrand tried hard to create a livelihood for Chuck. In the years that followed Chuck's return, the farm expanded to one thousand five hundred acres and five hundred head of cattle. Bertrand expanded the farm to create an operation he believed would generate enough income for Chuck to raise his children and support a family. Bertrand borrowed money from the bank to buy farmland, purchase top-line farm equipment, and construct two Harvestore silos which stood next to the barn feedlot area. Harvestore was a brand name for feed storage silos that had gained popularity during the sixties and seventies. Shiny blue-sapphire-colored silos were constructed using steel and fiberglass materials promoted to farmers as a superior crop storage method. At that time, the Harvestore sales pitch was that the silo retained crop moisture, thereby offering enhanced nutritional value. Gloriette told Kate that the Harvestores were expensive and cost around one hundred thousand dollars. Kate did not know if the cost was for one or both; she was attending college, and at that time, the amount of money was incomprehensible and not meaningful to her. The appeal of Harvestore silos was diminished during the decades that followed because newer, more efficient, and less expensive methods of storing crops replaced Harvestores. In hindsight, this purchase was an expensive expenditure for a small-scale farming operation. Beef prices remained depressed, and it was difficult to support the farm operation as well as the increased debt that had been accumulated to pay for new equipment and facilities, such as the expensive steel silos. The prime interest rate increased from 7 percent to 21 percent during the early eighties, and financial ruin appeared imminent because of heavy debt obligations. This was a devastating time for farmers and business owners who existed on borrowed money to pay for land, equipment, and livestock.

During the years 1982 to 1985, Kate was starting her career as a registered representative, which was another name for stockbroker. She saw the devastation that rising interest rates had on fixed income account valuations and investment grade bonds that sold at a fraction of their face value. Kate remembered her father being anxious during this time and asking her about a savings account she had as a child and inquiring if she still had it. Her mom told her they could not continue spending their income on the farm as they had every year since Chuck ran the operation. Kate did not know the extent of the farm losses; however, she knew they were stressful times because of the conversations she had with her parents and their voiced concerns about paying their debt obligations. Her mother spoke to her about selling the land and all the farm equipment. Gloriette hoped to recoup some of the monies that had been spent on expensive equipment over many years. Bertrand and Gloriette discussed their plans to retire, adamantly expressing their plan to stop farming. During 1985, Bertrand and Gloriette told Chuck that the farm operation was done, it was not profitable, and they were no longer able to finance his farming venture. They said, "You must find a job. We are unable to continue to support your family and lifestyle." Her father announced his retirement during 1986 and stated again that he was done financing Chuck's farming venture.

Chuck had been in charge of the farm operation since he dropped out of college and returned to the family farm during the early seventies. Her parents were private people and did not discuss financial matters with others; however, as their eldest daughter, their financial advisor, and her mother's confidante, Kate knew more about their finances than anyone else in their family because they asked her questions and discussed their financial concerns.

Several years following her parents' retirement, much of the original eighty acres where the farm stood was sold to a local developer. Chuck took credit for his part in this sale, often bragging about his cleverness in finding the developer who built large houses on the back sixty acres of the family farm. At their kitchen table, Kate questioned the wisdom and necessity of the sale, questioning her parents about their reasoning behind the decision. In hindsight, it was a poor investment decision because the land had become valuable over the next two decades that followed the sale of the property. By the early nineties, the majority of their farmland was sold and the related debt completely paid off. The land was purchased along with the family stone house and had its tax base dated back to 1958. There was no reason to sell this particular parcel to a developer because the property tax expense was not a financial burden to them and an inconsequential expense against their fixed income.

The hills of the farm had been scenic with the herd of Black Angus cattle and Chuck's two paint horses. Once the back acreage was sold for development, the topography of the farm changed. The large hill used for winter tobogganing and sledding was bulldozed and leveled. The black and red cherry trees were removed. The ski hill was gone, having been replaced by a housing development built on a slightly inclined hill.

Following her father's funeral, Kate surveyed the family farmhouse and buildings from a distance. The farm appeared as if it has been neglected for years, as if an elderly person lived there, unable to properly care for the property. A polo pony nibbled at tufts of grass in the weedy overgrown pasture. The once-active farm now reflected years of neglect and decline. Rusting farm machinery deteriorated around dilapidated buildings. The shrubs Kate had carefully pruned during her years on the farm were old and scrappy, reflecting of the entire property under Chuck's care.

Valley Egypt Road was the road to their family home, Kate's childhood address, and her parents' address for six decades. Back when the farm was purchased during the year 1958, Valley Egypt was an unpaved gravel road. The road was considered a natural beauty road. In the name of progress, much of it had been paved. For most of the last century, Valley Egypt Road had been considered rural country. Neighbors consisted of other large country farms and cow pastures. Neighbors were separated by twenty acres to several hundred acres of land. The farms and farmland now have disappeared, replaced by fancy golf country clubs and expensive housing developments. Kate's parents' farm property had previously bordered Oak Hills High School. Oak Hills School District was now considered one of the best school districts in the state, in part leading to the drastic rise in property value.

THE AMENDMENTS

In an airplane, flying back to California, Kate opened the large legal package which had been handed to her after the funeral. She was stunned as she read the cover page written by Chuck's attorney who was representing their parents' estate. The law firm—Cheetham, Steele and Morse LLP—represented Chuck. The letter stated that Kate was excluded from representation. "Why?" she asked aloud.

Kate's dad had passed away two weeks before at the age of eighty-nine years. Chuck was her older brother, and they were born eighteen months apart in age. Chuck and Kate were designated successor trustees of their parents' trusts and estate when the documents were established over twenty-four years before. At that time, their parents were of sound mind and had recently retired from their careers.

Kate had three brothers and two sisters: Richard Charles III (who was called Chuck), Ann, Cybil, Bertrand Alan II (known as Bert), and Phillip, the youngest.

A successor trustee's legal responsibilities became relevant after the passing of the primary trustee. After her dad's death, Kate was designated to be the co-trustee of her mother's irrevocable trust. In May of 1992, her parents had asked Chuck and Kate to be the successor trustees for each of their trusts. Immediately following her father's death, Kate learned that she had been removed as successor co-trustee of his trust without her knowledge. This was stated in the legal paperwork she had received following the funeral. Her mother had passed away eighteen and a half years earlier. Upon her death, her mother's trust document became irrevocable. An irrevocable trust means the trust language and document cannot be changed. Consequentially, Kate remained successor co-trustee of her trust and believed that she should have been represented by the law firm representing her parents' estate. It was Kate's opinion that she should personally hire legal representation if she were to execute her responsibilities as trustee.

The large envelope from the law firm included a cover letter prepared by Chuck's attorney, Cheetham, Steele and Morse LLP. The letter was addressed to the six beneficiaries of the estate, the six children: Chuck, Kate, Ann, Cybil, Bert, and Phillip. The letter stated, "Your sister Kate is named as co-trustee of the Gloriette trust to serve with Chuck. We are not representing her in that capacity." Shocked, Kate asked aloud, "Why aren't you representing me? You are retained to represent our parents' estate." She did not understand why she would be excluded from representation.

The legal letter upset her. Her hands shook. She was surprised by the tone of the cover letter and continued to read in disbelief. There were several new amendments and additions to her dad's trust that she was not familiar with, and shockingly, the second amendment dealt with her removal as co-trustee of his trust.

Kate's heart began to beat louder and faster. She was familiar with the original second amendment. She and her dad had met with her parents' long-standing family estate attorney, Ken Powler, to draft the new amendment to his trust at the request of the brokerage firm where she was employed during 2002. It became obvious to her that whoever drafted this amendment was not aware of an existing second amendment established years before. She began to suspect foul play.

Accompanying the letter were copies of the original trust agreements and wills she had read years ago. There was a second codicil to her father's will which appointed Chuck to serve as their father's personal representative. The document was dated November 24, 2006, and gave Chuck authority to make all decisions regarding settlement of their parents' estate. If Chuck was unable to serve in that capacity, Ann was named to replace him. Ann was Kate's younger sister, born two years after her. Ann did not have a college degree, professional financial expertise, and self-admitted she was financially and legally illiterate. Kate questioned why Ann was chosen to replace her as successor trustee. This was especially inconceivable to Kate who had over thirty-three years of experience in the financial services industry and held numerous prestigious designations. She had been involved in the financial settling of estates during her three-decade career, yet she was removed as trustee of her parents' estate settlement process. She wondered why she hadn't been informed of this major change to her parents' estate plan at any time during the past ten years.

Kate thought back to November 24, 2006, and remembered the date and time as the first Thanksgiving in ten years that her dad did not spend with her family at their home in the California desert. She also realized this was a few months before her dad transferred the investment trust accounts away from Gordon, her husband, who was her dad's registered representative and stockbroker.

During 1983, with less than five thousand dollars, her parents had started a small investment account, establishing the account as one of her first clients. The investment account grew to a substantial amount during the nineties under Kate's close attention and advice. After her mother's death in June of 1997, her parents' joint account was divided into the two trust accounts. Kate was her parents registered representative and stockbroker from 1983 to 2005, and her husband Gordon was cobroker and registered representative from 1995 to 2007. During 2005, she became a money manager and founded her own investment management company, White Point Capital LLC. Gordon became her dad's sole registered representative and stockbroker for the next two years before the accounts were abruptly transferred away, ending a twenty-three-year professional relationship. The recommendations Gordon made to his father-in-law were from joint research efforts with Kate and continued the investment strategies which had been successful for past accounts. The portfolio held the highest quality blue chip securities, carefully researched by Gordon and Kate and had been accumulated using sophisticated option selling strategies. Gordon and his father-in-law had a positive and cordial relationship and communicated on a regular basis. Kate and Gordon had assumed the trusts were transferred to a reputable registered representative in Minnesota, competent to continue with the investment strategies successfully employed twenty-three years prior to continue a good legacy. Following her father's death, Kate and Gordon realized this was an incorrect assumption.

The newer amendment to the restated trust agreement was dated November 24, 2006, and was unfamiliar to Kate. Prominently, the document listed a fifty-thousand-dollar loan she had borrowed from her parents when she and her husband purchased a home in California in July of 1996. She had paid back the loan and put the money in a separate account for her dad's access. Furthermore, her loan was not from or related to his trust. The new amendment stated fifty thousand dollars was to be subtracted from her share of her father's trust assets upon his death.

Kate recalled Chuck and Ann often asked for loans from her dad's trust the years immediately following her mother's death. Kate also knew that in 2006 both Chuck and Ann had loans outstanding, each in excess of the amount listed in this amendment because their loans were documented on the trust statements which she had reviewed on a monthly basis. Kate was her father's registered representative and received copies of all statements and had documentation regarding Chuck's and Ann's personal loans.

Kate believed this amendment was orchestrated by Chuck and executed by Finn Nash the day before Thanksgiving 2006 because the date was listed on the documents. This fact hurt because to her the holiday was about being thankful and appreciative for all they had individually, as a family, and as a nation. She was taken aback that her dad would sign documents that were not factually based. She wondered if he considered this would hurt her emotionally. His action was especially malicious in nature to occur the day before a holiday celebrating family and gratitude. She wondered if it was deliberate.

Finn Nash, an Indian Falls attorney, replaced the long-standing family attorney, Ken Powler. On November 24, 2006, Bertrand was in Finn Nash's office one week following the birth of Bert's son, his grandson. Bert was his second son and fourth child. He lived two miles from his home. Kate's father had not taken the time to see his son and new grandson; however, he did make a trip to Chuck's attorney to establish new legal estate documents. Kate wondered what had provoked her dad's intense anger toward her to draw up legal documents specifically and maliciously against her, his eldest daughter. She felt her dad's actions were intentional, which felt like a slap from beyond the grave that hurt her heart.

Beginning with the winter of 1995, Kate and Gordon gave their desert home to her parents to use during the winter months. Prior to 1995, they seasonally rented the property to a regular winter snowbird. A snowbird is a person who migrates from the colder climates to spend their winter in a warmer locale. They were amenable to forgo the extra income in exchange for Kate's parents' comfort during the harsh Minnesota winters. Sadly, her mother passed away two years later. They were happy to lovingly continue to offer it to Kate's dad and considered it a generous arrangement for him from their family. He used their second home for six months, over the span of ten desert winters, terminating his use of the property after May 2006.

After her mother's death and during the legal process of Gloriette's estate, Ken Powler listed personal loans of the children that were outstanding and suggested to Bertrand that he forgive his children's loans. He forgave Chuck's and Ann's personal loans up to Gloriette's death. However, Kate's loan was not forgiven. She continued to pay her dad monthly interest which was deposited to his joint checking account with Chuck. Kate set up a separate account in 1998 to pay off the fifty-thousand-dollar loan she had borrowed from both parents during 1996. She told her dad that it was important that he have funds to cover unexpected medical expenses or to afford assisted care if he needed it. Gordon had given her instructions to set aside her dad's money in a separate account because there was a fear Chuck might confiscate the funds. By this time, Kate knew monies deposited to her dad's checking account were already being used for Chuck's ventures. Monies from her dad's checking account were used to renovate Chuck's house, construct a new barn roof, and expand and improve the pond—three major expenditures. Her dad told her two motorcycles were purchased by Chuck using his trust funds. Gordon and Kate did not want to deposit their savings to an account that Chuck could easily access and withdraw the funds. Furthermore, her dad agreed that if the account was not used by him during his lifetime, the account would return to Gordon and Kate to defray some of the maintenance and property expenses associated with giving him the use of their second home for the winters he lived there. Therefore, he signed the "joint account with right of survivorship" brokerage paperwork and stated to Kate that he thought it was a fair agreement. Their agreement was in effect from the time the separate account was established in 1998, and he was living at their desert home six months out of each year. The agreement and account existed eighteen years until his death in January 2016.

The account, established at Prudential Bache and Company, was in 2001 transferred to Paine Webber and Company and then eventually in 2005 transferred to Charles Schwab Corporation, when Kate started her investment advisory company. Bertrand had signed three sets of brokerage documents over the span of eight years regarding the fifty-thousand-dollar account established and funded by Kate. Kate submitted proof of the deposits and funding of the account as well as three sets of brokerage account transfers and the value of his separate account as of his date of death to Chuck and his attorney, Mr. Morse, in June 2016. Mr. Morse was one of several attorneys hired by Chuck to defend his actions as trustee of both trusts prior to the death of Bertrand. Kate believed that she had supplied the account documentation confirming their agreement along with proof that she had paid back the loan and that it was legally titled in his name. Kate sincerely believed she had supplied concrete proof that her father was not of sound mind when he signed the new trust amendments, which made significant changes to his trust and estate. Chuck and the law firm representing the family trusts appeared to ignore and dismiss her substantial documentation as irrelevant, and they chose not to respond to it. Kate was dumbfounded by their patent rejection of pertinent documents which supported her charge that Bertrand was not mentally competent.

Both trusts contained legal language placing limitations on the trustees and a prominent provision against trustee self-dealing. This term means that the trustees were not to enter into transactions with trust assets that would financially benefit themselves. On November 24, 2006, Finn Nash and Chuck removed the language prohibiting self-dealing transactions, significantly changing the terms of her father's trust.

Her parents named Chuck and Kate to serve as trustees of their trusts in their legal documents, believing their intent would be honored. Kate realized that Chuck did not know that another second amendment existed which alerted her that something was amiss. She concluded her dad no longer possessed the mental clarity necessary to know what he was signing. That was her initial belief. With time and the multitude of legal documents executed against her, she realized that her dad was angry and intended to hurt her through his actions. Kate questioned what had occurred to provoke his intense anger toward her; she did not know what she could have done. She repeatedly asked herself why. Two new amendments indicated to her the change in legal documents were orchestrated by Chuck because the changes allowed him to manipulate assets and control the estate settlement process. Unfortunately, the twenty years following the funding of Bertrand's trust saw the majority of assets transferring out of his trust to the possession of either Chuck or Ann. However, Kate's nontrust asset found itself in more than one trust amendment drawn up years before her dad's death. More importantly, this occurred just prior to major changes to the handling of their family financial assets in over two decades. Three months following the legal amendment changes, the trust accounts were transferred to another brokerage firm in Minnesota, changing the investment oversight, advice, and strategies that had been in place for twenty-three years.

On January 12, 2012, a number of additional legal documents were drafted by Mr. Nash, Chuck's attorney, employed by this Cheetham, Steele and Morse LLP, completely changing her parents' estate plan from what had been in place for decades. This law firm had drafted the new later amendments during the final ten years of Bertrand's life. Unfortunately, her parents' estate attorney, Ken Powler, who had worked on their behalf for twenty-five years, was changed to Finn Nash during the 2005–2006 time period. This was the time her father became increasingly belligerent to her. Chuck often bragged to his brother Bert about the great attorney he had in Finn Nash. During this time, Bertrand transferred a percentage of his trust assets and his Simplified Employee Pension retirement account to insurance companies, purchasing two insurance contracts with the funds. He purposefully disinherited three of his six children by eliminating their names as beneficiaries of his new policies after removing the assets from his legal trust. Kate, Cybil, and Phillip were removed as beneficiaries as the assets were transferred out of the trust to insurance contracts.

Still on the plane returning home, Kate continued to read through the paperwork. Kate learned after her dad's death (in January 2016) that Ken Powler transferred to a new law firm during the latter part of 2004, noting the new amendments drawn up by the legal firm, Cheetham, Steele and Morse LLP. The fourth amendment to his trust agreement stated that Kate's 1996 loan was forgiven following the transfer of title of the legally described real property. Property previously designated to six children was to transfer directly to the sole property of Chuck. She read the document several times as she found the wording confusing. This land was the last real property parcel of farmland that remained of their parents' estate. At the time of her father's death, the land was valued in excess of two million dollars. The parcel of land was directly across from the increasingly valuable Huntington Golf Course and was larger than the entire golf course property. This was the remaining land purchased by Kate's parents over forty years before.

Kate put the stack of papers back in the large envelope and numbly sat on the airplane for the remainder of her flight. Why did the law firm state that Kate not be represented as co-trustee of her mother's trust? Why did Bertrand sign an amendment in 2006 which was based on incorrect information? Was her dad mentally aware of what he was signing? The final amendments were signed on January 12, 2012. The prior summer, Bertrand was eighty-six years old when Kate and her son spent a full week with him in July of 2011. She recalled her dad appearing frail; he walked with a walker and no longer tended to his personal finances because her sister Ann told her so. Ann carried his credit cards and handled all his expenses for the trip. He required a wheelchair to get around and required the help of a nurse to get dressed. Chuck controlled Bertrand's finances at this time because Ann made a point of telling Kate that Chuck paid for his nurse and his home expenses. She knew her dad was no longer capable of any deep, meaningful conversations because she spent a full week with him. They ate daily meals together and went on day trips and attended music events. It was clear to her that he was declining both in health and mental ability and often seemed confused, finding it difficult to engage in conversations because he could not understand what others were saying because his hearing was poor and he did not participate in conversations during their meals together.

It was Kate's opinion that Chuck believed she would not personally hire legal representation to question the many changes to their parents' estate. Kate lived on the West Coast, and the estate was in Minnesota. Chuck's actions indicated that he assumed it would be costly and difficult for Kate to oversee the estate settlement process as successor trustee. Kate realized that Chuck did not expect her to use her personal savings to go up against a large and powerful legal firm in the state. Furthermore, it became apparent to her that he had spent years working on his scheme to change their parents' estate plan to make himself the primary beneficiary of their estate assets.

Kate had told Ann on numerous occasions that she intended to ensure Gloriette's trust remained intact after Chuck and her dad transferred the trusts to their newly appointed Minnesota broker. Although she made these statements over the years, she did not realize that her mother's trust was being improperly accessed by both trustees. Kate had not considered that they would participate in self-dealing transactions and patently violate the trust agreement and their fiduciary duty. She had believed it was important that her mother's intentions were honored, and she assumed her dad and brother operated as competent and ethical trustees of her mother's trust.

Kate expected Chuck to honor their parents' plans and work together because they had verbally said they would when they signed the trust documents and were informed of their parents' wishes.

Memories flooded Kate about working on the farm over many years: daily farm chores and the hard seasonal labor of baling hay and picking corn from frozen snow-covered fields before spring.

She thought of Bert and Phillip, who devoted over twenty years of their lives working on the farm. They all labored long days, dawn to dusk, feeding cattle, milking dairy cows, plowing fields, harvesting corn, and baling hay. The difficult physical labor had been expected of them without commensurate compensation throughout their years working on the family farm. Shocked, she discovered the estate paperwork indicated all valuable assets were now transferred to Chuck.

Thus, the year and a half, emotionally painful, and legally expensive process began.

THE INVESTIGATION

Bertrand's funeral service was on a cold and cloudy Friday afternoon. He was buried the following morning on a sunny, crisp, and frigid day. His grave was next to Gloriette's tombstone at Findlay Cemetery. The country landmark was found at a corner intersection of two gravel roads. It was heavily wooded, surrounded by predominantly maple and oak trees. Prior to 2010, the cemetery was considered remote. For over one hundred and fifty years, the corner lot was peaceful and quiet. Common noises were chirping birds and rustling leaves. The day Bertrand was buried, Kate noticed several new homes had been constructed next to the cemetery perimeter. From childhood to later years when she returned for visits, she walked to the cemetery from their farmhouse and wandered around Findlay reading the tombstones. Some of the gravestones dated to the mid-1800s. She recognized the names of people who had previously occupied their family home and neighboring farms. Kate noticed the years they lived between the dash marks, date of birth to date of death, noting the dates that reflected a shortened life. Kate's memories included some of the deceased people buried at Findlay. The tombstones from the mid-1800s was worn and difficult to read as the dates had been carved into the stone over one hundred and fifty years before. As she surveyed the cemetery, she spotted the tombstone of a neighbor's child who died tragically when Kate was eight years old. The petite blonde-haired girl was climbing a sand mound at the local gravel pit off Crest Road. She was buried by the moving sand as it collapsed her lungs and she was unable to escape. Thereafter, Kate felt an intense sadness as she passed their small house located at the far end of their pastureland. She recognized the family tombstone of the elderly neighbor woman who was so kind to her during her childhood. She smiled as she thought of pleasant memories they shared during cozy afternoons having tea and shortbread cookies together.

As her father's casket was lowered into the ground, a jet flew directly above. At that moment, a murder of crows started squawking and causing commotion among the birds perched in the trees lining the cemetery. As the casket was lowered six feet below where she stood, Kate recognized a distinct bird call. She remembered how much her dad enjoyed watching birds. Strolling through the woods and pasture, she recalled his personalized bird call in which he attempted to impersonate a nighthawk. Kate thought of the bird feeders she filled for her parents outside their kitchen window. They enjoyed spending time at the kitchen table observing the birds excitedly fly and perch on the bird feeders hanging from a crab apple tree located next to their window.

Monday morning, following his funeral service and burial, Kate was back at her office, on the West Coast. She started her investigation into what had happened over the past ten years, the years that followed the transfer of her parents' trust accounts, the last years of his life. She questioned why estate documents prepared by Chuck's law firm, Cheetham, Steele and Morse LLP, were altered.

Gordon, Kate's husband, received the notices of the trust account transfers during March of 2007. At that time, she placed all her parents' files in a locked metal file cabinet. She had not looked at the files since that date. Kate slowly opened the cabinet that had been locked for a decade and carefully stacked the files on her large round glass office table. She methodically outlined a strategy for her investigation. She understood the history of specific assets that had been held by each trust because her parents included her in their estate planning execution. Kate reviewed one document at a time. She separated the Cheetham, Steele and Morse LLP paperwork into respective stacks. Gloriette's home and property, known as 12200 Valley Egypt, from the time the house was built (eighties) had been titled and held in the Gloriette trust. After her father's death, she was told Chuck and Mildred—Chuck's wife—owned the house. She questioned why Chuck did not purchase her property from Gloriette's trust after Bertrand's death. Bertrand had the legal right to occupy the home during his life; however, the home was owned by Gloriette's trust. Chuck and Mildred purchased Gloriette's house, titled in the irrevocable Gloriette trust, four years before Bertrand's death in January 2012 for a valuation of the property that was documented in June 1997, which was Gloriette's date of death. Kate did not understand why the transaction occurred without the beneficiaries of Gloriette's irrevocable trust being informed. At this time, Chuck and Mildred had been married for thirty-six years. Mildred was Chuck's spouse and cobusiness partner since the late seventies. Chuck and Mildred ignored the real estate appreciation which took place from the time of her mother's death and the years that followed, from 1997 to 2012, the year they transferred ownership of her home to themselves. Kate questioned the validity of the transaction since it appeared to be blatant self-dealing by the trustee.

Kate separated additional legal documents. She had possession of Chuck's land contract on the family stone house, 12100 Valley Egypt. The contract had been between her mother and Chuck and was signed in May 1992. The document was his agreement to purchase the family stone house, barn, buildings, and twenty acres of land. At the time, her parents discounted the value of the purchase because they believed the actual valuation of a half a million dollars would be financially difficult for him. As Kate separated his land contract from the other paperwork, she experienced a negative sensation in her stomach, and she felt queasy and nauseous. She believed there was something strange about the land contract paperwork although she did not know what it was. Kate set the 12100 Valley Egypt paperwork aside which was the second prominent asset that was held by her mother's trust.

Kate's objective was to obtain copies of all the trust statements since her mom's death, almost nineteen years before. She was her parents' registered representative for most of those years and had copies of year-end statements. She researched the current location of the trust accounts since they transferred from her oversight during 2007. Kate discovered the account numbers and address of the Minnesota brokerage company. She wrote a letter which requested access to statement copies and the original transfer paperwork. She sent proof her authority as successor trustee of the Gloriette trust. She requested copies of her dad's trust statements. Although she had been removed as successor co-trustee of Bertrand's trust, she had a legal right to the information as one of the trust beneficiaries. She stated this fact in the letter to the brokerage firm's operations manager.

Kate received the okay to receive all the statements since Chuck and Bertrand transferred the accounts, during 2007, away from Gordon as his registered representative. Her objective was to do an accounting of the trust assets from 2007 to 2016. In a short amount of time, Kate had acquired nine years of brokerage statements for both trusts. She obtained monthly statements of each year since the accounts were transferred. Kate gathered the prior year-end consolidated statements and pieced together nineteen years of activity for both trusts. She had worked for Prudential Bache and Company during the nineties, a decade in which many financial firms had merged. The consolidation of the industry after the banking collapse of 2007 and 2008 added to the difficulty of her effort because each firm required a separate request. Over a period of two months, she pieced together the history of account appreciation, deposits, and extensive history of numerous withdrawals.

Kate received statements from five brokerage firms during the initial two months of her investigation, and many statements were retrieved from dormant archives. Prudential Bache and Company was bought by Lincoln Securities. Lincoln Securities was purchased by Fargo and Company after the 2008 financial collapse. Kate also contacted UBS Group AG and requested the old statements. She had worked for major reputable Wall Street's firms since 1982. UBS Group AG acquired Paine Webber and Company during the year 2000 and surprisingly gave Kate what she needed to complete her forensic accounting of the trust activity during the entire nineteen years after her mom's death. She had twenty years of brokerage statements for both parents' trusts. Kate was impressed that she had retrieved the information easily; pieces were put together, and conversations occurred which revealed information that was useful. During this time, Chuck told his team of attorneys that he could not obtain copies of any statements or checks because the age of the documents exceeded the five-year statute of limitation and were no longer available. Kate's success in gathering over twenty years of statements and copies of cleared checks demonstrated that Chuck's statement had been a bold lie.

Kate reviewed the transactions involving her mother's home property, 12200 Valley Egypt. This house was built by both parents during the eighties and was located next to their family stone house. The family stone house had been sold to Chuck using a land contract agreement that had a legal document between her mother and Chuck, signed and executed in May of 1992.

The family farm pastureland was gradually sold in the latter part of the eighties and early nineties. Her parents had retired during 1986 and set up their financial estate plan initially that year and again reviewed and executed new legal documents in May 1992. The 12200 Valley Egypt house was legally an asset of her mother's trust. Her parents had planned to live their remaining life in the house. The property included a two-story log cabin with two massive woodburning fireplaces on each level. The small house was located on several acres of wooded land and backed up to a pond and wooded hillside. Trees surrounded the property with exception of the south side where the family stone house stood. It was a short walk between the houses. Chuck walked to the house daily to have coffee with her dad. Kate learned after his death that their visits usually consisted of complaints against her. Chuck repeatedly said, "Kate's a b—. She's a rich b—. She's ungrateful, and she hates you, Dad." She heard these statements repeated after her father's death by Chuck, Mildred, Cybil, and Ann. Ten years had passed since she was part of her dad's life, she questioned why they were calling her names.

The 12200 house was valued at one hundred twenty-five thousand dollars at the time of Gloriette's death in June 1997. The estate documents revealed that Chuck and Mildred purchased Gloriette's house and surrounding land for one hundred twenty-five thousand dollars, the exact value as listed by her estate valuation, fifteen years before. The value of property in Cain County had appreciated significantly over nineteen years following her death. The country land had become highly valued by doctors, attorneys, and professionals desiring to live away from the city.

Gloriette's trust owned the house and surrounding property. Chuck and Bertrand were trustees of her trust. Her trust specifically stated, "no self-dealing." As trustees of her trust, they sold her house for a valuation that indicated the property had not appreciated in fifteen years. She carefully reviewed all the brokerage statements for the past ten years. Chuck and Mildred purchased Gloriette's house and property on January 12, 2012. Kate did not see any evidence of monthly payments for their purchase of her mom's property which had been required according to the contract they both signed. The paperwork stated that Chuck and Mildred purchased her property by land contract valued at one hundred twenty-five thousand dollars and with no down payment. Kate noticed monies withdrawn from Gloriette's trust the month before Chuck and Mildred signed the land contract purchase. Kate recognized that the withdrawals from her mother's trust the prior month was for Chuck's renovation of the first floor of the home where her dad was living. Within two weeks, Chuck and Mildred purchased the property for zero monetary deposit or referred to as a zero down payment. Kate wondered why there were no deposits to Gloriette's trust for the monthly payments. Kate asked, "Where are the payments they promised to make according to the contract they had both signed?"

Kate completed the accounting of all deposits and withdrawals from both trusts for the ten-year period preceding her dad's death. She noted few deposits and alarmingly increasing withdrawals from both of her parents' trusts. She recognized the exact date Chuck took control of writing checks out of the two trusts because there was a significant change in the turnover of trust assets as well as number of withdrawals made on a monthly basis. A lump sum deposit was made in December 2014 to the Gloriette trust, which covered the exact amount of the 12200 Valley Egypt land contract payment that Chuck and Mildred owed her trust for that year. This was the first deposit that reflected a payment they owed her trust, and it was made two years before her father's death. It appeared that they made a lump sum deposit in lieu of making monthly payments as the land contract stated; therefore, one lump sum deposit was made approximately three years following the signing of their land contract. She requested copies of all deposited checks as well as checks paid from the trusts. The payment was made from Bertrand's trust, not from Chuck and Mildred's account, as the stated purchasers of Gloriette's property. In short, Chuck and Mildred purchased the trust property and paid two years of payments from Bertrand's checking account in December 2014 and December 2015. The questions remained: "Why were there no contract payments made during 2012 and 2013 to the Gloriette irrevocable trust? Why was the property valued at one hundred twenty-five thousand dollars on that particular day and year?"

Ann refused to give Kate any of the records stored in her mother's house. Ann tersely stated to her that she thought Chuck should get the house. Ann said to Kate that she refused to take sides. Ann stated that Bertrand wanted to keep the house in the family. Kate knew that it was agreed long ago between her parents, Ken Powler, Chuck, and Kate that her mother's house was to be sold after Bertrand's death. Chuck could have purchased it from the estate at a fair appraised value agreed to by all beneficiaries. However, no sibling knew about the transfer of their mother's house to Chuck and Mildred. Kate believed the sale of Gloriette's property to Chuck as trustee was an obvious corrupt self-dealing. In laymen's terms, Chuck and Mildred swindled the house and property.

Kate determined the price of one hundred twenty-five thousand dollars was set from a comparative market analysis, referred to as a CMA, prepared by a local nursing home during 2010. Chuck had requested Maybrook nursing home to consider purchasing the house in exchange for Bertrand moving to the elderly care home. Maybrook was a local reputable assisted-living home for aged people desiring to live their remaining life in a facility dedicated to an aging individual. The explanation did not make sense to Kate. She telephoned the real estate firm who had prepared the CMA. They had three offices in Indian Falls. She coincidentally phoned the office, and the first person she spoke to was the real estate agent who had prepared the document five years before. She wondered what the statistical probability of reaching this particular agent was.

The CMA was prepared using sales of property during 2008, 2009, and early 2010. The land contract purchase was recorded on January 12, 2012; however, a valid acceptable appraisal was not requested at the same time. The CMA was outdated by years, having been completed during 2008 to early 2010. The comparative property sales were listed from the depressed years of the financial collapse which occurred during 2008 to 2009. This was significant because few homes were sold during the time of the financial crisis since it was very difficult to receive bank financing. By this time, Kate was convinced of unmistakable self-dealing by Chuck and Mildred.

Kate prepared a letter which stated the transaction appeared to be self-dealing by the trustees and a violation of the Gloriette irrevocable trust. She requested a locally referred attorney to legally rewrite the letter and send it to Chuck's attorneys. She requested an explanation of the questionable property appraisal, lack of monthly payments, and the two lump sum deposits which had been withdrawn from her dad's trust. Kate's letter requested a confirmed history of monthly payments which were to have been made according to the land contract signed on January 12, 2012.

The second asset held by her mother's trust was Chuck's 1992 land contract. This was a contract between her mother and Chuck for the purchase of the stone house, twenty acres, barns, silos, and other buildings which were all known as 12100 Valley Egypt. The family farm was adjacent to the small home built by both parents known as 12200 Valley Egypt. The remaining assets allocated to her trust were securities from the stock portfolio acquired by her parents since 1983. She completed her work on 12200 Valley Egypt, her mother's home which had been her parents' retirement home. The letter drafted by the local attorney requested responses regarding the questionable transaction. Kate anxiously waited for a response from Chuck's lawyers at Cheetham, Steele and Morse LLP. Her next project was to determine the status of the land contract on what had been their family farmhouse, the stone house, known as 12100 Valley Egypt.

Instinctively, Kate knew something was wrong with the paperwork, although she did not know what had been changed with the second principal asset held by her mother's trust. Kate had a copy of the original land contract signed by Gloriette and Chuck in May 1992, attached to the original amortization schedule. She knew Chuck had borrowed additional funds from her trust after her death because she saw the withdrawals and the word "loan" written on her trust checks. Furthermore, there were three amendments to her land contract which decreased the value and the terms of the contract over the span of nineteen years. Kate was the financial advisor of her trust the year following Gloriette's death.

Her daily ritual included reviewing deposits and withdrawals made by her clientele, and she did not recall deposits being made to her mother's trust account. She noticed the new amendments were initiated by Chuck and his attorney and appeared to restate the principal loan amount outstanding as if each monthly payment had been made. The new terms were based on all past payments being paid, interest and principal paid on time, current, and in line with the amortization schedule as originally stated in the 1992 land contract.

Kate had copies of the first amendment to his loan contract dated May 1998. She researched the attorney who had legally executed the amendment. The correspondence was between Chuck and this attorney; Bertrand was not listed on the correspondence as a trustee of Gloriette's trust. Kate had a copy of this document because her dad had sent it to her along with all the legal information that had to do with both of their trusts. At the time, Kate did not study the document because she assumed Chuck and Bertrand were acting as ethical fiduciaries of her mother's trust.

Kate noticed the second amendment to the land contract was dated almost one year later, May 1999. Again, the amount of his principal loan owed decreased. Interestingly, the principal loan amount declined during 1998 and 1999 as if the monthly payments had been made. The principal amount owed on a loan declined each month resulting in a zero balance after all payments were faithfully paid over the term of the loan, providing the payments were actually made to the holder of the contract—real payments, not imaginary ones.

Kate located the monthly brokerage statements for 1998 and 1999. She reviewed each statement from January 1998 to December 1999. She confirmed no land contract payments had been made to the Gloriette trust during that time period, yet the principal amount declined for each loan amendment as if all payments were faithfully paid since inception.

There was nothing Kate could do prior to 1997. Any payments prior to 1997 were deposited to her parents' joint account prior to her mother's death. Kate had only anecdotal evidence of her mother telling her, "Chuck is not current on his land contract payments. Chuck is not making his land contract payments."

Kate continued to review the Cheetham, Steele and Morse LLP paperwork and noticed another amendment to her mother's 12200 Valley Egypt land contract which was dated January 12, 2012. The amendment did not state the principal amount due despite the fact that the land contract was in existence for twenty years. The document stated principal amount outstanding from the 1999 amortization schedule as if all monthly payments were made from 1999 to 2012. The most recent amendment dated January 2012 erased all principal and interest that had been owed for a thirteen-year period of time. At that moment, Kate realized that she had all the monthly statements in her possession. She asked herself, "Did Chuck make payments to Gloriette's trust during those years?" Kate carefully looked at the monthly and annual statements for her mother's trust. The statements showed zero deposits were made to her mother's trust. Kate could not find one land contract payment that was deposited during the previous nineteen years of statement records.

Kate concluded that Chuck renegotiated his land contract three times; each time, he erased the history of principal and interest owed as if each payment had been made. Kate had evidence that hundreds of thousands of dollars of principal and interest owed to the Gloriette trust had been erased by the third land contract amendment. This particular amendment was legally executed by Chuck's estate attorney, Finn Nash. Chuck indubitably had put his interests above the beneficiaries of the Gloriette trust. Kate was certain that Chuck violated his duties as trustee by brazenly restating a falsely revised outstanding principal balance, a self-dealing act by the trustee. She believed he committed fraud because the three new amendments to her land contract were unmistakably incorrect, and it was his intent to cheat the Gloriette trust out of his legal obligation. Kate concluded that Chuck did not intend to honor Gloriette's trust.

Kate believed her mother had insisted Chuck's land contract be held by her trust because she was concerned about Chuck's accountability. She remembered their volatile relationship and her mother's distrust of Chuck's manipulative dealings. Her mother recognized Chuck's devious nature and resented his constant disruptive interference in her marriage. Gloriette had hoped that having Kate as co-trustee offered the oversight that was needed to protect her assets. The Gloriette trust was legally worded to ensure Kate was named co-trustee in the event Bertrand died before she did. Her mother was intuitive and intelligent, and she was fair. It was important to her that her assets were distributed equally between all six of her children. Kate realized this was not possible if the trustees were corrupt or senile and the law firm representing the trust was unethical.

After Gloriette's death, 20 percent of her stock account was withdrawn from her trust to pay for the remaining debt to build her house. Kate stated that this was an improper withdrawal from the Gloriette trust because the debt should have been deducted from all assets before the house was allocated to the Gloriette trust. The amount withdrawn from Gloriette's legal trust and transferred into Bertrand's trust was the amount that legally should have been credited to the Gloriette trust. The withdrawn funds transferred to Bertrand's trust held approximately 85 percent of their joint net worth, clearly an unequal division of net worth. Her parents were married for almost fifty years. Two years following her death, Gloriette's trust reflected 15 percent of their net worth while Bertrand's trust held their remaining assets that had been acquired jointly. Kate knew this because she was copied on the complete statement of net worth as listed by their longtime estate planning attorney, Ken Powler. She realized that this was another instance of her dad not treating his partner and wife of forty-eight years fairly and with the respect she deserved.

Kate devoted almost every day for two months to complete an accounting of twenty years of trust statements as well as cleared copies of checks that had been written and withdrawn from trust assets. She carefully pieced together the monthly financial activity. The local attorney was slow to rewrite her composed letter, requesting responses to pertinent questions and notifying Cheetham, Steele and Morse LLP law firm of her legal representation. During this time, she realized she required Minnesota legal representation. She began a search for an estate attorney who understood trust fraud, misappropriation of trust assets, breach of fiduciary duty, and use of trust assets for personal benefit, essentially a legal professional competent to expose the wrongdoing.

Kate woke up early one warm April Friday morning and began researching law firms specializing in trust fraud in the state. There were three law firms who advertised taking specialized cases in this area. Kate sent an e-mail to each firm outlining the general facts that she had uncovered and her concerns regarding her parents' estate. Before sending inquiries to each firm, Kate researched the individual principals of each firm. Jack Napp was an up-and-coming lawyer and had received accolades for his estate cases. As she read Jack's bio, she was impressed with his résumé. Mr. Napp specialized in trust fraud. Kate sent both him and his law firm an inquiry e-mail.

Joseph Stone was the principal and partner of the law firm Wright, Coolidge and Stone PC. He immediately responded to Kate's inquiry by e-mail. Mr. Stone stated that he was available to briefly talk to Kate about the case. When she arrived at her office early that morning, she telephoned his office. Mr. Stone said to her, "Jack is in my office and will be assessing your case too." During their conversation, she mentioned she was concerned about her brother depleting her parents' trusts, using their funds for his litigation expenses. Mr. Stone's response was that there was one county in Minnesota where the judge required a defendant charged of trust fraud to pay all legal expenses until he was proven innocent by the legal process. She had a sense of relief when Mr. Stone explained this to her; however, during the following months, Chuck managed to charge the trusts over one hundred thousand dollars prior to a court ruling. The process had taken five months of legal expense. At the end of their second mediation, Chuck again began writing large checks out of the trust accounts, and there was nothing Kate could do to stop it. On November 24, 2006, Bertrand had signed a document which made Chuck the personal representative of his trust. As the trust's personal representative, Chuck was allowed to write checks and control the legal process. Kate came to understand this was the reason the lawyers ignored her and explained why they were only concerned with Chuck's instructions.

Kate's initial conversation with Stone and Napp impressed her; they were the Minnesota law firm specializing in trust fraud cases. Kate believed Chuck would be receptive to a settlement if he was required to pay his own legal expenses. In time, this proved to be a false assumption. Kate paid her legal expenses from her personal savings as her objective was to represent Bert and Phillip, her brothers. Following Bertrand's funeral, Ann specifically stated to Kate that she did not want Phillip to get anything. Ann and Phillip had an acrimonious relationship throughout their life. Kate recognized this by the stories Ann told about Phillip to others. Ann had a strong opinion that Phillip was not a good steward of money and should not be allowed to have an inheritance. Kate firmly believed Phillip was entitled to an equal one-sixth inheritance because her parents told her specifically that their remaining assets were to be divided equally. At that time, Kate intended to carry on as successor trustee of her mother's trust. She did not know the extent of the undertaking she was committing to. She assumed that Chuck was using the trust funds to pay for his legal expenses. Kate did not understand why he was able to write checks from the trusts with no questions being asked by anyone.

During their initial conference call, Mr. Stone mentioned they were agreeable to meet with Kate the following week, in their office, to discuss the case further. Kate said, "I live on the West Coast, and I want to make a decision immediately." She asked Mr. Stone to review specific information and planned to call him within hours for another short conference call.

After she hung up from that first telephone call, she looked up Internet information on Mr. Stone. His law firm had a unique specialty and expertise in the area of trust and estate fraud, and it was one of the few in the state that advertised its expertise in this niche area of the law.

For these reasons, Kate believed that Wright, Coolidge and Stone PC were the attorneys to handle her case. During the months that followed, she believed that she had hired competent attorneys. That day, Kate told Mr. Stone he was hired and asked that he immediately go to work on the case. Mr. Stone told her that he was going out of town for a week; however, Jack has the case and was to notify Cheetham, Steele and

Morse LLP of her legal representation. It had taken her local attorney two months to notify Chuck's law firm that she was legally represented. Wright, Coolidge and Stone PC notified Cheetham, Steele, and Morse LLP the week following their conference call.

As she told Joseph Stone he had the case, she simultaneously asked if he had similar cases against Chuck's law firm. Mr. Stone said to her, "We actually have had three cases within the past year, on both sides. We represented a sole trustee in one case and beneficiaries in the other two cases."

"How did the cases end?" she asked.

Mr. Stone replied, "We won all three cases."

POLO CHUCK

Chuck was Kate's older brother; they were eighteen months apart in age. As a child and teenager, Kate admired him; after all, he was her brother. Eventually, as an adult, she realized that Chuck was manipulative, negative, and not trustworthy. When Chuck's life came to a figurative fork in the road, he chose the dark and twisted path.

Chuck was their dad's favorite son, named after his grandfather, Richard Charles II, nicknamed Dick. There were numerous photographs of Chuck as a baby, toddler, and young boy, which confirmed her dad's love and admiration for his son. Kate admired the photo albums containing pictures of Chuck while noting considerably fewer pictures of her other siblings. At an early age, she recognized her dad's favoritism toward him because he responded to his many requests and catered to his interests, whether it was buying toy guns and chemistry sets, funding his youthful business ideas, such as raising exotic chinchillas or arranging music lessons with well-known Indian Falls instructors.

They moved to the country when Kate was three years old and Chuck was approaching kindergarten age. Chuck's first day of school was captured on one of the family's few home movies. Chuck's disdain toward his sister was evident, reluctantly allowing her to kiss his cheek as he walked out the front door to his first day of school. As children, Kate and Chuck set up rows of toy soldiers, horses, covered wagons, taking a large section of the third floor attic of their new home; they were gifts to Chuck from her parents. They played cowboys and Indians and practiced basketball shots on Chuck's court; occasionally, he allowed Kate to shoot his BB gun in the open pasture fields.

Even so, Chuck was a personable young boy and often had a smile on his face. He was active in 4-H during his adolescent and teenage years. 4-H was a national organization that promoted after-school clubs intended to expose rural farm kids to agriculture and animal husbandry. Their logo was one of the most widely recognized; the four-leaf clover and the annual club efforts were displayed at local summer fairs. As a young boy, each year, her dad chose cattle for Chuck to show at the Lawrence 4-H Fair. Chuck haltered his black steer and led the animal around the show area as the fair judge observed, deciding his ribbon award. Smiling with pride, her parents watched as Chuck walked the cow or steer around the open ring, always receiving blue ribbons for his attractive Black Angus cattle. As he turned eight years old, her parents purchased a splendid paint-quarter horse for him. The chocolate-brown-and-white horse was named Duchess, and within two years, she had a colt; Chuck called her Lightening. A special horse trainer was hired for his new colt, as she was exceptionally temperamental, requiring extensive training and a complicated bridle. Chuck rarely saddled his horses because he lost interest in them while Kate often saddled Duchess and galloped through the neighboring pastures and cornfields after school. Duchess often tried to knock Kate off her back by galloping through tree stands with low-hanging branches, trying to return to the barn to her beloved companion. Sadly, the horses were eventually removed from the family farm by the Society for the Prevention of Cruelty to Animals. She was told by others this occurred because of the poor care they received from Chuck. Chuck had owned the horses since his dad had given him the horse and colt as a boy. Chuck was responsible for their lifetime care. Kate learned the horses were removed from the farm pastureland long after she had moved far away from her childhood home.

Chuck was sent to youth basketball camps to improve his game and prepare him for his junior and high school team. He regularly practiced his shots and technique on his court which had been built on the entire second floor of their large red barn, specifically for him.

During elementary through high school, Chuck was shorter than his classmates, and his high school coach told him that his height was too short for the team. Kate remembered Chuck's disappointment as he told his dad that he wasn't chosen to be part of the team even after he had diligently practiced shooting baskets working toward his goal of being a valuable team player. Eventually, he reached his adult height when he was nineteen years of age, after receiving his high school diploma.

Bertrand played the trumpet as an adult and gave Chuck a new trumpet and lessons the year before he attended junior high school. Chuck excitedly took up the instrument and enjoyed the attention and accolades he received for his performances. During his summer vacations, Chuck was sent to White Lake Music camp and a prestigious Summer Music Academy. Soon after, Chuck became his school band's designated first chair trumpet player. Throughout his junior and high school years, he won numerous blue medals for music competitions and was often chosen to play featured solos. His dad bought him a shiny silver trumpet as a young teenager, often boasting to others that it was a coveted musical brand for its musical pitch and tone.

Chuck was ten years old as he wrote about his aspirations, listing his lifetime goals. Kate discovered his handwritten essay in a box of her documents and gave it to him. At that time, Chuck was in his thirties and was a father to four children. His goals were ambitious as he had dreamed of becoming a star basketball player like Jerry West and sought fame as a trumpet player, comparing himself to Louis Armstrong. Chuck listed his goal to eventually attend medical school, becoming a surgeon, just like his dad had been. At ten years of age, Chuck had ambitious goals.

Bertrand bought numerous books for Chuck during elementary school, and Chuck collected stacks of paperback books from his monthly school book club. Although Kate never witnessed him reading, her parents often commented about the library Chuck was acquiring. As an adult, Bert thought his brother Chuck was an avid reader because he frequently made specific comments about the books he was reading.

Bert was fond of Western theme books written by Louis L'Amour. Mr. L'Amour was an American novelist who wrote historical fiction. Chuck made condescending remarks to Bert, such as, "Why are you reading that? Those books are all the same. They are not worth reading. You are wasting your time." Bert dismissed Chuck's opinions because he read the books and knew that they were not the same because they were well-researched historical fiction. Louis L'Amour made a living as a writer which was something that was rare during the era Mr. L'Amour was popular. The year following her dad's death, Kate found it difficult to believe Chuck was well-read or educated because his lifelong trail of squandering money and opportunity revealed to her that he was instead ignorant, lacking common sense, and devoid of wisdom.

Although Kate observed her dad's physical abuse to her younger brothers, she never witnessed him being physical toward Chuck. One evening, Chuck, Ann, and Kate came to the dinner table with what he claimed were dirty hands. He said, "Go out and get a plate of dirt. Your hands are dirty, so you must like to eat dirt." He was a general surgeon and washed his hands often because he understood the importance of cleanliness. Kate believed this particular incident was his effort to stress the importance of clean hands and fingernails; however, she now realized that discipline without love was abuse. She now understood the psychological term for his treatment was emotional abuse. Whenever Chuck mentioned this particular incident to Bert, his voice was laced with angry tones, conveying that he thought his dad's treatment had been unjust. Kate believed Chuck's personality was shaped by Bertrand's criticisms which may have been labeled as emotional abuse. A favorite colloquialism of Chuck was a phrase he attributed to his dad saying, "If all else fails, intimidation prevails."

Chuck was two grades ahead of Kate in high school, and during the years 1969 through the seventies, he grew his hair long to shoulder length and played his trumpet in a rock band for parties and school dances. Her classmates told her she was lucky to have Chuck as her brother, gushing to her enthusiastically, "Chuck is the coolest, best-looking guy at school."

Her girlfriends excitedly asked her, "How do you remain calm living in the same house as Chuck? He's so cool."

Chuck had crystal clear Paul Newman blue eyes. Others found Chuck's eyes to be unusual and striking. Also, Kate recognized that they commanded notice whenever he looked directly at her. As a teenager, Kate expected Chuck to be successful because he was usually one of the best students in school. He was personable, and she recognized that everyone seemed to like Chuck. Kate often helped with farm chores. The summers were hot and humid; she physically exerted herself with hard manual labor—baling hay, stacking the bales to the barn rafters while suffering from sunburn, heatstroke, and scrapes caused by the stiff field hay and straw. Standing on the hay trailer, inhaling the strong scent of freshly cut alfalfa in rows along the hills, she looked over the valley below and dreamed of swimming in the neighbor's cold pool next to their fancy house. Chuck and Kate were countryfolk, working the fields among the wealthy homeowners with beautiful swimming pools.

The summer of 1972, her parents planned a wilderness horseback trip to the Bob Marshall area just south of a well-known national park. Kate turned sixteen during the trip while Chuck was seventeen years old, having graduated from high school the month before. Her parents, Chuck, and Kate spent ten days horseback riding in the remote and wild mountains of Montana. Cowboys were their guides while their wives were the group's cooks. Chuck and Kate were the only teenagers among several wealthy couples who came from different parts of the country for the unique wilderness experience. Chuck and Kate's pleasant conversations were short during walks through the mountain meadows. Kate was enthralled by the sights, sounds, and smells of nature. She always assumed she and Chuck had camaraderie and naively believed that Chuck was her ally. In retrospect, they had not been close as children or teenagers because Kate had never shared her deeply personal thoughts or goals with Chuck. As children, they had separate interests. As a teenager, she was often working various jobs away from the farm and their home. At high school, Chuck pretended Kate wasn't his sister because she was not popular or considered a "cool" person among his peers. Kate overheard Chuck tell one of his classmates that she was not his sister. Later as an adult, Kate was grateful she had been shrouded from his influence during her adolescent and teenage years.

Chuck left for an out-of-state college the following fall. Kate's mother mentioned to her that Chuck did poorly in his freshman year of college. Kate knew her mother was concerned about Chuck's use of alcohol and recreational drugs because her mom had asked Kate about the small rectangular packages Chuck was regularly receiving in the mail at their Valley Egypt home. Kate visited her parents during the years she was a college student, returning to their home for occasional weekend visits because she lived less than an hour's drive away and attending Corinth College the fall of 1974 after graduating from Oak Hills High School the previous May. By this time, Chuck had quit college and returned to live at the stone house with her parents, Cybil, Bert, and Phillip. While Kate attended college, Chuck mentioned to her that he was considering enrolling at Corinth, which would have given him an opportunity to receive a college diploma. Kate remembered the gleam in Chuck's eyes as he shared this idea with her; however, Chuck did not return to college.

During the years 1974 to 1978, the hobby farm became a full-time expanding money pit. Kate referred to the family farm operation as such because her dad's medical practice income was devoted to supporting their farm venture. After Chuck quit college and returned home, several years passed until at the age of twenty-four, he married Mildred. Her dad purchased a mobile home trailer for his eldest son and new daughter-in-law, parking it next to their stone farmhouse. Chuck and Mildred lived in the trailer during the early years of their marriage while their family grew to include four children. The farm expanded as Bertrand's medical practice income was used to cover the numerous farm expenses, Chuck's salary, and Chuck's family's financial support.

Year after year, the farm was unprofitable because her parents regularly complained to Kate about it not being able to sustain itself without monies from Bertrand's medical practice. Kate's parents used their small savings account, borrowing money from their bank for land and equipment purchases. Kate believed they made an earnest attempt to create a successful livelihood for Chuck because they continued to buy and lease more farmland and purchased expensive farm equipment claiming they needed new machinery to improve the efficiency of the farming operation.

During this time, Chuck bitterly complained about his cramped living quarters and told Bertrand that he deserved to move into the stone house with his family. During the latter eighties, her parents built a cabin home a short distance to their stone house, eventually moving to their newly constructed home while Chuck, Mildred, and their children moved into the four-floor, five-bedroom stone house, what had been Bertrand and Gloriette's home for the previous thirty years.

During the eighties, Chuck's children were young, and Gloriette often mentioned to Kate that she was disgusted that Chuck spent his evenings at the local bar. "Why does Chuck go to the bars while his four children are left at home?" Kate asked her mother. Chuck and Mildred often left their children to fend for themselves while they went to friends' parties and saloons. During those years, Phillip was in partnership with Chuck and regularly took care of their children while Chuck and Mildred went to nightclubs with their friends.

During the early nineties, Kate returned to Minnesota with her husband, and while visiting their family farm, Gordon was taken aback by Chuck's six polo ponies grazing in the pasture. Chuck was known as the farmer who played polo during the eighties, the years while they ran the dairy operation. The local news ran a news clip about Chuck, which Gloriette videotaped and replayed often. Years later, Gordon told Kate that he knew Chuck could not pay for his expensive hobby without taking the money from her parents. By that time, Gordon mentioned Chuck's weight of approximately 250 pounds. Gordon asked Kate, "How do you play polo when you are so fat? Chuck is the fattest polo player in Minnesota. He needs five ponies to get through one match." Gordon added, laughing, "Chuck can't figure out why he can't make it to the puck fast enough." Kate believed that Chuck was doing what he enjoyed—farming and playing polo. Bert was Chuck's groom during the years he was living lavishly and traveling to his polo matches. Bert took care of Chuck's horses, his farm chores, and usually milked the dairy cows with either Bertrand or Gloriette while Chuck was away at polo matches. Kate didn't know the cost of owning polo ponies or his competition expense; she did not question her parents about the expense of his hobby nor did she really give it any thought.

During her visit, Chuck asked Kate if she wanted to ride one of his polo horses. Kate responded affirmatively, excitedly recalling her fond memories riding Duchess as a teenager. She eagerly agreed as Chuck saddled one of his horses. As she stepped up into the horse saddle stirrup, the horse jumped and took off running. She squeezed her thighs against the horse and held tightly to the bridle reigns. The coal-colored horse was so fast that she was scared to death she was going to fall off and break her neck as she galloped through familiar pastureland. As the horse increased his speed, she wanted nothing more than to remain in the saddle, alive. When she returned to the barn, still in the saddle, Chuck appeared startled and surprised. Bert later told her that his polo horses were retired racehorses and said he was surprised she rode that particular horse because he was wild, unpredictable, uncontrollable, and rarely ridden because of the physical risk. At the time, she thought it was strange that Chuck encouraged her to ride a dangerously wild horse; however, she thought he considered her a better horseman than she was. Years later, she realized that her assumption was naive.

Kate pursued her professional career, first as a sales representative, eventually becoming an Account Executive with a major Pharmaceutical Company while enrolled in night courses at a local state university. Although her position with a major pharmaceutical company was a well-paid job with many benefits, she chose to change careers to become a stockbroker, giving up a defined salary and agreeing to a commission-only income, forgoing a guaranteed salary. It took several years for Kate to earn more than a meager living, existing her first year on less than one thousand dollars per month. Kate developed her clientele through cold-calling and personally calling on business owners in the industrial areas of Southern California. During these years, Bert briefly lived on the West Coast before moving to Nebraska for several years. Bert returned to Minnesota periodically to help Chuck with the farm and building the 12200 Valley Egypt home. Bert moved permanently back to Minnesota during the later part of the nineties. Phillip lived his entire life in Indian Falls.

During the early nineties, Kate visited her parents in Indian Falls over the Christmas holiday and purchased a large television for their living room. Kate and her parents traveled to three major stores until they chose a TV from a friend of theirs, Lon Decker. Her parents were touched by Kate's gift and told her they considered the television purchase extravagant. Her dad said, "I did not expect any of my children to be as generous as you have been to us." Her dad had the television at the end of his life, watching it in his living room almost thirty years later, although by this time it was outdated and he was unable to operate its remote control. Her dad depended on Chuck, Bert, or Phillip to turn the television on as he no longer had the dexterity to operate it himself.

Often, Gordon and Kate vacationed with her parents. During the later eighties and the nineties, they spent their Christmas holiday in California with Kate's family. Just prior to her mother's death, they spent their winters in the California desert, enjoying their winter months away from Minnesota, particularly when they were able to play golf in the desert. During the mid-eighties and throughout the nineties, Kate was professionally successful, receiving an annual award designation called the Executive Club. Kate and Gordon invited her parents to travel with them for their business trips and to help care for their young daughter. Their first trip was to St. Petersburg, Florida, where Gloriette cared for her three-month-old granddaughter who had a bad case of croup. They all attended the Louis Rukeyser's Money Conferences in Las Vegas. Louis

Rukeyser had a popular business show called Wall Street Week with Louis Rukeyser. The show had a faithful following and was watched religiously every Friday night by stock investors during the seventies to the time of Mr. Rukeyser's death two decades later. They all were big fans and usually talked about his show each week. It was during this time that Bertrand sent Kate a personal note; he wrote, "I am proud of you. Love, Dad."

Gloriette died on June 16, 1997. Kate was forty-one years old, seven months pregnant with her second child, and her son was born three months after her mother's funeral. Her dad volunteered to take care of Kate's son during that year's executive club trip to Boca Rattan, Florida. Although the four had a pleasant trip, Kate realized it was difficult for Bertrand to take care of their three-month-old baby. He became flustered while Kate noticed his nervousness when he knew he would be alone with the baby for a short time. Kate's dad resided for ten consecutive winters in Palm Desert. Following Gloriette's death, he occasionally drove a couple of hours to spend time with Kate's family in Los Angeles. After her mother's death, Kate made it a point to telephone her dad regularly, usually a couple of times every week up until the latter part of 2004 when he became increasingly antagonistic toward her, later learning this was the time Ken Powler's legal firm dissolved and reopened at a new location.

After her mother died, she recognized a change in Chuck's personality; he became increasingly critical and negative. The family farm operation had been sold and terminated years before her mom's death. Afterward, during the nineties, Chuck worked in telephone sales, repackaging phone minutes. His employer sold the telephone business during the late nineties, leaving Chuck without any interest in the buyout, agreeing to take over the remainder of the business, which had questionable value. He continued to operate the business as if it was profitable, although by common sense and appearance, it was not. Bert told Kate that Chuck continued to pay the high office rent despite that the majority of the business had been sold and his remaining accounts generated significantly less revenue. Diana, Bert's wife, questioned Chuck's business, routinely asking, "Isn't everyone getting rid of their landline phones?"

During the nineties, Chuck was often found at the Dirty Shame Saloon. The locals often referred to the establishment as "Chuck's office." Chuck regularly took Bertrand to have lunch there after his mother's death and introduced him to Doozy. Bert and Phillip called her a "gold digger" and a "floosy." Subsequently, Doozy spent several winters with Bertrand in California. Kate did not question him about his relationship and chose to assume it was friendly companionship. Aunt Faye, her mother's sister, questioned her about his live-in relationship with Doozy; Kate naively replied that they were just friends.

Kate recognized that Chuck borrowed large sums of money from the trust each year following her mother's death—1998, 1999, and 2000. Chuck's land contract was refinanced two times during the late nineties. It was during this time when he became co-trustee with Bertrand for both the Bertrand and the Gloriette trusts. For the first time, Chuck was able to study the brokerage statements and recognize the monetary value of the trust holdings. Kate believed that Chuck schemed to gain access to the trust assets; however, his obstacle was Kate because she was the financial advisor and oversaw the trust activities. Chuck knew he could not access the funds without her scrutiny.

During 2001, Chuck sold the valuable thirty-eight acres of land her parents had held since the seventies. Gordon asked his father-in-law to call Chuck and confirm that it had been sold. Chuck confirmed the sale. Bertrand told Gordon that Chuck was paid a commission for selling the long-held farm property. "Why did he sell the property for what appeared to be below market value?" Kate asked Ann. Kate knew the proceeds were not deposited into Bertrand's trust because there were no deposits that matched the amount of the land sale. During the months of legal discovery, Kate reviewed the checking account statements and confirmed that the payment for her parents' thirty-eight acres of land went directly into another joint checking account that had been opened between Bertrand and Chuck. The property was sold by Chuck, and the proceeds were deposited to a newly established joint account which Chuck controlled. This fact, stated in the petition Kate filed with the court, supported her charge that assets were systematically removed from Bertrand's trust and transferred to Chuck's possession.

After Kate moved to the West Coast in June 1978, she distanced herself from Chuck. On the few occasions she spoke to him, she recognized that he was negative, critical, and talked despairingly about her siblings. Their conversations involved her countering his litany of negative criticisms with positive attributes. She did not enjoy the conversations she had with him, confining exchanges to her Minnesota visits or her annual telephone call to extend birthday wishes to him. Cybil, Bert, and Phillip were considerably younger than her in age, and while Kate was a young adult, slanderous comments Chuck made about her to others were repeated to Kate directly. She knew his backstabbing statements were untrue, hurtful, and occurred after Gloriette's death. Kate did not appreciate his extraction of Bertrand's assets from his trust because she knew that he was taking advantage of him. Bertrand became agitated if she questioned him about Chuck's expenditures, and she felt powerless to protect him from the large withdrawals from his trust. After the sale of Bertrand's set-aside trust land during 2000, Kate decided to completely ignore Chuck, believing her best course of action was to avoid communicating with him. Kate stopped communicating with Chuck after she had heard another one of his offensive and scurrilous comments about her. Kate incorrectly thought that if she stopped talking to him, he would leave her alone and no longer slander her. Her thought was as a child—if she closed her eyes and ears to what she did not want to see or hear, the slanderous statements would stop. Later, Kate realized that her silence toward Chuck intensified his vendetta. In hindsight, her decision allowed Chuck's narrative about her to be accepted by her siblings as the gospel truth for the years that followed.

During 2004, her telephone conversations with her dad were positive and pleasant, as she told him about her family activities. Later, her anecdotes were repeated to her by Ann into twisted, negative, critical, and complaining tales about Kate's husband and children. Kate asked Ann why her conversations were different from what she had told her dad. Ann admitted to her that Chuck was very negative and spoke despairingly about others, mentioning Chuck and their dad twisted things during their daily coffee at the kitchen table.

Kate realized that the timing and sequence of events made sense, and what had transpired was because of Chuck's manipulation. After Bertrand's death and during her investigation, Kate realized her dad had trusted her more than Chuck because he had told her confidential financial information that he had never disclosed to Chuck. Chuck's attorney, Finn Nash, authored the amendment removing Kate as cosuccessor trustee of Bertrand's trust. Within months, he transferred the brokerage accounts away from Gordon, removing her oversight. Kate realized that Chuck had financial troubles and his business didn't generate the revenue needed to cover his expenses. She had been aware of his numerous credit cards and credit card debt. His April 2007 credit report confirmed this fact. She had believed Chuck wanted to maintain his facade of success and consequently lived on Bertrand's assets to the time of his death. Her parents supported Chuck and his family from his early twenties. As Kate reviewed the brokerage and bank statements, she recognized that her dad supported Chuck with his retirement income until he died in January 2016.

As Kate read the Cheetham, Steele and Morse LLP paperwork during the plane ride home after her dad's funeral, she realized Chuck despised her because of the numerous legal documents drawn up maliciously against her. After months of research, the facts substantiated that Chuck manipulated Bertrand into getting sole control of his brokerage and bank accounts and tormented him by his extravagant spending of the trust and checking account money. Chuck controlled his dad's checking accounts for both the trust and the Lloyd's Bank accounts. Bertrand rarely spoke during his last years and often suffered from confusion, and

Kate recognized his mental deterioration during their brief encounters, which was substantiated by her brothers, family, and a few close friends. Dan Canfield, his favorite nephew, visited him prior to his death, relaying later to Kate that Bertrand expressed anguish over Chuck's extravagant spending of his money. Dan Canfield said that Bertrand was disappointed and said to him, "Chuck squandered his life and that he has nothing to show for what he was given."

Chuck took charge of Bertrand's checking account and finances after his second hip surgery in October 2011, and his dad became a shut-in. A shut-in is a person confined to the indoors as a result of a mental or physical condition. After his second hip surgery, Ann and Chuck took over all health and financial decisions for their dad. Throughout the legal process, they both claimed he was capable of making financial decisions, writing large checks and giving away his personal property. Chuck and Ann emphatically made this statement as the legal process churned on a year after his death, ignoring the facts. During the last years of his life, he was unable to read, write, use his phone or TV remote, and could not drive an automobile. They claimed that he could make complicated financial decisions and readily give property away—financial assets which were meant for his aged care. The case Kate made against Chuck was built on her dad's lack of mental capacity and Chuck's undue influence.

Following the death of Gloriette, Bertrand's conversations were short, and he did not discuss his finances with others. Chuck's manipulation of Bertrand's assets during those last years was considered "financial elder abuse." Financial elder abuse is a concern for aging people who own property and have financial assets. Elderly individuals may be preyed upon to separate them from their many years of work, investment, and savings. Chuck's scheme worked well since he had a partnership with his sister Ann and his wife Mildred. The facts showed that Ann was as interested in getting Kate out of Bertrand's life as Chuck was (i.e., betrayal). They conspired together to gain full control over his decisions and their parents' assets.

Kate thought about the years after her mother's death and prior to her estrangement with her dad. She had completely forgotten about the stroke he had suffered during the early nineties. After her parents retired, fulfilled their Ethiopia missionary commitment, and finalized their estate documents, they embarked on their lifelong dream of traveling to New Zealand and Australia. While exploring the farthest ends of the North Island of New Zealand in a rented motor home, Bertrand suffered a serious stroke. Fortunately, Gloriette was driving at the time. Realizing he needed emergency medical care, she drove the large motor home several hundred miles, nonstop, along the winding and steep cliffs of New Zealand. After many hours, she reached the hospital of the largest metropolitan city, Auckland. Bertrand was admitted to intensive care and spent several weeks there, eventually camping additional weeks in the motor home outside of the hospital awaiting clearance to return to the United States. His stroke caused paralysis of one side of his body. Approximately two years after suffering his stoke, he regained his ability to use his arm and leg. He suffered numerous minor strokes over the remaining years of his life which caused slurred speech and jumbled word sentences. He sometimes cried during conversations with others, showing an emotional side that he had never publicly expressed before. Kate forgot about the significance of his major health episode because she had been overwhelmed by documents, statements, and the forensic accounting that was required to figure out what happened to the trust money. She believed Bertrand's stroke and ministrokes might have left him vulnerable to Chuck and Ann's manipulation. Years later, after her dad's first hip surgery, Bertrand believed a mistake was made during surgery with a clamp and often complained about his botched operation. He was reticent to have a second hip surgery because of his negative experience. His second hip surgery, performed in October 2011, left him immobile and troubled him the rest of his life.

Initially, Kate dreaded to find out if what she had uncovered was true because the charges she accumulated against Chuck and Ann seemed fantastical to her. She found it difficult to believe a brother and sister would do these things to her dad, affecting the care he should have received during his final years of life.

Phillip told Kate, "Chuck ordered him to do something, and he obeyed his instructions. Chuck verbally reprimanded and humiliated him." Phillip lived with his dad for over a year, sleeping in the basement. Chuck controlled his dad's finances and his daily activities. Often, Phillip heard him up in the middle of the night and would check on him and find him confused and having forgotten where he was, repeatedly asking why he was there.

Phillip told Kate that Chuck turned Bertrand against him too, especially during the time Phillip lived in his basement. Chuck was afraid Phillip was getting too close to his dad and plotted against him. Phillip occasionally brought home special treats for Bertrand, causing Chuck irritation because Chuck would also bring him ice cream shakes, donuts, and other treats; and he did not want Phillip gaining favor with him. Chuck walked over to his cabin home and sat with Bertrand each morning. It was his brainwashing time. One day, Bertrand confronted Phillip, holding a knife in his hand and said, "Are you planning to kill me and take all my money?" Coincidentally, Chuck told Phillip that Kate was going to steal all his dad's money years before. This occurred during 2006. After this occurrence of Bertrand turning against Phillip, Phillip packed his things and left his dad's house, not returning for a year, realizing Chuck was threatened by him. Phillip was the youngest child but knew Chuck had turned Bertrand against another one of his children. Phillip revealed to Kate, only after Bertrand's death, that Chuck had continuous tirades against her during his daily coffee time with Bertrand.

Phillip worked for Chuck during his teenage years while attending high school and later during his twenties for a brief time after his landscape business was sold. Phillip explained to Kate that Chuck repeatedly said to him, "You must play the part, and to play the part, you must look the part. You must know how to orchestrate the story." Kate came to understand that Chuck was an actor and master manipulator.

During the months following the funeral service, Phillip helped Kate understand what had transpired during the years that she had been estranged from her dad. Kate asked Phillip why he didn't intervene during the time Chuck was turning her dad against her. He apologized, explaining that he couldn't have done anything because he was never taken seriously and whatever he said was ignored. Kate came to believe that Chuck was a con man and a bully. During the legal process, Chuck listed many witnesses he claimed agreed to testify that he was an excellent caretaker of Bertrand. Kate spoke to several of his witnesses during the fifteen-month legal process and realized he did not have their permission to use them as his witness.

Chuck knew how to present himself to certain people. Bert explained to Kate that Chuck was a narcissist. A narcissist is a person who has an excessive interest in themselves. Chuck used profanity often, easily flew into a rage, and was hypercritical of others. His brothers and neighbors said that he was distrustful and paranoid. Bert lived two miles from Chuck and frequented many of the same stores and restaurants. Business owners mentioned to Bert that Chuck asked the whereabouts of his brother because he didn't want to run into him. Bert told Kate that Chuck had a few admirers, women who smiled at his flirtatious behavior toward them.

After her dad's death, Ann immediately sided with Chuck and ignored Kate. She told others repeatedly that Kate was wrong to sue Chuck and that she was breaking up their family. Ann called Jack Napp, Kate's attorney, and had a several-hour conversation with him. Kate received a new legal bill in excess of eighteen hundred dollars for their telephone conversation. Kate called Jack Napp and said that she did not authorize their conversation as part of her billing agreement. Jack said that it was a productive conversation because Ann made many contradictory statements. He said, "Her statements are beneficial for her deposition or a court hearing. Ann said that she knew Chuck was manipulative and he did things that were questionable. Ann stated repeatedly that she didn't think you should be suing Chuck." Jack said he took copious notes of their conversation.

Gordon said to Kate, "Send her the bill and tell her to pay it." She did; however, Ann ignored the bill and Kate.

Phillip told Kate that her dad was bewildered by Chuck's actions during the last several years of his life. She learned that her dad was disgusted with his manipulative behavior and called Chuck a crook and a liar at the end of his life. He told Dan Canfield and Phillip he was angry at Chuck for squandering his life. After his funeral service, a childhood friend told Kate that Chuck was passing out recreational drugs to his friends. "Was he celebrating?" Kate asked her friend.

Chuck's brother said he was a blasphemer, disrespectful of God, often violating the fourth commandment: "You shall not take the name of the Lord your God in vain, for the Lord will not hold him guiltless who takes His name in vain" (Exodus 20:7, NKJ). According to Bert, he had been a lifelong blasphemer. He religiously made fun of churchgoers with contempt, calling them Bible beaters. Chuck did not like women because of the way he treated his mother, his sisters, and his girlfriends who Kate had witnessed as a young woman. Bert said that Chuck was paranoid because he was distrustful of everyone he knew and hypercritical of neighbors and friends. He showed his disdain for his brothers and sisters by his elaborate scheme of changing their parents' estate plan after their mother's death. His animosity toward Kate was evident by the numerous legal documents specifically against her.

Kate came to believe that Chuck made Bertrand's final years sad and unpleasant because it was stated throughout the years of medical documents Kate carefully reviewed. She was told that Chuck did not allow him to enter a quality retirement home where he would have received excellent care. Kate questioned whether Chuck was punishing him or just being cruel. The evidence she uncovered showed that Chuck and Ann systematically transferred their parents' assets over the nineteen years following Gloriette's death to themselves. Chuck's repeated justification was that he stayed and everyone else left the family home. The final amendment to Bertrand's trust gave the last parcel of valuable land to Chuck. Chuck's first grandson, Alden, was named after the road where the land is located.

Kate heard from others that Chuck continuously discredited her work and brainwashed her dad into thinking that she had enmity toward him. Kate realized the treatment she received from him was because he was manipulated by Chuck. Bertrand either called her a "b—" or hung up the telephone on her. He did not reply to any of the cards or letters Kate sent him. Ann knew what Chuck was doing because she often drove to Minnesota to get checks from him. She actively promoted the idea that he did not want a relationship with Kate. Chuck and Ann worked together to create a painful, emotional barrier between Kate and his other children. The tragedy was that Kate would not realize this until after he had died.

Bert and Phillip had many complaints against Chuck because they worked under his direction for decades, hard manual labor, often without any compensation. Throughout their teenage years, they covered for Chuck's misdeeds, often telling lies to their parents for Chuck's benefit, while Chuck was verbally and physically abusive to them. After their father's death, they realized that according to Chuck, all was his, pretending that he did not have two brothers. He repeatedly stated to others that he stayed while everyone else left. His statement might be true if he didn't have two brothers who lived within two miles of their family farm.

During the litigation that followed his death, Kate believed Chuck's attorneys were afraid of him, refusing to challenge his withdrawals from the trusts, which paid his legal expenses. Kate discovered that Bertrand was afraid of Chuck from the conversations she had with relatives and friends who had witnessed their interaction. Kate realized her father's submission to Chuck's requests as she studied the numerous shaky check signatures. She did not believe her father would have done what he did unless forcibly coerced because it was against all that had been planned and agreed upon decades before by both he and Gloriette.

Kate thought of David in the Old Testament who went up against Goliath, a giant man. At that time, no one thought the small boy David could defeat the giant Goliath. Going up against a large and powerful law firm and their aggressive tactics to get Kate to give up reminded her of David's story as told in the book of Samuel in the Bible. Kate understood why David said, "Can't I even speak?" (Samuel 17:29, NIV). She did not understand why her questions were dismissed and ignored by her siblings. She was reminded of David during the litigation process and came to her personal meaning of this particular Bible story.

The last time Kate saw Chuck, he was morbidly obese, and his skin color was pale. He had white hair and walked with a limp. Years of recreational drug use, excessive alcohol consumption, gluttony, and lack of exercise had taken a toll on his health. One look at him and one may have surmised that he suffered from poor health. Chuck appeared to be an old man at sixty-two.

BETRAYAL

Bertrand died in January 2016 in Arkansas. Ann discharged him from his retirement home during the fall of 2014 and drove him to the rural outskirts of Augustine where she lived with her husband, Leonard, and her many children. Chuck finally allowed Bertrand to move to the retirement home during the spring of 2014; therefore, Bertrand lived at the retirement home for less than one year. At that time, Kate was grateful he would be at a loving home for his last years. After the move, Ann stated to Kate and others that this was where he wanted to live. She believed that he was unhappy at the home and stated that her children would learn how to care for an elderly parent. Emphatically, she stated this was her justification for moving him to Arkansas to live with her family. Periodically, Kate spoke to Ann and asked about Bertrand's health and whether he was content. Months after his death, she discovered that her younger brothers were not informed of Ann's plan to move him miles away from his home of six decades. Bert and Phillip had visited him regularly at Maybrook retirement home. This was no longer possible with him so far away. On Bertrand's last birthday in December 2015, he was driven back to Minnesota by Leonard. Kate did not know about the birthday celebration until after her dad had returned to Arkansas and Ann said to her that the winter trip was cold and he developed pneumonia. He died one month later. In time, her story changed and was eventually revealed to Kate. Kate was told that Ann and Leonard could no longer care for him and admitted him to a local nursing home where he tried to escape one evening without shoes and proper clothing. He developed pneumonia and was admitted to the local hospital where he died. Ann and Chuck took care of the funeral arrangements.

Two years prior to their estrangement in March 2007, Bertrand became increasingly belligerent toward Kate. He spent his winters in the California desert, and Kate's family drove from their home to the desert for periodic weekend visits. One visit in the fall of 2004, he complained that he was disappointed in her and she had been a "rotten" child. She had no idea what he was talking about and found his rants offensive because she did not remember anything she did to justify his derogatory statements. He treated her with contempt and dislike and became increasingly angry and hostile toward her. His antics continued into the next year. His behavior upset her because he disrespected her as an adult. She was offended that he treated her as a child. Twelve years later, during the legal litigation following his death, she realized what had turned him against her and why he had treated her as he did.

Kate had numerous financial discussions with her dad which took place during the eighties, nineties, and the first part of the two thousands. She became an account executive and stockbroker during 1982. Her parents started their stock account with her beginning May 1983 and accumulated a profitable stock portfolio from her recommendations and advice for twenty-three years. They communicated, typically once or twice a week. Specifically, her dad followed her advice and accumulated quality dividend growth securities, allowing him to have an increasing annual income. After her mother's death, they worked together to divide the assets into their two trusts: the Gloriette irrevocable and the Bertrand trusts.

The year following her mother's death, his father began making changes to his trust that didn't make sense to her. Chuck borrowed money from Gloriette's irrevocable trust, and simultaneously, over one hundred thousand dollars was withdrawn consecutively for three years from his trust. In the spring of 2001, the land held by his trust was sold by Chuck. Kate was alarmed that he agreed to sell the property that was giving him extra annual income. In the presence of Gordon, he telephoned Chuck and asked whether the land had been sold. Chuck confirmed during the phone conversation that it had been sold. Kate remembered her dad's silence, and he did not mention it again to either Kate or Gordon.

Almost two years had passed since the sale of her parents' set-aside land, Kate sat at the kitchen table with her dad and had a conversation about his money. By this time, she realized a sizeable amount had been withdrawn from his trust for Chuck's benefit. She knew he had also made loans to other siblings after her mother's death. Kate was concerned about the constant transfers of funds from his trust to the joint checking account he held with Chuck. She said, "You may need more money as you age because of medical expenses, or you may need to go to a home." It was after this conversation that their relationship turned decisively negative. She believed her dad's increasing acrimony was caused by Chuck's efforts to turn him against her and remove her influence. At that time, Kate was increasingly concerned about funds being withdrawn from his trust and deposited to his local Lloyd's checking account because she thought all income and expenses should be from his trust, for proper accounting and oversight.

During the fall of 2004, her dad became increasingly difficult to talk to. From 2004 to the time he transferred the accounts, March of 2007, he repeatedly hung up the phone on her and often called her a "b—." This corresponded to the time that he complained about her as a child, teenager, and adult. He continued to spend his winters at the desert home.

Her dad enjoyed Thanksgiving 2005 with her family in the California desert as he had done the previous nine years. The following year, he stayed in Minnesota. Her dad traveled to the West Coast and resided there during the winter of 2006 with his companion, Gwen, at her desert home. Kate appreciated his new arrangement because her dad had become unbearably mean and unpleasant to be around, refusing to give her any explanation for his increased hostility toward her. She had grown tired of his name-calling and his antagonistic behavior. Her dad transferred the trust accounts away from Gordon, three months following November 2006, terminating their twenty-three-year professional relationship.

Gordon was a financial advisor for both the Bertrand and Gloriette trust accounts. Kate had formed her new investment advisory company in the spring of 2005. She had explained to her dad that her business was changing to discretionary—meaning, she was no longer a broker. She explained to him that the trusts would remain with Gordon as his advisor because he was not a discretionary client and she was no longer a licensed stockbroker or registered representative. He was grateful for their recommendations, and together, they had implemented option strategies to accumulate quality stock positions. In Kate's new position, she no longer executed option transactions, which was her dad's method of acquiring securities. At that time, her dad understood he would continue to work with Gordon as he had the past twelve years. She believed it was a positive relationship since they had been amicable toward each other.

Following months of research, she pieced together the sequence of events that led to their estrangement. Her parents' long-term family estate attorney changed firms during 2004. The dissolution of Ken Powler's firm coincided with her dad's initial incidences of belligerence and noncommunication toward her.

Kate believed that Chuck opened his mail, realizing this was his opportunity to figuratively poison Bertrand against Kate while changing the attorney who had counseled her parents' estate and legal affairs for over twenty years. During this time, Bert and Phillip admitted that they witnessed Chuck's constant negative rantings against Kate. They did not know what was behind his plot; however, having witnessed his negative rants against others, they categorized it as his typical behavior. They witnessed Chuck exerting unrelenting pressure on Bertrand to sign the transfer paperwork. Bert repeatedly said to him and Chuck, "So what if

Kate is a b——? What is the relevance? Kate and Gordon are good at what they do and have done well for you. Why are you going to change what has clearly worked to your advantage?" Bert mentioned his hesitation and reluctance to sign the papers that Chuck aggressively shoved in front of him repeatedly, week after week until he eventually signed the transfer forms. After his death, Kate was told that the following statements were often made by Chuck, Ann, and Cybil—that Kate was ungrateful, Kate is a b——, and Kate hates Dad—to anyone who would listen. She did not know this took place on a regular basis, intensifying from the years 2004 to 2007. Beginning the fall of 2004, her dad became cold and dismissive to her. As she pieced together the sequence of events, she realized that Ann had assisted Chuck in turning her dad against her.

Gordon received the "account transfer out" instructions in March 2007. He called his father-in-law and asked why. Bertrand said, "I want to try something different."

Kate called him immediately after Gordon's conversation and asked, "Why are you doing this? You have done very well with our advice. What you are doing is not ethical. You have significant capital gains from our recommendations, and another broker will be compensated for our many years of advice and research. We have not been compensated for our work. What you are doing is wrong!"

Her dad screamed into the telephone, "You are a b——!" He slammed the phone down, simultaneously terminating the connection.

Kate immediately redialed her telephone and asked, "Why are you removing my oversight? I am successor trustee for both trusts. What would Mom say?" Her dad refused to talk to her or answer her questions and again slammed down the telephone, ending their phone call. Kate was distraught because she knew this was a significant change in their relationship, a termination because her dad removed her as his financial overseer. She expected to be compensated for their advice when the securities were eventually sold; now, their years of work were gone.

To her, he was a thief! Immediately, she called Ann, sobbing over the telephone. The years following this incident, she repeatedly questioned Ann, "Why did Dad do this? I don't understand why he would make this drastic change." Ann listened and said nothing. Over the following ten years, Kate brought up the subject to her during their numerous conversations. Later, Ann repeatedly responded, each time saying Kate didn't do anything with the accounts; that's why he transferred them. Kate replied, "That doesn't make sense." Ann repeatedly stated the same response during later conversations about the subject.

Gordon and Kate were not given a credible explanation for the transfer of her parents' trust accounts. She heard more about her dad's reasons nine years later during the petition and discovery process revealed during the estate trust litigation (see "Exponential").

During the years from 2004 to 2007, Kate regularly communicated with Ann. Ann unequivocally knew Kate was both angry, hurt, and concerned about her dad's decision. Ann was aware Kate had tried repeatedly to talk to her dad and that he had called her names and hung up the phone each time she called. The derogatory names he angrily said to her were the names she repeatedly heard nine years later. Chuck had a narrative about her as she realized that he shared it with everyone he knew. Ann never mentioned that her dad regretted how he treated Kate. Ann occasionally said, "Dad is unhappy that he doesn't have a good relationship with some of his children."

Kate repeatedly asked her, "Who is he referring to?"

Ann responded each time, repeating, "Bert, Phillip, or Cybil."

Years passed, and eventually, Kate questioned why Ann had never acted as her advocate. Ann did not talk about their estranged relationship although she knew Kate was hurt and angry by her dad's unjust actions. Ann said nothing. Kate did not understand why her dad no longer valued her advice because it had been extremely profitable to him for many years. Ann's silence told her that he did not want anything to do with her or her family. Ann's silence contributed to Kate's feelings that her dad did not love her as his daughter and was indifferent whether she was in his life or not. Kate lamented many times to Ann about the loss of the relationship and his unjustified treatment. Ann listened; however, she never indicated he was even slightly unhappy about the estrangement. After her dad's death, Kate came to understand the depth of Ann's deceit and her own naiveté when she had confided her feelings so openly to her. Kate had confided to Ann because she seemed closest to their dad and was in a position to understand as she often traveled to Minnesota.

Kate never forgot her dad's cruelty toward her during her childhood. One particular incident haunted her throughout her life. Kate was eleven years old. Her family drove a motor home to the West Coast for a monthlong summer vacation where they visited the national parks and their California cousins. One outing, they picked up their cousins, Aunt Etta, and Uncle Jay in Northern California and drove to Santa Cruz. There was a landmark amusement park right on the Pacific Ocean. Kate remembered the noisy, roaring roller coasters and the excited screams from the park. The families arrived early in the morning with their motor home full of children and adults. Her dad stopped her as each person excitedly exited the bus. "You are not going into the park," he said. "You upset and hurt Chuck. Your punishment is to stay here on these steps for the day." Kate cried for hours. What did she do? Why was she being punished? The end of the sad day finally arrived when the excitedly happy children reminisced about their day. Kate sat in the back of the motor home, sadly staring out the window with tear-stained eyes. She remembered Aunt Etta looking at her with pity. Aunt Etta did not have the confidence to question Bertrand, her cruel brother. Kate recalled sitting on the steps of the motor home as an eleven-year-old girl was equivalent to being stationed in the Disneyland parking lot, forbidden to enter because of an unknown wrong. This particular incident affected her personality. The years following this incident, she often remained a silent observer, purposefully refraining from conversations because of her low self-esteem.

Kate's earliest memory of her dad's cruelty was as a small child sitting in her high chair. She remained in the chair for hours because she did not eat her food. She cried until she fell asleep while her parents and Chuck were out of the house during their usual Sunday walk. She remembered the large cast on her leg when she was three years old. The cast was set to straighten her crooked leg. Her dad angrily complained when she reached her arms toward him and asked him to carry her. He angrily scolded her, saying, "I refuse to carry you because there is no reason you cannot walk." This occurred just prior to moving to their country home. She believed her father did not like her because he did not treat her with kindness during her childhood and teenage years. Years later, as a young teenager, her dad taught her to iron a dress shirt. During one of his instructions, he became irate and beat her on the head and her upper torso with a shirt hanger. He said, "I know you will become pregnant and be a disgrace." Kate did not know why he made this statement because, at the time, she had no interest in boys. Kate believed her dad had a distrust and dislike toward her that she did not understand. He treated Chuck and Ann differently. She accepted this fact; however, inwardly, she desired to create a life different from what she experienced at a young age.

This childhood memory along with many others pushed Kate to mentally accept what happened as one more incident of her dad treating her with unjustified disrespect and injustice. Kate did not know the reasoning behind her dad's belligerence until she had spent months researching the time line. The year following his death, she uncovered what had occurred to cause his anger toward her during those years. Kate diligently worked to develop a good relationship with him especially the years following her college graduation and subsequent move to another state. However, her dad's actions during 2007 supposedly confirmed that he wanted nothing to do with her. She and Gordon gave Bertrand their second home along with their professional advice. They paid for the trips together and enjoyed many holidays. Their acts of kindness, consideration, and love didn't seem to matter. He terminated Kate's position in their family, and he disregarded her professionally. Her dad rejected Kate as an adult, and he made it clear she was not to be part of the last phase of his life.

From the time Kate was a teenager throughout adulthood, she regularly called her parents, wrote letters, and sent Hallmark cards and postcards from her travels. She religiously sent her dad his birthday card and telephoned him with greetings each December 8. She spoke to her parents regularly and always on holidays. She shared stories about her career on the West Coast because her dad seemed to have a genuine interest, and she sensed her dad respected her work ethic. Following his transfer of the trust accounts and his slamming the telephone down on her, she no longer telephoned him or sent him a birthday card for several years.

A spring day during 2009, Kate was driving to work, upset and angry because once again she was thinking about her dad's outrageous actions against her and Gordon. At that moment, she decided she was going to discontinue her daily emotional turmoil, a combination of hurt and anger. Her anger toward her dad was stoked because of his unethical actions; he had financially cheated her as a professional, and she was indignant that he terminated his relationship to her family as her father and children's grandfather. Kate made up her mind to turn off her emotions toward her dad; her pain was great, and her heart toward him was gradually turning to stone. During her lifetime, she had too many memories of his unjust treatment. She realized that her focus had to be directed to her family and business. She was an involved mother of two children, devoted to her family, and was developing her new business as an investment advisor representative. Additionally, their family was in the midst of a large home construction project. Her goal was to conduct her daily life positively.

Four years later, June 2011, Kate saw her dad at a family wedding of Ann's son. Bert drove her dad's car to Arkansas. Her dad was old and frail, and he needed a wheelchair to get around. He could no longer drive and was unable to change his clothes and wore adult diapers. He was indifferent to Kate at the wedding. He did not speak to her and seemed to ignore her entirely. Following that weekend, Kate had a deep sadness within her about what had happened years before.

Kate planned to spend a week in northern Minnesota the month following the wedding. She encouraged Ann to invite her dad to visit. His friend, Nurse Foe, drove him north and tended to him. They spent a week together, enjoying meals, daily concerts, and short-day trip excursions; however, her dad's conversation was minimal. Kate was cordial each time she saw him; however, it was her impression that the time had come and gone for apologies or understanding. By this time, she had accepted their relationship would never be what it had been. She truly believed that he did not care for her as a person or as his daughter. She had a lifetime of memories which supported her belief. No one told her different the last ten years of his life. As the years passed, she sadly accepted that this was the way it was to be, and this remained a deep and sad hurt within her the remaining years of her dad's life.

The following summer 2012, Kate rented a cottage in northern Minnesota for one month. This was the second consecutive summer she had spent in the state. Her dad, Ann, and her son planned a barbecue at her summer cottage rental. While they explored the area and had meals together, she recognized her dad suffered from short-term memory loss and senility because he seemed easily confused and sometimes forgot what he was saying. He had difficulty getting around, needing the assistance of a walker or wheelchair. Kate noticed a decline in his health from the year before. The following summer, 2013, her dad was unable to travel north. Kate and her son had dinner with him at a local restaurant on a nearby lake in Indian Falls. They had minimal conversation which she considered pleasant, focused on her son's activities and the weather. That meal was the last time she saw him before his death.

Years later, Kate resumed occasionally sending him cards for the remainder of his life, always signed, "Love, Kate." Her dad did not send her correspondence or call her from 2005 until the time of his passing,

January of 2016. It was the year following his death, during the eight-hour deposition, that she learned what had transpired to change their relationship for the remainder of his life.

Following her dad's death, her emotions came flooding back. She had one question: "Why?"

Surprisingly, Ann snapped at her after their dad's death. Ann harshly scolded Kate that she should have made up with their dad. Kate thought to herself, *What was I supposed to do when he hung up his telephone after he repeatedly called me a b——?* Ann's comment was deeply hurtful because she had tearfully confided to her what had transpired during their conversations. At that moment, she realized Ann was never her advocate. Ann knew exactly what had occurred, and she fully supported their estrangement.

After his death, Ann said to Kate, "Adrien Van Stern didn't understand what happened between Dad and you." Ann stated to Adrien that their estrangement had to do with a land deal. Adrien was Bertrand's male friend the last four decades of his life. Kate was shocked to hear that Ann's explanation of their estrangement had to do with selling a parcel of farmland that had been part of their parents' estate. After Ann's statement, Kate realized she was part of the scheme to turn her dad against her. She realized that it was in Ann's interest for her to be out of the picture. Ann realized that if Kate was no longer involved in his care or giving him financial guidance, she would take her place. Ann was Chuck's coconspirator in removing Kate from the trust's oversight. She was always excluded to events that involved her dad and her siblings. Chuck and Ann had a narrative about Kate and repeated it behind her back for years.

Kate was not close to Ann during her childhood because she was always sneaking into her bedroom and taking her clothing, candy, and money she had saved. If something was missing, she eventually discovered that Ann had absconded with it. As a teenager, Kate called

Ann a tattletale and actively ignored and avoided her.

Kate recalled an incident when she was a high school senior, seventeen years old. She was driving Ann, a sophomore, home from school using the family van. Kate drove out the back parking lot and turned left onto the road behind the school; it was a cold winter day as she was driving the remote, rough, gravel road. The road sharply turned left at the top of a hill. As she made the required forty-five-degree turn, the tires hit a patch of ice with increasing downhill speed. As Kate slammed her foot to the brakes, the van slid sideways, coming to a stop only after driving into the ditch and hitting a lone sapling on the other side of the road. Ann jumped out of the car and ran to the front of the van stepping in the snowbank to survey the damage. Kate was relieved it was minor, although she was upset and shaken having just experienced her first automobile accident. The car was pulled out of the ditch and was drivable. Eventually, her parents arrived at the scene. Immediately, Ann began bawling and complaining loudly that she had hurt her leg. She was limping around and crying loudly. She told others that Kate was driving fast, and Kate almost killed her by her reckless driving. The following week, her family drove to northwest Iowa to visit their relatives. At the time, Kate had nine uncles and aunts and many cousins living in northwest Iowa. While visiting each family, Ann hobbled around and loudly exclaimed that her injuries were caused by Kate's reckless fast driving. She exaggerated her pain by limping and crying each time she told her story while Kate remained silent. She was disgusted by Ann's continuous attempts to discredit her in front of her relatives. Kate was embarrassed, and she was angry with her exaggerations and her purposefulness in demeaning her. She witnessed Ann running, skipping, jumping, and laughing when others were not watching. A couple of months after this incidence, Kate left their home, attended college, and had minimal contact with her for the following decade. Ann was married and began her large family. Once Ann had three children, Kate visited the Arkansas family. She forgave and completely forgot about this incident and Ann's childhood manipulations because she was interested in her nieces and nephews and assumed Ann had outgrown her tattletale and childish behavior.

During the months following her dad's passing, she realized Ann harbored envy and resentment toward her because of the things she said about Kate behind her back that were later told to her by Bert, Phillip, and her cousins. During Kate's childhood and teenage years, she was aware Ann often excitedly blurted stories to her parents to discredit Kate. As an adult, she realized that Chuck operated similarly, trying to discredit her by telling ugly tales about her. By her early fifties, she realized Chuck was untrustworthy and a backstabber. The year following her dad's passing, she realized that Ann and Chuck had spent their entire life going behind her back to turn her parents and her other siblings against her. Her mother had mentioned their devious attempts as a teenager. During those years, she had no interest in their manipulative behavior because she was focused on her education, career, and her personal goals. Both Ann and Chuck badmouthed Kate as children, and she recalled being angrily questioned by her dad about incidences that were told to him by either Chuck or Ann. This happened repeatedly during her years living at their Valley Egypt home. Kate realized the extent and the damage of their lifelong manipulation after her dad's passing.

Ann went to a music academy during her senior year of high school while Kate was completing her college degree. Once she received her degree, Kate moved to the West Coast. Chuck was working on the farm while her parents supported his lifestyle and his family. Ann later attended one year of university, married, and moved to Arkansas. Cybil, Bert, and Phillip were fifteen, fourteen, and ten. Kate turned twenty-one years during the first summer she spent in California.

Chuck often repeated the following trite phrase, "Keep your friends close and your enemies closer" (a quote from the character Michael Corleone of *The Godfather Part II*). Kate believed Ann took this phrase to heart and worked diligently to make sure Kate believed that she was her ally.

For those who knew Ann superficially, she was considered a sympathetic figure. She had eleven children and many grandchildren. This was relevant because she had incessantly instructed her children to be kind and thoughtful to one another. Kate realized she taught her children to do as she said, not as she did. Ann was elaborate in her demonstrations of unselfish giving to her family and relatives. Kate did not imagine she was conspiring against her until after the death of her dad. She realized that Ann's devious and manipulative actions the year following his death revealed her true nature.

Kate wrote a tribute she had planned to read for her dad's funeral service. They had spent many holidays together. Her parents—and later her dad—traveled with Gordon and Kate. She fondly remembered the good times and gradually realized what happened to her dad after the death of Gloriette. Chuck instructed the minister that Kate was not allowed to be a part of his service. Despite Chuck's interference, she went to the podium and read her tribute to him, honoring his life. Their estrangement caused a deep emotional hurt which she experienced only after his death, prompting her to deliver his eulogy. At the end of the tribute, Kate thanked Chuck, Ann, and their families for taking care of him during his final years. The year following his death, Kate realized that appearances are not always what they seem.

After his death, Kate was told that the house which was owned by her mother's irrevocable trust had been sold or given to Chuck years before. Kate explained to Ann this was not their parents' plan. "Why didn't Chuck and Mildred purchase the house from the estate? It was to go to their six children equally," Kate pointedly asked Ann. Ann took charge of cleaning out Gloriette's house. Kate told her repeatedly that the possessions of their parents were to be equally divided among their children.

Ann stated, "The remaining contents will go to the grandchildren."

Kate said to Ann, "You must talk to each sibling, and they may distribute to their children if they choose to." Ann ignored her instructions. Kate was not included in her siblings' meeting after his funeral. Although she briefly stopped by her mother's house after her dad was buried at the cemetery, she had not been welcome years before because of her dad's harsh treatment toward her. During the brief time after the burial, Ann tersely told Kate who was getting their parents' remaining personal property there were six antique rockers acquired over their lifetime and there was one for each child; several were over one hundred years old. Kate mentioned that she would like to have one of the antique rockers.

Ann stated, "They are taken." Ann stated that she and Chuck had taken the majority of the home furnishings. Kate had given her parents household gifts over their lifetime. Ann stated everything else was given to her and Chuck's children. Bert's, Phillip's, and Kate's children did not receive any of their parents' furniture or possessions that had remained in the home. It was Kate's opinion that Ann was disrespectful of their parents' legacy by her selfish handling of their tangible property during her father's life and after his passing.

Ann adamantly stated that Bertrand wanted Chuck to have their mother's house because he wanted to keep the house in the family. She said to Kate, "I'm happy with everything I got."

At that time, Kate thought her statement was odd. Her parents had legal documents which involved six children. "Why was the estate execution completely different than what was spelled out years before? What about our mother's legacy? Was it to be disregarded?" Kate asked repeatedly to anyone who would listen. Kate was dismayed by Ann's treatment of her younger brothers. She ordered Bert and Phillip to pick something from the house. "They are our parents' children too!" Kate stated emphatically.

The actions of Chuck and Ann before, during, and after the funeral raised figurative red flags. Their actions were incongruent. Kate was determined to understand what happened between her and her dad. She wanted to understand what happened to her parents' estate plans and why they were changed the last years of his life.

The months following the funeral, Kate researched years of records. During this time, she received verbal and written attacks from Ann. She did not want Kate to question Chuck. Ann's repeated acerbic statement was "Everything is as Dad wanted it." Ann repeatedly stated, "Chuck stayed and cared for Dad, and he deserves to get everything." Kate wondered why Ann didn't instruct her parents not to bother setting up an estate plan because she planned to get their assets at the end of their lives. Kate realized Ann resented her parents' naming her as successor trustee. She believed that Ann harbored animosity toward her and conspired with Chuck over many years to eliminate her legal authority. Kate believed they did what they could to eliminate her financial position in their family. They disregarded the terms of their parents' trusts and schemed to transfer assets from the trusts to their possession. The estate plan and trust documents were changed during the final years of her dad's long life.

Ann told Kate repeatedly that her dad was happy with his new financial advisor. After reviewing ten years of monthly brokerage statements, Kate realized that her dad did not have a professional relationship with the person designated as his registered representative and broker of the trust accounts. Her dad did not transact business as he had the past twenty-three years. Furthermore, he did not execute another stock option transaction with his new broker. An important aspect of his life was watching current events and tracking his stock portfolio. During the decades Kate and her dad worked together, they had weekly conversations discussing the financial markets, politics, and current events. Fred Schafte was a bond broker, touted his fixed income expertise, and self-proclaimed that he did not follow the stock market for investment purposes. They transferred the trusts to a person who was not licensed or qualified to execute the sophisticated stock option strategies he had previously used exclusively to purchase securities. In hindsight, the strategies used the prior twenty-three years acquired the several of the best dividend growth securities to have owned over the following twenty years. Fred Schafte gradually churned highly appreciated dividend growth securities into illiquid, thinly traded bonds at a high cost, cannibalizing the accounts over time. In addition to Chuck's and Ann's principal withdrawals, the results the following ten years were destructive to her dad's wealth, and funds meant for his care dissipated. Kate confronted Leonard and Ann about what she discovered three months following the funeral. Leonard and Ann closely followed everything her dad did the last ten years of his life. Kate directly asked, "Did you know Dad's broker was not licensed to transact business as he had with us for twenty-three years? Did you know he was a bond broker? Why didn't you tell me he was unhappy that we were no longer part of his life? Did you know he was no longer following the stock market?" Ann and Leonard refused to answer any questions and ignored Kate's repeated questions.

After his death, Ann admitted that Chuck turned their dad against her during a time period she had tried to persuade him to move to Arkansas. Ann told Kate that her dad hung the phone up on her and refused to talk to her for some time. Ann failed to mention this information to Kate before. Ann told Kate that Leonard wondered if Chuck's pressure to transfer accounts from her and Gordon's oversight was an effort to confiscate his money and purchase houses for each of his children. In the presence of Kate, neither Ann or Leonard questioned the termination of Kate and Gordon's professional relationship and resulting estrangement during the ten years leading up to his death.

Leonard made an insincere and crafty attempt to show interest in their estrangement after her dad's service. Leonard pretended he had no idea of the issue and stated so directly to Kate. She hadn't suspected that self-proclaimed, apathetic Leonard was a coconspirator with his wife, absconding her parents' assets under a cloak of self-sacrificing righteousness. Leonard had a pious demeanor and often walked around with his Bible tucked underneath his right arm. Their actions following the funeral and the following year were desperate and vicious toward

Kate, Bert, and Phillip.

Ann and Leonard seemed closest to her dad, spending weeks at a time with him. Leonard drove him to California and Minnesota on numerous occasions. Ann often drove him to Iowa or Minnesota. Kate asked why they never questioned the change in their relationship, his reasoning, and not extending any effort to repair their broken relationship. Kate wondered why they did not question her dad about the credentials of his new broker in Minnesota compared to Gordon's experience, professional record, and accolades. Kate asked pertinent questions repeatedly, receiving silence in return.

In hindsight, Kate realized that Ann and Leonard spent a tremendous amount of one-on-one time with him the last ten years of his life. Both Ann and Leonard knew Kate was unhappy about the estrangement. Kate realized that Ann knew Chuck pressured her dad to transfer their trust accounts away from Gordon's oversight. Ann was purposeful in not disclosing the truth to either Kate or Gordon. Kate confronted Ann after five months of reviewing trust documents and ten years of brokerage statements. Ann blurted, "Yes, I knew, but I never said anything bad about you!" Ann's silence allowed her to be placed in a position of power along with Chuck. During the last nine years of her dad's life, Ann traveled to Minnesota numerous times. Each trip, she departed with a van full of their parents' possessions. She received money for family trips, her children's education, home construction projects, and music lessons and expensive musical instruments that included two five-thousand-dollar harps. After reviewing twenty years of brokerage statements and many years of bank statements, she concluded Ann never visited her dad without leaving his house with a check in her pocket, usually thousands of dollars.

Ann persuaded her dad to name her as primary beneficiary to the life insurance her parents purchased for each child equally. Kate's parents bought these policies over twenty years before her mother's passing. After her mother's death, the policies were changed, giving half of the policy proceeds to Ann and the remaining amount divided among six children. Over 50 percent of the policies went solely to Ann. Kate knew that her mother would have been adamantly opposed to changing the beneficiary to one child because she told Kate that she wanted each child given equal treatment in regards to the division of her property. Ann persuaded her dad to sign the beneficiary change document less than one month following her mom's passing. Kate had the original policy information and realized what had transpired. She confronted Ann, "Why weren't the changes honestly disclosed?" Ann's response was silence. Kate, Bert, and Phillip believed that Ann should have been transparent about her actions and the change to the insurance policies that she manipulated her dad to sign. As the history of events unfolded, Kate realized Ann knew that she would have questioned her actions had she been aware of the extent of her extraction of assets. Ann knew that Kate would have tried to prevent her from taking advantage of her dad financially.

Kate carefully reviewed the trust accounting the months following his funeral. Chuck did not telephone or e-mail Kate. Her questions remained unanswered. At that time, her option was to file legal petitions. She told Stone and Napp that she was interested in mediation. They told her that Chuck could not be compelled to cooperate with the process without filing a legal petition. It was apparent to Kate that Chuck was not going to cooperate because he refused to answer her questions regarding all the changes. He did not answer her telephone calls, and he actively avoided any attempts to discuss the numerous discrepancies. Six months after her dad was buried, Kate filed petitions for her parents' trusts. Although Kate had nothing to do with the date the petitions were filed with the court, the official court filing date of the legal documents was June 16, 2016, nineteen years to the day of the death of her mother.

The months following Kate's court petition filings, she received numerous caustic letters and texts from Ann. Another name for her correspondence was hate mail. Ann emphatically stated to Kate that she was wrong to sue Chuck because she was breaking up their family and holding up the estate and causing shame to their parents' memory.

Kate chose not to respond to her accusations and went forward trying to initiate a process that would provide transparency to the estate settlement process. She believed that Ann had no reason to be objective and no interest in considering the facts. Kate believed she was acting properly and conducting herself as a proper, ethical successor trustee. Ann tried to pretend their parents had no plan and sanctioned the wrong actions of Chuck and his corrupt dealings as the co-trustee of the two trusts after the death of her mother. Kate did not file petitions for herself but for all the beneficiaries, each one of her siblings. Most importantly, Kate believed she was honoring her parents' legacy. It was evident that her younger brothers were not being represented by the process. Kate knew her parents intended her younger brothers to inherit something of what was left because they had expressed that intent to her years before. She believed she had an obligation to represent her younger brothers because it was immediately apparent that they were being dismissed and ignored as children of her parents.

Up until the first mediation and later prior to their second mediation, Ann actively worked to discredit Kate's petitions. Kate talked to one of her dad's long-time friends, Nurse Foe, following her dad's funeral service. During a long conversation, Nurse Foe gave Kate anecdotal stories which convinced her that her dad was afraid of Chuck. Nurse Foe stated to Kate that Bertrand was afraid of Chuck; he did what Chuck told him. Chuck shoved papers in front of him and told him to sign. Bertrand needed Chuck's approval for everything. Nurse Foe told Kate that she stopped by the evening of January 12, 2012, and found him extremely upset. She asked him, "Doc, did you do something that wasn't supposed to be done?" He nodded his head yes, affirming a nonverbal yes. He told her it had to do with Gloriette's house being sold. He told her that the house wasn't to be sold during his lifetime. During the settlement process, Nurse Foe gave a notarized affidavit. She stated, "It was clear to me during the two occasions I met Kate that she was cold to her dad and demanded more of him than he was physically capable of." Nurse Foe stated, "He wanted to give the two houses and the remaining land to Chuck. Kate and her dad had a negative relationship. She stated that she was certain Bertrand would be embarrassed and ashamed by Kate's actions." Her statement was almost identical to statements Ann made in her affidavit during the time their affidavits were submitted to the court. Kate wondered why she altered what she told her. Nurse Foe did not know Kate. Kate wondered what Chuck and Ann had on her. Other than their long conversation after her dad's funeral, Kate had not had a one-on-one conversation with Nurse Foe the two brief times she met her during the four years prior to her dad's passing. Bert mentioned that Nurse Foe had made a strange comment to him years before his death. Nurse Foe asked Bert, "Who are the players in this family?" At the time, Bert thought her comment was bizarre. Upon reflection, Bert said that Nurse Foe had to have known that he was being manipulated for monetary gain.

Ann worked tirelessly to discredit Kate during the petition, mediation, and settlement process. Kate was taken off the Christmas card list by all of Ann's children and many relatives. Kate was shunned. Kate was shocked that her relatives readily aligned themselves with Chuck and Ann. Phillip explained to her that Chuck had spent years disparaging her, and they believed his repetitious narrative about her.

Kate did not understand why Ann refused to let the legal process unfold without manipulating and pressuring named witnesses. The only explanation she could think of was that Ann did not want the truth disclosed.

Kate, Ann, Chuck

PETITIONS AND MEDIATION

Kate was interested in using the process of mediation to settle her charges against Chuck and plainly stated her intention to attorneys, Stone and Napp. Mr. Stone explained to Kate the potential "statute of limitation" arguments which may arise and advised starting the proceeding by petition. A petition is a legal document which starts a legal process. Without a legal court process, there was no reason for Chuck to cooperate and supply the documents needed to provide transparency regarding her parents' estate distribution. Essentially, if a court petition was not filed, Chuck could decline to answer questions, decline to provide documents, and let the statute of limitations time run out.

Kate spent three months researching and acquiring documentation which supported her claims to submit a compelling legal petition to the court. This process required Chuck to respond to the methodically organized and documented claims. The *discovery phase* required additional research, documents, and responses and followed the filing of her two petitions. Five months into the legal process, Chuck's response to Kate's petitions was his filing of counterclaims followed by interrogatories. An interrogatory is a list of questions one party sends to another as part of the discovery process. The interrogatories are followed by witness lists, signed statements by select witnesses, affidavits, and deposition requests. A deposition is a written record of oral testimony used for discovery evidence and potentially for court testimony. Chuck's responses to Kate's petitions was mentally exhausting because it was a transparent attempt to avoid responding to her questions and claims. He actively avoided providing documentation that had been requested, specifically proof that he made land payments for 12100 and 12200 Valley Egypt legal contracts. His outright refusal and avoidance to provide documents convinced Kate that they were using stall tactics, hoping she would give up and go away because of her mounting legal expenses.

After her father's death and just prior to his funeral, Kate called Nash with questions about the newer amendments to her dad's trust. Immediately, Finn Nash turned her parents' estate file over to a fellow attorney, Mabel Snatt. Kate believed he turned the case over because he realized the trust changes he had implemented were going to be challenged by her. Several hundred thousand dollars were spent following her dad's death because of Finn Nash's work, executed under Chuck's direction. Five months after Kate's petitions were filed, Mabel Snatt turned the case over to their pit bull attorney, Mr. Morse. Mr. Morse was an expert paper generator. Kate's petitions were countered with Mr. Morse's numerous legal filings, which stated that she had no rights under the statute of limitation legal definition. Subsequent egregious legal expense could be attributed to the trustee Chuck and Finn Nash, the attorney listed on the paperwork. Ann vocally and unequivocally supported Chuck and Nash and disparaged Kate for questioning Chuck's actions. Bertrand was eighty years old, did not drive, read, couldn't operate a phone or TV remote, and suffered from severe depression and loneliness; and he did not sign one of the numerous checks written to Chuck's law firm. One year passed since the legal petitions had been filed and Kate was incensed that nothing had been accomplished other than increasing legal bills which depleted her savings. Why weren't any of the trust beneficiaries informed of the changes made? Chuck and Mildred were the financial beneficiaries of the new amendments, and they were solely aware of the changes to the legal estate documents. If her dad's intention was for Chuck to receive his entire estate, why hadn't they all been informed that this was his intent? Why the secrecy and nondisclosure? Kate asked these questions to deaf ears.

As of November 2016, Chuck successfully avoided responding

to every one of Kate's questions and claims as stated in her petitions. Previously, Kate requested authorization to receive the joint checking account bank statements. Eventually, her request was granted by the judge; however, his authorization was met with more objections by Chuck's newest attorney, Mr. Morse. The legal documents confirmed Finn Nash of Cheetham, Steele and Morse LLP was Chuck's attorney since 2005 and was responsible for drafting new amendments to her dad's trust.

His legal work and the documents he generated completely changed her parents' estate covering the last ten years of his life. The legal documents drafted by Finn Nash were signed after her dad had turned eighty years old. Gloriette, Bertrand's wife of forty-eight years, had passed eleven years earlier. The condition of her dad's health did not stop Mr. Nash from drafting new amendments altering the parents' estate plan from what they had intentionally put in place when they were healthy and of sound mind.

Kate was told by Ann one week before his funeral that Bertrand's long-serving estate attorney, Ken Powler, was replaced by Finn Nash. Finn Nash worked for Cheetham, Steele and Morse LLP. Kate called Chuck and asked why Ken Powler was removed as their parents' estate attorney. Chuck stammered and said, "I'm not going to get into it with you!" He ended his phone call with her. This was the last conversation Kate had with Chuck during the entire legal process. Chuck told Bert that Bertrand and Ken Powler got into a "knock-down-dragout fight," and their dad terminated their relationship. Chuck told Ann a different variation of the story. Kate had spoken to Ken Powler in the past and had sent financial and legal correspondence back and forth to him after her mother's death. She had spoken to him during the time they were separating securities into the two trusts and during the time the second amendment was drafted, which was early two thousands. Kate knew he was a kind man because her mother had trust in him because of conversations which had given her confidence that her estate would be handled properly. Chuck refused to give Kate the information she asked for, and Mr. Morse made increasingly slanderous statements in the legal documents, defending Chuck, causing Kate to conclude that Chuck had orchestrated the changes. She examined ten years of her dad's cleared checks payable to Cheetham, Steele and Morse LLP, signed by Chuck. Kate believed Chuck coerced her dad to change his attorney to Finn Nash.

An important aspect of Kate's petition claims was that there was a lack of mental capacity to make the legal changes along with Chuck's undue influence on her dad to make the many changes. A presumption of undue influence arises when (1) there exists a confidential or fiduciary relationship between a grantor and a fiduciary; (2) the fiduciary or an interest that he represents benefits from a transaction; and (3) the fiduciary has an opportunity to influence a grantor's decision in the transaction (see "References").

The two opposing attorneys agreed to use Jacob Broader as the mediator. The mediation date was set for November 22, coincidentally Chuck's sixty-second birthday. The mediator was respected by both sides—Cheetham, Steele and Morse LLP and Wright, Coolidge and Stone PC. Kate hoped they were close to reaching an agreement because she had provided all documentation that her claims were backed by facts. Chuck had not provided any evidence to support his defense that he had made the payments and had acted as a proper trustee. Mr. Morse scheduled a court date for the end of December. If the mediation was unsuccessful, their case would proceed directly to court. Kate was informed by Jack Napp that if the case proceeded to court, additional depositions would be required, and his estimated cost was an additional three hundred thousand dollars.

Kate's legal bills increased each month. She was aghast as she opened her October bill which included her attorney's preparation for their November mediation. The case took time from her business and personal life, causing her periodic nausea, headaches, and insomnia when she thought of Chuck's and Ann's betrayal and deceit. She realized the abusive treatment her dad had endured under their care while they transferred his financial assets to themselves. Kate recognized that they each partitioned him from his other children by their slanderous statements and manipulation. They were both physically and emotionally abusive to their dad, and they prevented him from receiving the care he deserved by a competent care facility.

Kate researched the meaning of *financial elder abuse* and realized Chuck's and Ann's actions were textbook examples. Chuck stated the estate was rightfully his, and he gave him no option but to remain a prisoner in his own home. Her dad was dependent on Chuck who forced him to change legal documents. Chuck was relentless in his pursuit to have transfer paperwork signed, and he did not stop until everything was signed. Phillip said he witnessed Chuck standing over their dad until he signed documents being shoved into his hands. Chuck stated that he despised his father and complained to Ann about his work as caregiver. Ann had failed to mention this to Kate over the years before her dad's death. Bert and Phillip mentioned the vulgar slang name he routinely called their dad. Chuck's scheme was elaborate, complicated, and executed over many years; he was doing whatever he needed to ensure his long-term plan wasn't thwarted, and his aggressive legal tactics to get Kate to go away confirmed his intent.

Kate questioned why changes were made in the figurative dark of night with no sibling informed of the alterations to the trust documents with transactions affecting everyone. Ann worked with Chuck to ensure she would get her share. She remarked to one of the assisted-living clerks at the home when she removed Bertrand, "I want to get the money that is going to Maybrook."

The documents and statements made by others confirmed that her dad was bullied, threatened, and demeaned by Chuck. Kate listened to Phillip's accounts of what went on during the time when he lived in the basement. Conversations with different people revealed that her dad was afraid of Chuck. Ann told Kate that her dad was restless and tormented in his last years because of changes made to documents. Kate questioned her comments; however, Ann's statements were vague, and Kate didn't really know which documents.

Bertrand mentioned to Phillip that he was forced to sign papers transferring his assets. He said, "I am in no position to do anything about it, and I have to accept what has been done."

During the spring of 2017, Aunt Janelle told Kate about a visit she had with Bertrand during 2013, repeating their conversation, during which he told her, "Chuck will get Gloriette's house because Chuck is taking care of me." Chuck effectively brainwashed and manipulated him into thinking he had to do what Chuck told him to do. He believed no one would bring him food or take him out occasionally unless he followed Chuck's instructions.

Kate's dad talked about going to a retirement home in Indian Falls by the river already when Kate was a young girl. Kate recalled him talking about his future plans several times at the dinner table. Her dad mentioned living by the river, looking out at the falls, and living in an active and growing city, smiling at the idea. Bertrand was a social person; he enjoyed being around people. Prior to his retirement, he often said, "I would like to work at Disneyland as a street sweeper. I think that would be a fun job around lots of people every day." Kate surmised he made the statement as a sharp contrast to the high-pressure, stressful work he experienced as a general surgeon. Kate realized that if her dad moved to the assisted-living home before he became an invalid, he would have been happier because he would have received the proper care required by an aging person.

"Did he want to be home alone?" Kate asked Bert. Bertrand's trust generated enough dividend income to pay for the highest-quality assisted-living care available in Indian Falls after following his increasing dividend assessments during 1998 and 1999. Kate told Bert that he could have had around-the-clock care with his portfolio income. Instead, he was confined to a dark, cold house because he was told he could no longer afford the assisted care home. He was dependent on Mildred to drop off his food. "Did she sit and talk to him? Did she spend any time with him?" Kate asked Bert and Phillip.

"No, she did not. Mildred dropped off his food and left," Bert replied.

Chuck came in the morning to write checks from his checkbook. "Chuck was negative and abusive to him," stated Phillip's affidavit. The affidavits from Chuck, Ann, Mildred, and Nurse Foe stated, "Mildred brought Dad nutritious meals."

During her 2013 visit with Bertrand, Aunt Janelle was alarmed by what she witnessed and later said to Kate, "He should not be left alone. He cannot get up on his own or dress himself."

Kate telephoned Ann to discuss Aunt Janelle's concerns. Ann stated emphatically that he was fine and he was happy. Ann convinced Kate that he was where he wanted to be and was receiving proper care. As long as he was at home, his costs were minimal as Chuck used his monthly income to pay for his personal expenses and lifestyle. Kate realized the low cost of his care after reviewing years of bank records. For all appearances, Chuck and Ann were taking good care of him. Ann said to Kate, "Dad is happy. He likes his new financial advisor, and he says he is very happy with the new arrangement." Kate confessed that she did not believe they were capable of doing anything other than making sure he was receiving proper care and treatment.

In hindsight, Kate wondered why her dad wasn't admitted to Maybrook years before, after his second hip surgery. Kate visited her dad's sister, Aunt Etta, in California during December 2011. Aunt Etta did not speak to Kate; however, she appeared to recognize her. Aunt Etta lived in a nice retirement home, and it was observable to Kate that she was well cared for by the staff and her large family, particularly her daughter who lived close by. Kate sent a picture of her visit with Aunt Etta to her dad along with her personal December 2011 letter she had mailed to him. Additionally, Kate visited her uncles and Aunt Irma during August 2013 at their assisted-living home in northwest Iowa. Interestingly, Bertrand's youngest brother rarely spoke as he aged. He was known as a man of few words during his lifetime. A common characteristic of each sibling was a quiet personality, speaking few words. Bertrand's conversations became more limited as he aged (see "The Last Chapter"). They were of Dutch heritage; a quiet disposition was considered an elderly Dutch personality trait.

Kate thought back to their conversation regarding the handling of the trust accounts. Her dad nodded his head and said little, and she had assumed he was in agreement with her. Bert often spent Sunday afternoons peppering him with questions while receiving stares and silence in return. Bert was a music volunteer for Maybrook, mentioning that it was a five-star hotel compared to the Iowa home where his uncles and aunt lived. Several of Bertrand's lifelong neighbors and doctors who he had professional referral relationships with lived at Maybrook. Kate did not understand why Chuck and Ann made the decision for their dad to live alone in a cold house instead of an active assisted-care home where he would have professional care and social interaction. Kate reviewed his extensive medical records which covered a period of ten years.

Her dad's care was planned according to Chuck's and Ann's scheme, and they both refused to cooperate with the document requests. Ann had all of Bertrand's tax returns, bank statements, and trust documents and adamantly declined to give any to Kate. Chuck would not supply any documents until he was forced by court order to turn over the most recent five years of bank statements, but this required five months of legal expenses.

As of November 2006, Bertrand's trust portfolio generated enough income to easily support the monthly expenditures required by a first-class facility. Furthermore, the dividend income was increasing each year before the assets were transferred and eventually sold by their self-interested broker, decimating his trust income from 2011 to the time of his death. The third petition charge was Chuck's breach of fiduciary duty.

> Fiduciary duty is the obligation the trustee owes to the beneficiaries, undivided loyalty and impartiality.[12] expenses. As of November 2006, Bertrand's trust portfolio generated enough income to easily support the monthly expenditures required by a first-class facility. Furthermore, the dividend income was increasing each year before the assets were transferred and eventually sold by their self-interested broker, decimating his trust income from 2011 to the time of his death. The third petition charge was Chuck's breach of fiduciary duty. Fiduciary duty is the obligation the trustee owes to the beneficiaries, undivided loyalty and impartiality..[13]

Chuck breached his duties as a fiduciary. The trusts were damaged by his actions. The foundation of Kate's petition against Chuck was Bertrand's lack of mental capacity, Chuck's influence, and his breach of fiduciary duty as trustee of the trusts.

Chuck became enraged when Bertrand talked of his bowel complaints and berated him in front of others when he had an accident. Phillip witnessed Chuck's verbal abuse toward him regarding his irregularity and witnessed him crying after Chuck's repeated humiliations. Bertrand said to Phillip, "What can I do? I am just a child." He repeatedly said, "I am just a child."

Often, Chuck was irate and complained to Bert, "I am dealing with a child." Bertrand confused his telephone handset with his television remote control. He tried to make telephone calls with his television remote control device. Bertrand's age and dementia were apparent; his poor vision along with the normal loss of fine motor skills made using

---

12   From the state of [redacted] in the probate court for the written petition by the law firm hired to represent the successor trustee of the mother's irrevocable trust.

13   See note 12 above.

both the phone and remote impossible. He was not allowed to have a fire in his fireplace because he had come too close to starting a house fire more than once. Chuck and Ann had access to their dad's medical and financial records and did not discuss them with any of their siblings.

Bert mentioned to Chuck that he would help pay for Bertrand's care in an assisted-living home. Bert asked Chuck, "Why don't you put him into a professional care facility?"

Chuck responded, "I want to do it." Chuck was often exasperated, complaining of having to care for his dad; however, he did not want to relinquish any control. Chuck appeared to others to be the long-suffering and dutiful son.

Chuck called Bert to check on his dad regularly. "Will you go check on Dad? He fell down and cannot get up."

Kate asked Bert, "How did you know he fell if Dad was unable to use the phone?"

Bert told her that he had not thought about that question before. "I did what was asked of me. Even though I saw Chuck beat Phillip, Theodore, and torture animals throughout my life, I did not consider any physical actions toward Dad until you brought it up. I was naive and trusting," Bert sadly replied.

The petitions were filed in June 2016; eventually, their mediation was scheduled during November 2016. Kate was tired of the entire legal process and wanted it to end. She was shocked by the increasing monthly cost. Unknown to her at the time, the legal process would continue for eight more months, and each month, she was presented with a new legal bill. At the time, she thought Chuck was in financial trouble, as he has been in for decades. She had seen his credit report the spring of 2007 and was aware of his reliance on credit cards and revolving debt. After the conclusion of the case, following the second mediation, April 2017, Kate realized her assumptions had been incorrect because he had a high credit score and he no longer had any credit card debt.

Kate realized any settlement would entail forgiveness of what would have been the inheritance because the market value of the trusts had been significantly depleted from what it had been ten years before. Chuck's land contracts had been restated, erasing hundreds of thousands of dollars owed to the Gloriette trust, and it all made a complicated record for the average person to comprehend. Kate lost interest in spending more money to take the case to court, and she assumed Chuck didn't have the money to restore the trusts to amounts they should have been worth under proper oversight and guidance. The money was gone. Unfortunately, two of the assets had been confiscated; the land contracts were improperly handled, and her mother's house had been transferred to Chuck and Mildred without payment to the trust. Kate's intent was for Chuck to be held accountable for the two transparent self-dealing transactions as trustee. Kate telephoned Chuck, hoping to reach an agreement prior to their mediation date. She had spent significantly more money than she thought would be needed to expose Chuck's self-dealing and theft from the trusts. She knew another two months would add thirty thousand dollars to eighty thousand dollars or more to her legal bills. Additionally, she had invested her time accounting for the trust's transactions at a significant personal and professional cost.

She telephoned Chuck. His cellular phone rang twenty times. She left a message on his voice mail, "Hey, Chuck, we have mediation next week. Let's come to an agreement." She did not receive a return call. The next day, she left another phone message. This time, the call went directly to his voice mail. She realized that Chuck would not answer her calls, so she wrote him an e-mail, stating he would be responsible for the legal fees and attached her October bill to his e-mail, a bill in excess of twenty thousand dollars.

The next day, she e-mailed him an article which clearly defined financial elder abuse. The article described Chuck's actions toward his dad. The following day, Kate sent Chuck a picture of one of the farm doors with the name 4B. 4B stood for the name of the farm: 3 brothers and Bertrand. Kate's intent in sending him sequential e-mails was to coax him to negotiate with her. The following day, she received an e-mail from Jack Napp stating that she was not to contact Chuck. Soon after, she received a legal document from Chuck's attorney accusing her of harassing Chuck. The document stated, "Kate's voice messages and e-mails show her extreme level of paranoia. Kate's hatred of Dad and of me is evident." Kate realized her mistake telephoning and e-mailing Chuck, urging him to reach a compromise with her.

Bertrand's bank and brokerage statements were evidence that Chuck and Ann financially manipulated him for nineteen years following Gloriette's death. To friends, acquaintances, and relatives, Ann and Chuck appeared to deserve everything. After all, they told relatives and friends they had sacrificed themselves caring for their dad. Sadly, Bertrand's medical records stated he was lonely, depressed, and crying. Kate recalled her conversation with Ann two months after she had moved her dad from Maybrook to her home in Arkansas and stated that she could no longer care for him, giving Leonard responsibility for her dad's daily care. Ann occasionally took him out in public to show she was a loving and doting daughter. For their service, Ann and Leonard paid themselves the same monthly amount that Maybrook had received for his twenty-four-seven professional care. "Were they able to give him the same level of professional care he received at Maybrook?" Bert asked Kate.

Kate told Bert, "Had he lived at Maybrook the last seven years, he would have had proper care, and his children would have been around him."

Ann did not want his other children around Bertrand. She repeatedly told her children and Phillip, "I want the credit for his care at the end of his life."

Kate carefully read eight years of medical records just prior to the November mediation. Each medical visit, year after year, listed complaints of intense loneliness, isolation, loss of short-term memory, sadness, and frequent crying spells. The medical records stated that her dad did not read after his early 1990 stroke. Bertrand stated to his medical doctor that he was dependent on Chuck and others to read for him. Finally, Kate understood why Chuck was able to have her dad readily sign documents.

Prior to returning to Minnesota, Kate reviewed Chuck's witness list and noticed her ninety-eight-year-old aunt listed. Aunt Irma was Bertrand's oldest sister and his closest confidante. Kate telephoned Aunt Irma, "Did my dad tell you what he wanted done with his estate at his passing?"

She said, "Your dad told me everything was to be divided equally. He didn't want no trouble after he was gone." She verbally lashed, "Why are you taking your brother Chuck's love? You have no business taking your brother's love."

Kate thanked her and said, "Aunt Irma, you have known me my entire life, and you know I am a good person; you have known me my entire life." Kate said goodbye, but as she hung up the telephone, she realized that Aunt Irma had also been poisoned against her.

Prior to boarding the airplane to Indian Falls, Kate was told that several siblings had prepared affidavits and would not attend the mediation. The purpose of the mediation was to reach an agreement among all the siblings, so Kate was disappointed.

Ann's affidavit stated, "Chuck was a loving, dutiful, respectful son. Mildred prepared and delivered nutritious meals." Ann stated, "Dad transferred his accounts away from Kate and Gordon because Kate was mean and said he could no longer stay at their desert home during the winter."

Kate read her claim in a letter from Cybil (see "Sisters II"). "Who said Dad could not stay at our desert place?" Kate asked Gordon. Later, Bert told Kate that Chuck constantly complained about their desert home not being properly set up for their dad to get around and often complained to others that his dad was too old to continue to stay there. No one had ever shared this information with Kate and Gordon, and both Ann and Cybil told others that Kate kicked her dad out of their desert home.

Bertrand's favorite niece, Lydia, told Kate after her dad's death that Bertrand had complained to Lydia of falling by the community pool. Complaining to Lydia, Bertrand stated, "Kate wasn't there to help me after my fall." Lydia was Dan Canfield's sister and Kate's cousin. Kate hadn't heard his complaint before; however, she heard the story repeated by others only after her dad's death. Kate lived one hundred and twenty miles away from where her dad spent his winter months. A conveniently omitted fact was that her dad had a companion staying with him most years her dad resided at Kate and Gordon's desert home. After Gloriette's death, Bertrand shared the home with Doozy, Gwen, and, one winter, Bertrand's sister, Irma. Bertrand said to Lydia, "I am afraid I will lose money with Kate. That is why I transferred the accounts away from her."

After Lydia told Kate what her dad had said years before, Lydia said, "Come on, Kate, you knew what was going on. You know, you were never any fun as a teenager. You were so sullen." Kate was shocked by Lydia's statements. However, after some thought, Kate assumed Lydia meant that Kate deserved the treatment she got because Kate was not a fun and outgoing person. Lydia was four years older than Kate. Lydia went to college in Indian Falls during the time Kate was in high school. Lydia visited with Bertrand and Gloriette during her college breaks because the school was close by. Kate realized that the false statements Bertrand made to others were to justify his hostile actions toward her, which he knew was unjustified. At the time, Kate knew that Chuck was behind Bertrand's actions; regardless, he chose to do what he did. At the time, Kate thought about flying back to Minnesota to confront her dad. However, Kate instinctively felt there were powerful unseen forces against her. Bertrand was irrational, and the reason for his behavior wasn't explainable, so Kate chose to walk away because she knew to do anything different would be as difficult as being a lone soldier going into the inhospitable landscape of Afghanistan only to be swiftly taken out by enemy forces. Additionally, Kate was exhausted trying to understand his behavior. At the time, Kate thought Bertrand may slander her to justify his unethical and wrong action. Lydia confirmed that this was exactly what he did. At that time and the years following, Kate had assumed the trust assets and their growth were sufficient for Chuck and Ann to reimburse the trusts their outstanding debts using their inheritance to properly reimburse and treat all siblings fairly. She knew the assets were sufficient to pay for Bertrand's care for as long as he lived. In hindsight, had Chuck and Ann operated ethically and properly, Kate's assumption would have been correct and even underestimated. The rapid liquidation of assets and withdrawals over the last years now prevented any possibility of reimbursement and fair accounting.

Kate was prepared for mediation, having assembled a listing of all the facts she had discovered in documents and interviews prior to the mediation. She looked forward to presenting her organized documentation to the mediator and Chuck's attorney.

Each day, she received more and more documents issued by Chuck's attorney, Mr. Morse of Cheetham, Steele and Morse LLP. She was overwhelmed by the volume of paper, affidavits, legal motions, and witness lists. A few days prior to mediation, Kate finally received Chuck's discovery documents. A court order had been issued in October requesting five years of bank statements. She received a zip drive (computer storage device) by Federal Express, which contained two thousand three hundred pages of relevant documentation. Ten months had passed since her dad's death. Kate had concrete proof that Chuck used Bertrand's trust and checking accounts for his personal expenditures. The documents just received were equivalent to one case of paper, and Kate had one day to review the statements, medical records, and checks to determine what was relevant before her flight to Minnesota to attend the mediation.

Included in the two thousand three hundred pages were Bertrand's medical records covering his last eight years of life. She had reviewed over one thousand scanned pages of documents and recognized the last five years of his monthly bank records. The statements confirmed what she had previously surmised months before. Chuck's erratic land contract payments briefly deposited to Bertrand's checking account were countered with withdrawals and transfers back to Chuck and Mildred's personal bank account. Year-end deposits were made from Chuck and Mildred's account, followed by withdrawals debited from Bertrand's checking account and transferred to Chuck and Mildred's account the first week of the New Year, occurring annually. Bertrand and Chuck's joint account and Mildred and Chuck's account were at the same Lloyd's Bank branch. Apparently, Chuck had instructions to transfer funds between both accounts with a standing letter of authorization on file at the bank. Checks were written to Chuck for personal expenditures which included his credit card balances, dental expenses, clothing and food purchases, and other repetitious expenditures. Chuck made numerous cash withdrawals. Large withdrawals and corresponding missing copies of the actual checks listed on the statements were missing. Kate found plenty of proof to support her claims. She was prepared for mediation.

Kate arrived in Indian Falls late in the evening. The following morning, she drove to the downtown Indian Falls mediator's office. His office was the entire top floor of a new downtown high-rise. She looked out at the city and saw the area where the Medical Arts Building previously stood, the location of Bertrand's medical office. She recalled the sparkling clean marble floors and the building's strong antiseptic smells as she rode the modern elevator up to her dad's office. She had worked in his first medical office during her junior and high school years. Kate often walked with her dad downtown to have lunch at one of his favorite restaurants, the popular German restaurant next to the hospital or his favorite Chinese restaurant. She recalled the polite barber who smiled at her from his first floor glass shop and the handsome plastic surgeon who drove a sporty silver Jaguar car having his office on the fourth floor. Bertrand routinely referred cancer patients to him for reconstructive surgeries. She slightly smiled as she thought of her teenage years, assisting Virginia, his office manager, with administrative tasks—pleasant memories she had experienced many years before.

The entire day was spent in mediation. Chuck, Mildred, and their attorney, Mr. Morse, were in one room while Kate and Jack Napp were in another room at opposite ends of the top floor law office. The mediator traveled between the two rooms. All day, back and forth, Chuck's offer was to receive the remainder of the estate, his personal loans forgiven, his land contracts forgiven or considered paid off, and the remaining farmland was to transfer to Chuck. His legal expenses were to be paid by respective trusts. Kate made her final offer to Chuck. She wanted the remaining farmland divided between Chuck, Phillip, and Bert. Chuck refused to compromise. The mediator came back into Kate's room and stated that when he gave Chuck her offer, Chuck jumped out of his chair, muttered obscenities, and he and Mildred stormed out of the building. Mediation was over. Kate gathered her documents and numbly rode the elevator down seven floors, leaving the building, and coldly walked several blocks to where her rental car was parked. That day, during mediation, she learned Bertrand and Chuck transferred a significant amount of money out of the Bertrand trust in the summer of 2005. During that particular week, Gordon was in the hospital for a heart procedure, and Bertrand's trust funds were transferred to American Investors Life Insurance Company. Through the mediator to Mr. Morse, Kate requested information about this particular transaction she had discovered while reviewing the brokerage statements. Mr. Morse responded to Jack Napp. Bertrand transferred the assets to an insurance company, removing Kate, Cybil, and Phillip as beneficiaries. Chuck told Mr. Morse that he did not want three children to inherit his trust funds, and Mr. Morse repeated this statement to Jack Napp. Additionally, during the same week, he transferred his retirement plan to another insurance company, also removing three children as his beneficiaries.

Kate had established her parents' self-directed retirement accounts over twenty years before, and their two accounts were combined after Gloriette's death. At the time, they were valued in excess of one hundred thousand dollars.

After Kate returned to California, she discussed the account transfers with Gordon. He reassured her, "Your dad was a bad man to have done such a thing. He had no reason to be angry with you. We were always very good to your dad."

The legal documents generated during 2006 and 2007 were directed against one child, Kate. The asset transfers were initiated to disinherit three of his children.

After reviewing twenty years of trust statements, Kate noted that checks were written to Chuck, Ann, or her dad. The checks payable to Bertrand were deposited to the Lloyd's Bank account which was held jointly with Chuck. Kate wondered why her dad failed to tell her that he wished to disinherit her from his estate. The trust accounts increased in value by one million dollars during the nineties because of Kate and Gordon's advice and recommendations. The stocks held at his death had appreciated substantially after the trusts were transferred. Kate figured that amount was at a minimum another million in asset growth. The majority of the funds had already been distributed to the two children, Chuck and Ann. Kate and Gordon did not know about the transfer of assets to the insurance companies because Gordon's hospitalization occurred during the time Kate was establishing her new business. The trust security holdings continued to dramatically increase in value, masking any transfer of assets and cash withdrawals by Chuck.

The day following mediation, Kate gave her required deposition on November 24, 2016. The day was exactly ten years from the day Chuck, Finn Nash, and Bertrand signed new legal documents which removed her as successor trustee, removed the provision against trustee self-dealing, and additionally added a new amendment which subtracted assets from

Kate's inheritance. These documents were signed on November 24, 2006. The entire deposition involved eight hours of grueling questioning by Chuck's attorney, Mr. Morse. Chuck and Mildred were seated at the end of the long conference table. Mr. Morse was directly across from her; Jack Napp sat next to her. The court reporter was between Mr. Morse and Kate. Mr. Morse began the questioning with an aggressive angry tone. Mr. Morse was a large muscular man; he used threatening body language as he leaned toward her and angrily repeated questions. Kate had command of the historical facts and was confident in her responses; she had thorough knowledge of the twenty years of relevant documents. Kate had been a registered representative and investment advisor for thirty-four years. The industry was one of the most regulated, and compliance meant regular interaction with attorneys. Kate was not intimidated by him nor did she have trouble responding to his aggressive tone and threatening demeanor.

During her deposition, she learned the precise date and incident which began the "poisoning" or "brainwashing" of her dad against her. Although twelve years had passed, the incident was repeatedly cited by Mr. Morse as evidence that Kate hated her dad. She realized this statement had been repeated often by Ann, Cybil, Chuck, and Mildred. This incident initially stoked Bertrand's anger toward Kate, a purposeful brainwashing tactic to accomplish their manipulation of father against daughter.

Bertrand spent the winter of 2004 in the California desert. April 2004. Gordon, Kate, and her children drove to Death Valley along with her dad. Their spring break involved driving through the blossoming floral desert during their road trip. August 2004 was Kate's thirty-year high school reunion, and it was the first and last reunion she attended. Kate had two days to fly to Indian Falls, attend several events, and return home. She was told by Ann that Gwen was spending that particular weekend with Bertrand.

Gwen was Bertrand's female companion from approximately 2003 to

2008. Kate wasn't interested in seeing Gwen in Minnesota at Gloriette's home because she had just spent a week with him three months before. Kate called Ann and discussed whether she thought it was okay for her to attend the reunion and bypass visiting her dad and Gwen. Kate planned to cram several events together and return home Sunday to attend other business and family commitments. Kate played in a Saturday golf tournament, attended the evening event, and left from Indian Falls airport the following morning. It was after this incident that her dad became increasingly angry at Kate.

During the mediation, Mr. Morse repeatedly asked, "Why were you so cruel as to visit Indian Falls and not see your dad? Do you realize how much you hurt your dad?" Mr. Morse's questioning was angry and repetitive.

Kate remembered back to that time and realized that Chuck made a big deal about Kate not visiting her dad. Kate telephoned Ann. "How did Dad and Chuck know I was in Minnesota for two days? You are the only person who knew?" Kate asked. She fumbled and blurted out that Chuck ran into Ted Black and Ted told Chuck. Ted Black was the only person in her class Ann could think of on the spot. Kate played golf with Ted and his wife that weekend. Ted didn't know Chuck and certainly would not have had such a conversation with him. Kate knew Ted because they sat next to each other during four years of high school band class. Ann overtly lied. Kate did not know that Chuck repeated this incident to Bertrand, emphatically stating, "Kate hates you. She visited and didn't even stop by to see you, and she hates you!"

During the harsh questioning, Kate was stunned and realized this incident had been drummed into her dad's psyche and heart. In hindsight, she felt she probably had made a mistake. She routinely telephoned her dad and had just spent their spring break with him. She didn't think he would ever find out. She was flabbergasted that Chuck and Ann repeated this to him as a way to make him feel angry and hurt. Ann's tattling was behind their entire estrangement. Twelve years had passed and it continued to be used against Kate. Following his funeral, Cybil said to Kate, "You hated Dad so much." Kate was astonished because she did not know why Cybil would made this statement. Her statement was based on this event, which had been repeated by Chuck to Bertrand and her siblings for years. Ann was the initiator and promoter of the poisonous lie which accelerated all the manipulation of her dad and stoked his anger toward Kate. It was following this incident that Bertrand removed Kate as beneficiary of trust asset and as beneficiary of his retirement plan, eventually making the other changes which resulted in their estrangement. Interestingly, Chuck visited Southern California twice a year for several years, never calling Kate or visiting her home. Chuck and Mildred purposefully snubbed her family, yet Kate was called names for over a decade for one explainable incident.

Until the day of her deposition, Kate didn't know this was the incident which caused her dad's anger and belligerence toward her. The time period was well-defined from 2004 to 2007. However, she did not discover why her dad was so angry at her until after his death. Ann was Chuck's partner, manipulating him against her. Their goal was to sever their relationship and terminate her financial oversight of her parents' trusts. Simply stated, they wanted the money. This incident was followed by others. Kate was innocent, but whatever she said or did was twisted by Chuck and Ann to appear she was uncaring, mean-spirited, and sinister to her dad.

Toward the end of the deposition day, Mr. Morse's tone and demeanor changed. He realized Kate was operating from honesty and facts. Close to the end of the long day, Kate showed Mr. Morse bank statements showing sporadic deposits Chuck made for his land contract payments. His deposit was made the last week of the month, typically in December, and was followed with a withdrawal of the same amount transferring the funds back to Chuck and Mildred's checking account. What appeared to be land contract payments actually were reversed on the next page, transferring the funds right back to their bank account. Kate was confident this was the case when she reviewed the deposit bank statements several months before. She confirmed the fake payments, showing Mr. Morse numerous monthly and annual statements—the "transfer-in" deposits and "transfer-out" withdrawals. Shocked, Mr. Morse jumped to his feet, signaling to Chuck and Mildred to leave the room. They abruptly left the room. Mr. Morse was white-faced and shaken by the disclosure. He returned to the room, stating that the deposition was over; everyone was excused. The following week, Mr. Morse canceled his objections and, pending court actions, intended to block Kate's discovery requests. Mr. Morse realized Kate had facts backing her claims. He told Stone and Napp he wanted to settle the case. Unfortunately, Chuck wasn't ready to reach an agreement. When going against an adversarial opponent, a court petition was necessary.

Mr. Morse demanded Kate to give a deposition. She was billed for the court reporter, her attorney and his preparation as well as rental of the conference room. Although she was personally billed over ten thousand dollars for her one-day deposition, they did not request a court transcript of her testimony in any of their legal documents that followed.

Following Kate's deposition, Mr. Morse called and e-mailed Mr. Stone repeatedly. Kate was billed for the numerous hours that they discussed settlement options. Although Kate was exasperated by the October bill, it was dwarfed by the November and December bills. Kate was informed by Jack Napp that Chuck was getting a settlement offer together. Toward the end of January, Kate received new affidavits from Nurse Foe and Fred Schafte, Chuck's and her dad's Indian Falls broker. Nurse Foe's expanded, updated affidavit stated, "Doc was a great conversationalist. He told long and elaborate tales." Nurse Foe revised her affidavit just before the second court-ordered mediation. Kate knew Nurse Foe witnessed Chuck's abuse of Bertrand. Nurse Foe told Phillip that she did not like Chuck. She had mentioned the slang, vulgar names that Chuck called Bertrand, and she had witnessed Chuck putting checks in front of him to sign. Nurse Foe knew that Chuck was committing financial elder abuse. She had witnessed it, and she had remained silent. Kate believed that her slanderous statements were an effort to deflect her participation in Chuck's abuse of Bertrand. Kate believed Ann convinced Nurse Foe that if the facts of Chuck's manipulation came out, her medical license would be in jeopardy.

That was the only explanation Kate could think of to explain Nurse Foe's silence regarding conspicuous elder abuse, or it could have been Nurse Foe's interest in Bertrand's money. The arduous mediation and deposition explained in part why the legal progress was lengthy and costly.

THE HOBBY FARMER

Bert's birthday was two days before Kate's; he was the fifth of six children. Kate recalled the day he came home from the hospital on July 18, 1963. Her grandmother traveled from Iowa. The drive from northwest Iowa to Indian Falls was approximately ten hours by car. Her grandparents traveled to Minnesota prior to the birth of her brothers and sisters to help her mother. There was excitement when he arrived home from the hospital, the adults gushing, "What a beautiful baby." He had a thick head of jet-black hair. In time, he became a good-looking blond boy with bright blue eyes. Everyone called him Bert; he was named after his dad, Bertrand. Although he was named after his father, his personality, temperament, and values were disparate.

Bert was a happy baby and child. He often cycled around the yard on his pedal push tractor with a big smile on his face. Kate did not have much in common with him during his childhood because of their seven-year age difference. Her mother combined their birthday celebrations because they were only two days apart. Each year, Kate requested homemade angel food cake. Her mother's recipe called for twelve egg whites, using her remaining twelve egg yolks for Bert's sponge cake. Bert and Kate shared homemade ice cream and birthdays throughout their years together on the farm. Although Bert and Kate were separated in age, she considered him an ally and appreciated his sense of humor and intelligence.

As a child, Bertrand and Chuck were often verbally and physically abusive to Bert. He was beaten as a toddler while Kate cringed, feeling helpless and confused by their treatment of him, not understanding their anger toward her smiling blond-haired brother. They hit the cute, happy boy, justifying their violent actions by shouting that he was stupid or did not follow orders according to their commands. Kate regretted not defending him because she was afraid of the unpredictable response of her dad and Chuck. Despite the unjust childhood treatment of Bert, he kept his sunny disposition, possessing a positive attitude throughout his adult life, often fondly reminiscing about his childhood. He recalled trudging through the fields with Phillip, shooting Bertrand's revolver at objects in the fields, laughing together. During his later years, being retired, Bertrand expressed regret to Bert for not taking him fishing. Their times together, during Bert's youth, were spent working in the fields, feeding the cattle and walking the farmland. After Bertrand's death, Bert and Phillip were told their dad's revolver went to one of Ann's son's and that his .22-caliber rifle went to Chuck. Kate asked Bert how he felt about not being included in the distribution of his guns. Bert said, "I can go out and buy a gun. I have a problem with the way they went about getting his possessions. Chuck and Ann conducted themselves as if they were our parents' only children. They went about getting their possessions, circumventing the proper process. I would have gladly given her son the gun if it had been given to me."

Bert was five years old as he hiked up the hill east of the family farm to neighbors, the Wilders, a routine he repeated during his childhood. Dr. Wilders was a retired family physician. Bert knocked on their door. Mrs. Fredericka, Dr. Wilder's wife, answered and said, "Dr. Wilder is downstairs doing his woodworking." Bert excitedly ran down the stairs to find him casually in robe and pajamas, working on his custom boot boxes. Dr. Wilder was fond of Bert and spent time patiently teaching him all he knew about woodworking. Bert developed his love of carpentry while he was working with this neighbor during his youth. Dr. and Mrs. Wilders were special, particularly to Kate and Bert. Kate's fond memories include cuddling with Mrs. Fredericka on cold winter Sundays against her warm mink coat as they returned home riding in their comfortable car after Sunday church service.

The Wilders married after World War I. Unable to have children of their own, they spent their years traveling the world. As nature enthusiasts, they were passionate bird lovers, spending hours listening to phonographs of bird calls. Kate remembered the peaceful afternoons spent in their living room, listening to National Geographic records, guessing bird species from their recorded calls. They enjoyed afternoon walks through the woods, identifying birds and listening to the sounds of the woods. Kate often ran up the hill to their home for a visit which included tea and the homemade scotch bread cookies that Fredericka kept in her emptied instant coffee jars. Mrs. Wilders was a petite woman with a pretty face. She wore gloves to church and dressed impeccably. She met Dr. Wilders during the war while they were both stationed in Germany. Kate did not know why they never had children; however, she sensed a sadness in her voice when she talked about not having children, and she was a kind and quiet lady. Kate daydreamed living with them in their peaceful home perched on top of a hill that overlooked the family farm. Their home was peaceful while hers was turbulent with her dad's tyrannical tirades and the persistent quarreling of her younger siblings. Dr. Wilders liked to talk about subjects he was familiar with. They were both avid readers; numerous books lined their living room shelves. Dr. Wilder was retired for as long as she knew him, periodically traveling to Scotland, returning with beautiful wool scarves they gave to Kate and her mother. She treasured the gifts and enjoyed wearing the scarves during the winter months throughout her life.

Fredericka died of heart failure while Kate was away at college. Dr. Wilders died years later after he remarried. The Wilders were buried at Findley Cemetery, not far from Bertrand's and Gloriette's graves. "Dr. Wilders left all his woodworking tools and skill saws to Dad and Mom," Bert said. The extensive collection of woodworking tools and skill saws he had lovingly used were transported to Arkansas, hauled away by Ann after her mother's death. Bert said to Kate, "I have lots of tools, and I do not need more tools. Ann took the tools without consideration or consultation with anyone else as if she was the only child entitled to our parents' possessions."

Growing up, Bert fondly remembered his farm chores—planting and harvesting—as a small child to the day he graduated from high school. Bert and his mother worked together, appreciating their time working when Chuck was away at college. They shared a common love of outdoor work and farm animals and had a close relationship, sharing a kindred spirit. Gloriette preferred driving a tractor to pushing a vacuum cleaner or a mop.

Gloriette often reminisced about working in the fields with her own father, plowing the fields, preparing to plant their crops. Her father was a gentle, kind, quiet, and loving man. Kate recalled her grandfather spoke few words but always in a kind, low voice. Gloriette's sisters did housework and baking while she preferred to be outside, helping her father with his farm chores. As a young teenager, her friends all called her Roy instead of Gloriette. She enjoyed playing outdoor sports. She was a favorite pitcher for their church softball team, known for her strong pitching arm and ability to strike out players. Gloriette wasn't interested in makeup, frilly dresses, and high heel shoes, preferring simple attire and wearing her straight hair in a short simple cut throughout most of her life. Kate admired her ability to be herself without the need for makeup, fancy clothes, and jewelry.

One fall day, Chuck was driving the farm's white Ford tractor and commanded Bert to hitch the trailer to the tractor. Bert was in grade school, approximately seven years old when his finger was caught between the two hitches. The heavy trailer hitch was impossible to hold steady. As Chuck backed the tractor drawbar to the hitch, Bert's finger caught between the bar and the hitch, pinching and severing the tip of his pointer finger. Bertrand tried to salvage it by reattaching the severed finger to the remaining stub. Kate recalled the day her dad amputated most of the dead flesh, leaving Bert's finger as a stub. As an adult, Bert wore his wedding ring on his right hand to lessen the attention to his partial missing finger on his left hand. Coincidentally, their younger brother Phillip lost his finger and a partial finger while standing on a grain truck. He caught his fingers between the chain and sprocket of the auger filing the truck. Bert and Phillip joked they were members of the "missing digit club."

Over the years, the family farm raised beef cattle. Calves were bought at auction, fattened by eating corn and hay, eventually reaching a weight of one thousand five hundred pounds, ready for slaughter. The brothers corralled the fattened steers and led the cattle into a truck to be taken to the slaughterhouse. This was a high-pressure and tension-filled time for Bertrand and his sons as they loaded the fat cattle. Bert wore a snowmobile helmet to protect his head from purposeful beatings from the sticks they used to herd the steers into the truck. The cattle seemed to instinctively know they were headed to their death while Bert took the brunt of the blame for cattle jumping over each other and being difficult to load. Chuck made fun of Bert for wearing his helmet. Regardless, Bert knew he had to protect his head from the blows he was sure to receive from Bertrand and Chuck.

Beef cattle were raised for two decades, and pigs were fattened for slaughter. A few years following raising cattle and pigs, Chuck attempted to earn a living raising sheep. Chuck thought he could make money selling his sheep's wool, buying his friend's sheep, and combining their sheared wool to receive a favorable market price. Phillip recalled Chuck's surprise by the meager amount of money he received from his first wool sale; shortly thereafter, he abandoned the venture complaining it was too much work to shear sheep. Chuck had hoped he would make enough money to support his privileged lifestyle as a doctor's son. During this time, the family had three dogs: an English shepherd, Shep, and a handsome Norwegian elkhound, Fido, accompanied a scrappy dog named Wolf. Wolf was a gift to Chuck from his high school girlfriend. Wolf was a big gregarious dog; part husky and part Samoyed, his coat was dirty white caused by rolling in the dirt. Wolf was a happy and friendly dog, a companion to Shep and Fido, playing and running through the fields together.

Chuck often disagreed with his neighbor, Clyde Pettis, during the years that Chuck raised sheep, openly despising Clyde. Chuck often accused Clyde's dog of killing his sheep. One day, Chuck stormed over to Clyde's house with his .22-caliber rifle. Chuck yelled, "Your mangy dog killed my sheep!"

Clyde replied, "You are wrong, Chuck. Your dog killed your sheep!" yelling back.

Chuck spun around, lifted his gun, and pointed it directly at Wolf. Wolf had followed Chuck, patiently waiting for his master without hesitation; Chuck fired his gun, shooting the dog directly between the eyes. Wolf was shot dead. Chuck turned to Clyde and hollered, "Now we'll see which dog is killing my sheep!" Chuck drug Wolf home, burying him beneath an apple tree in the orchard which separated their two properties.

Phillip read Kate's account of Wolf's death. Telephoning her, Phillip stated, "Bert's story of what happened isn't accurate. What actually happened is much more gruesome." He proceeded to relay the following tale: Chuck spun around and confronted Wolf. Enraged, he beat Wolf with the butt of his rifle. Breaking his rifle stock during the beating, Wolf was beaten unconscious. Chuck drug his dog to the barn and left him to die. Phillip brought the dying dog water and tried to arouse him the following two days. Phillip was devastated because he loved animals and was especially fond of Wolf. Forty-eight hours passed, Wolf barely moved. Chuck shot him and buried the poor dog in the apple orchard next to his house. Phillip had witnessed his brother kill innocent animals before; however, this was something he could not forget, never mentioning the incident to anyone until he read what Kate had written, approximately thirty years later.

The next time Kate spoke to Phillip, she asked, "Phillip, in your memory, did Chuck ever show his rage to you?"

Phillip replied, "Not often. I saw Chuck's rage at Bert and his own son, Theodore."

Kate asked, "Why did Mildred allow it?" Phillip was silent. They each said good night and simultaneously ended their telephone call.

Phillip told Kate about a horrific incident involving Chuck and Bert. Bert was approximately eight years old as Chuck beat him. Bert was lying in the cornfield dirt, down the road from their farm. Each time Bert struggled to stand, Chuck kicked his stomach and ribs until he again collapsed to the ground. Phillip witnessed Chuck kick Bert across the entire cornfield. Bert was severely beaten, bleeding, bruised, suffering serious rib injuries which he felt each day thereafter to this day.

Their farm used an electric fence instead of the traditional attractive wood fences. A simple wire was used to border the pastures. The wire was connected to an electrical pulse which sent shocks throughout the wire. The cattle learned not to go near the wire because the resulting shocks were not pleasant. Periodically, Bertrand and Chuck told Bert to test the electric fence. He tested the wire because it was expected of him. He didn't like it however, and shocks appeared to be a part of his farm chores. Bert recalled a time that Chuck sent him out to fix a broken wire fence. As he was connecting the broken wires, Chuck turned on the electrical current, knocking Bert off his feet, sending powerful shocks through his body. Returning to the red barn, he saw the gleam in Chuck's eyes, explaining Bert's strong dislike of electric fences to this day.

Bert helped Chuck milk dairy cows during the years he was trying to make a living as a dairy farmer. Often, Bert and his dad were milking the dairy cattle while Chuck was absent. The dairy operation came after raising cattle, pigs, and sheep. The farm lost money year after year. "No more," Gloriette said. The next effort was known as their dairy years. The brothers, and occasionally their parents, milked dairy cows for a local farmer. They arrived at the milking barn early each day and at dusk for the second milking.

"The young calves were removed from their mothers at an early age to promote the cows producing optimal quantities of milk. The calves bellowed loudly when they were pulled away from their mother because they were hungry," Bert explained.

One morning, a calf was bellowing incessantly. Chuck had a hangover; his mood was foul as he picked up a heavy stick. Clubbing the calf over the head, the calf dropped down to the ground, appearing dead. Chuck exclaimed, "It's a goner! Get it out of here!"

Bert stated "It's a goner" was one of Chuck's favorite expressions. Bert dragged the calf to another barn and proceeded to nurse him back to health over the next several months, naming him Crazy Charlie. The calf became a steer and appeared to have brain damage because he stuck out his long tongue and gazed upward toward the sky. The steer eventually grew to weigh one thousand five hundred pounds. Bert assumed he would receive some of the auction proceeds when Crazy Charlie went to the meat market. Chuck forgot about the animal he had claimed "It's a goner," happily collecting the auction proceeds and never mentioning Bert's part in saving Crazy Charlie as a calf.

Bert said he looked forward to the day he would be strong enough to return Chuck's beatings. Eventually, Bert was in his prime at twenty-five years of age, having just completed a triathlon. Bert returned to Minnesota permanently, building his new home while working several jobs which included his unpaid job of milking the dairy cows for Chuck. Chuck drove over to Bert's trailer and turned on his electric lights, his usual method of waking Bert for their morning milking job. Bert came out of his trailer and saw Chuck trudging through a thick mud puddle, corpulent, being one hundred pounds overweight, and having his usual scowling facial expression. Bert broke into his heartiest laugh because he realized he could overtake Chuck, losing his desire to return past beatings. Bert found the turn of events amusing, and following this day, Bert pitied Chuck.

A talented musician, Bert played the trombone during his junior high and high school years, graduating from Oak Hills High School in May of 1981. Shortly thereafter, he drove West, spending a few years in California studying trades, primarily building and carpentry. During those years, he continued to play his instrument with the Long Beach Symphony. Bert left California, returning to Minnesota, and helped with farm chores and needed manual labor, never receiving a paycheck from his dad or Chuck. A friend asked Bert to help with a historical building project in Nebraska, and once again, Bert moved from Minnesota to work on the project. He had many friends in Omaha and knew Warren Buffett on a first-name basis. Bert devoted several years renovating the landmark building; a plaque was inscribed with his name as the primary building renovator. Bertrand and Gloriette even cried tears of pride when they saw the tribute to his work during their visit to Omaha, Nebraska.

While Bert lived in Nebraska, he secured a piece of property from the family farm and immediately began to make monthly payments to his parents for the purchase. Bert knew on some level he would someday return to Eudora to build a custom home for his family. Eudora was the small town outside of the big city of Indian Falls and the address of the family farm. Gloriette told Bert to faithfully make his payments and encouraged him to pay off the property as soon as possible.

Bert was a carpenter and farmer; he enjoyed working outdoors and was joyful raising his cattle, pigs, and chickens. He permanently returned to his childhood town during 1999 to build his own dream home. He had bought additional acreage from Bertrand and Gloriette during the eighties from what had been the second farm property known as "the other place" and located a couple of miles from the family farm. Bert built his home on a hill overlooking the field that Kate had worked her spring college vacation, picking up frozen corn from the muddy field, salvaging what was left of last year's crop that was buried under the winter snow. Bert's home was built on a hill overlooking rolling pastures. It was a unique custom log home, each piece of wood carefully selected by him and artistically planned to create a unique log cabin. This was a source of pride and happiness for his family because of the many years building and designing the home. Bert's cabin floors were heated by hot water pumped through the pipes laid underneath the wood planks and stone flooring. Water was heated by the woodburning facility he personally designed and operated.

Bert was a diligent and thoughtful father and generously allocated time to raising his son, Daniel. They often went fishing, camping, and swimming. His goal was to ensure Daniel had the childhood memories that he did not have. Bert, his wife, Diana, and Daniel spent most of their time together enjoying their family farm.

Bert was an accomplished musician and performed with the Indian Falls Symphonic Band. As an adult, he volunteered his time as conductor for his church boys' choir, youth band assemble and men's choir and played his instrument when asked. He volunteered his musical talent for various charitable organizations and accompanied other musicians playing both the trombone and/ or piano, using his left hand for the trombone while reading the bass cleft sheet music. He transposed bass music to treble cleft and sang alternate verses. He usually conducted his choir using his right hand to play piano melody while his left hand was used for direction. Bert had a nice baritone bass voice, inheriting his vocal talent from his mother. His mother enjoyed his singing voice and told him often. Gloriette had a musical funeral service, but the day she died, Bert was bicycling through the mountains of Montana and sadly missed her last days of life. While Ann and Kate planned the funeral service, Kate focused on her mother's tribute which she read during her service. Bert told Ann he would appreciate the opportunity to sing, but Ann quipped, "You must audition for me to determine whether your voice is adequate." Following his audition, Ann said to Bert, "Your voice is not good enough." Bert was not allowed to sing, and Ann's family took his place in the church program. He recalled this incident as a blessing because Bert returned to Omaha and immediately enrolled in singing lessons while studying the German language. The conductor gave him a vocal supporting role in a well-known German opera that was performed by the Omaha Symphony and later performed with the Omaha Symphonic Chorus. Bert credited his vocal progress as a direct result of failing Ann's audition.

Bert was a dedicated volunteer, inheriting his generous trait from Gloriette. Kate's childhood memories included accompanying her mother during her routine visits to "shut-in" members of her church. Gloriette regularly visited women who were unable to leave their home. Kate typically sat quietly off to the side of the room, daydreaming or casually listening to their conversations. Kate sympathized with the women confined to their homes by unfortunate situations and saw their gratitude for the pleasant visitations. Kate recalled one kind lady taking unselfish care of her quadriplegic son, solely responsible for his twenty-four-hour care, unable to attend church and live a normal life. Kate thought of another elderly woman who was no longer able to get around, smiling broadly during her mother's visits. Gloriette said to Kate, "These women are lonely. They just want company and to know someone cares about them." Kate knew of her mom's Christian service because of the years she accompanied her as a young girl, but Kate never heard her mom mention her Christian service to anyone. The week following her mom's death, over five hundred people attended her service, held at a beautiful prominent church in downtown Indian Falls. Kate was surprised by the number of people who came to her mom's visitation at the funeral home as well as the large number of people who attended the service. There were friends and relatives standing in the back of the church because all the seating was taken. Kate realized these were people her mother had touched during her life with Christian actions carried out with a loving and kind heart. Her mother's church guild friends prepared an exceptional luncheon following the funeral service and remained faithful friends to Bert, Phillip, and Kate.

Bert continued to entertain residents at Maybrook assisted-living home after Bertrand's death. Before, during, and after the time he lived there, Bert arranged special musical events for the enjoyment of elderly residents. He regularly visited him during the brief time he resided at Maybrook. Bert lived two miles from the family farm, his parents' home, often stopping by for visits, cooking breakfast, delivering lunch, or helping his dad with what he could during the last years he lived at home before his move to Maybrook.

One cold November morning, Bert, his wife Diana, and his son Daniel brought his favorite donuts to Maybrook for their routine family visit. Upon arriving, he was told, "Your dad is gone, and your sister took him away."

Bert exclaimed, "What sister? I have one in California, Colorado, and Arkansas."

The orderly told him, "Ann took your dad to Arkansas." Ann didn't mention to him that she was removing his dad from Maybrook. During the last year of his life, Bert was not given the courtesy of a telephone call regarding Ann's sudden removal of his dad from the state he had lived for over sixty years.

Bert worked on the family farm from the time he could walk until he graduated high school, even losing a finger while helping Chuck. He helped with Bertrand's care during the last years of his life. Immediately following his funeral, Chuck coldly informed him, "Everything goes to me. That's what Dad wanted." Bert and Phillip were not to inherit any of the remaining land as had been stated by both parents at the close of the farm in early nineties and as stated in their trusts. Chuck had sold the thirty-eight-acre parcel in 2001. "The remaining 160 acres will be transferred to Chuck upon Bertrand's death," stated the fourth amendment to Bertrand's trust. Gloriette's property, 12200 Valley Egypt, was given or "purchased" by Chuck and his wife Mildred. Ann said, "Chuck owns the original family farm because that's what Dad wanted."

Bert had a land contract which was pushed and orchestrated by Chuck covering the land where his home was built. The legal papers he received shortly after his death stated, "You are required to pay off the contract within two months of Dad's death." After months of research,

Kate uncovered Bert's land payments; each month for ten years were deposited to Bertrand and Chuck's joint checking account. At his death, the bank account became Chuck's because it was a joint account with right of survivorship, legally becoming Chuck's account. Chuck instructed Bert to continue making payments to this bank account, failing to disclose it was his sole account.

Bert remained objective during Kate's petition process. He was wary to believe what Kate initially uncovered regarding Chuck's schemes. Kate trusted the facts would come to light during the petition and discovery process, and the complicated shenanigans and years of crooked dealings would become transparent.

During Kate's investigation, Bert shared a story involving the last acreage of farmland when he was helping Chuck on the back 160 acreage, harvesting corn during the first fall Chuck had planted a small crop. Coincidentally, this was 2014, two years prior to Bertrand's death. The corn-growing scheme was Chuck's effort to make others believe he was devoted to working the land and entitled to ownership of it. The corn combine machine was not working properly, and Chuck asked Bert to climb between the blades of the combine to fix the jammed blades. Following the ordeal, Bert realized he had been close to either losing his limbs or death. He asked Kate, "What if Chuck turned the combine on when I was working in those massive dangerous blades?" He clearly envisioned a struggle between the heavenly hosts of angels holding the gear shift while Chuck pulled hard, trying to put it into motion.

Bert shuddered as he vividly remembered the time Chuck said, "I would have been better off if I was the only child and none of you were around." Bert realized he had survived an enormous struggle between good and evil and was grateful for his angelic protection. However, during the entire petition and discovery process, Bert was fearful and insecure, worrying about the safety of his wife and son. Returning from his church each week, he wondered if he would find his custom-built home burned to the ground. He often thought to himself, "What will

Chuck do?"

Bert recalled his sincere question he posed many years before: "Dad, will you help finance some of my house building expense?"

Bertrand responded, "Wait until I die. You will get plenty of money."

Fortunately for Bert, he built his home with his own hard work and limited funds, not waiting or expecting an inheritance that was not to be.

The year following his death, little mention was made of Bert by Chuck. Chuck did not mention the many years that Bert worked on the farm, never receiving a paycheck for his labor. Bert had thought that one day he might inherit a piece of the farm. Chuck often called on Bert to do things—bring Bertrand lunch, take him on errands, and generally help him get around. Bert helped build the 12200 Valley Egypt house their parents lived in from the late eighties. Bert was grateful he was able to help his father during the seventeen years he lived close by, down the gravel road from his dad's place.

Bert recalled the last time he saw his father; it was his eighty-ninth birthday party at the 12200 Valley Egypt house. Leonard, Ann's husband, drove him to Minnesota from Arkansas where he was living the last year of his life. The date was December 8, 2015. He died the following month, January 2016. Chuck casually waved at him from the kitchen chair he occupied as Bert helped him to the door. "See ya," Chuck said, not bothering to get up.

Bert kissed his dad goodbye as he helped him get into the car. He said, "This will probably be the last time I see you," with tears in his eyes.

Bertrand mumbled, "Yep, think so," crying softly.

The only reference Chuck made regarding Bert stated in the legal filings was "Bert—the occasional hobby farmer."

PHILLIP

In January 1967, Kate was ten and half when Phillip was born; he was the youngest of six children. He was a good-looking child with a full head of blond curly hair. As a baby, he was often sick, and the doctors were unable to figure out what was wrong with him when he became listless without warning or explanation. The periodic episodes occurred until Phillip was three years old. Following numerous tests and weeks in the hospital, Phillip's eventual diagnosis was weak and malformed kidneys. Phillip later showed Kate the large scar encircling his abdomen where exploratory surgery had been performed.

Phillip was a happy and gregarious child; all attention turned to him when he entered the room. He was cute, funny, and had a pleasant personality, making others laugh. Kate believed Phillip would have a great future as a successful salesman, rising in the corporate ranks to reach a top position because he had it all: personality, looks, intelligence, and likeability. Kate worked several jobs during high school, often away from their home, and her memories of Phillip were mainly as a toddler and young child. He was seven years old when she permanently left home to attend college.

Phillip's childhood memories involved working on the farm with his older brother Chuck. An early memory involved riding the old tractor, called M4, over the hills to a hay field a couple of miles from the farmhouse. Phillip was barefoot and wearing his pajamas as Chuck lifted him up to the tractor seat, preparing to drive to the field. Gloriette said to Chuck, "No, do not take him. It is too late." Ignoring her request,

Chuck drove the tractor up the last rolling hill to the hay field, and Phillip, having fallen asleep, fell off the tractor fender onto the gravel road. Bert vividly remembered seeing Phillip, scraped and bleeding, as Bert was waiting in the field for Chuck. Despite being banged up, Phillip was happy to share adventures with his older brother.

During his childhood, Chuck became his father figure because Bertrand was rarely around because he was too busy working at the hospital. Phillip said to Kate, "By that time, he seems tired of raising children."

One day, Phillip followed his big sister Ann out the front glass door of their house. Ann wasn't paying attention and allowed the glass door to slam behind her. Too short to reach the metal door handle, Phillip held his hand up to the glass to stop the door from closing. The impact caused the glass to shatter over Phillip, and he had glass cuts from head to toe. As an adult, his scarred chest and legs reminded him of this accident, and he preferred to wear a moustache to cover his facial scars.

Phillip and Chuck were often together, working the endless tasks that were required to care for the animals. Phillip enjoyed the hard farm labor, working outdoors and driving tractors and trucks from a young age. Chuck taught Phillip to drive the old M4 tractor, each switching from riding fender to seat and seat to fender. One time, Phillip took the wheel from Chuck, and the tractor took an immediate ninety-degree turn, driving up a large tree. Phillip was four years old. He drove the full grain trucks to Lawrence before he had a driver's license, beginning his professional driving at ten years old.

Phillip's painful experience with a large grain truck resulted in losing one finger and a section of another finger. Gloriette stated the accident occurred because Chuck was negligent in following the safety procedures for farm equipment. Phillip was sixteen years old; Chuck had worked on the auger chains the day before, failing to replace the safety shield. The following day, borrowing his dad's Cadillac, Chuck left on vacation. A large semitruck arrived to pick up the load of corn their company had purchased, and Phillip was in charge of overseeing the transfer of the corn to the semitruck bed. It was the semitruck's driver's first day on the job and his first time loading a truck with corn. The truck bed was backed up to the silo, and Phillip set the auger to transfer the feed corn. The corn was being unevenly distributed, so Phillip jumped into the truck bed to position the auger, attempting to distribute the feed to the front of the truck. Suddenly, the driver moved the truck. Phillip lifted his arms, attempting to balance himself on the load of corn. In shock, Phillip did not initially feel anything; however, as he lowered his arms, he realized that the tip of his index finger was gone and his middle finger had a bone protruding out of his knuckle with chewed flesh surrounding the bone. Immediately, he positioned his bleeding hand under his armpit, squeezing and holding tight as he jumped off the truck bed and went to the driver and said, "Hey, dude, why did you suddenly move the truck?" He briefly showed the driver his bleeding hand before clamping it under his arm to reduce his blood loss.

The driver shouted, "You have to go to the hospital!" The truck driver was visibly shaken and bent over from his waist to vomit. Phillip proceeded to tell him how to shut down the equipment and remove the auger to complete the transfer of the crop. Phillip was at one end of the farm where the feed was stored and proceeded to walk the distance to Gloriette's house and entered the front door as he removed his hand from his armpit.

Gloriette became hysterical, jumping up and down as she shouted to Phillip, "I have to call your father!"

Having been out on a farm errand when she reached him, he said, "He will be fine. I will come home and take him to the hospital."

Phillip left her house and went back to the semitruck to oversee the shutdown of equipment and departure of the semitruck, eventually returning to her house as he lay down on her living room floor, saying,

"I feel sick."

Eventually, Bertrand arrived, changed his clothes, and drove to the hospital using Chuck's diesel truck. The remainder of his life, Phillip carried his distinct memory of diesel fume and his resulting nausea as he lay on floor of the truck being transported to the hospital.

Bertrand telephoned the hospital, calling for a hand specialist surgeon. However, the surgeon did not return his call. The emergency room scheduler said, "There is a resident surgeon who can work on your son's hand."

Using many expletives, Bertrand said to her, "Do you think I want a resident to practice on my son? Get me the head surgical nurse and give me a room. I'll work on him myself." He proceeded to give the surgical nurse a list of what he needed and took Phillip into an operating room where he worked diligently, surgically repairing what was left of the damaged fingers.

Phillip said, "He was a different person in the operating room. He was kind, compassionate, and professional."

Kate asked Phillip if Chuck was ever held responsible for failing to engage the safety mechanism on the auger after he had knowingly disengaged it. Phillip said that no one ever discussed the fault of the accident in his presence.

Bert said, "Chuck said that it was his dad's fault because he shouldn't have sold the load of corn when he was gone." That particular day was the semi driver's first and last day working for the feed company. Bert said, "Farming is one of the most dangerous occupations. Chuck's failure to engage the safety mechanism or shield on dangerous equipment was indicative of his work on the farm. Chuck was careless, hasty, and reckless in his operation and maintenance of farm equipment."

Phillip later said to Kate, "I do not blame anyone for the accident." He paraphrased the Bible verse from the Old Testament: "Vengeance is mine saith the Lord, for the Lord will judge His people according to their deeds" (Deuteronomy 32:35, NKJ).

As an adult, Phillip had a torn hip socket, requested copies of his medical records, and was advised to have repair surgery. As a young teenager, Phillip was throwing bales of straw down from the second level of the barn when he slipped and fell twenty-five feet through a hole in the floor. Following the accident, Bertrand said to him, "You will be fine. Go to bed, and you will feel better in the morning." He endured the night by crying and screaming in pain. Bertrand said to Gloriette, "You take Phillip in for an X-ray." The pictures showed Phillip broke his foot in five places and his leg in two places. He had a leg cast and used crutches for six months. Eventually, Phillip received an apology from his dad while admitting he should have been taken to the hospital because immediate attention to the injury might have reduced the permanent damage to his hip. Phillip suffered daily hip pain throughout his life because of this particular fall through the barn floors. Despite these memories, Phillip considered his early years on the farm to be happy years.

During his junior year in high school, Phillip applied to the high school board to receive permission to work his senior year on the farm. The high school authorities granted Phillip permission. Phillip graduated with his class at the end of the year. He spent each day of his senior year doing manual labor for Chuck with an agreement to be paid seventy-five dollars a week for his work. His days were long and hard, starting at five o'clock in the morning and ending at sundown with the exception of Friday, having the night off after eight o'clock in the evening. However, Phillip was expected to be up early to milk the cows by five o'clock in the morning. In his final year working for Chuck, Phillip's salary was raised to one hundred twenty-five dollars per week. Chuck handed Phillip his paycheck and immediately asked to be paid for the cost of feeding the dairy cattle because Phillip owned three dairy cows. During the summers, Phillip was out in the fields, cutting alfalfa and converting the dry hay to bales, often by himself, having no help, setting the tractor to drive very slowly as he operated the baling machine and stacking the hay bales on their flatbed trailer. He slowly accomplished the job of two to three laborers because Chuck was nowhere to be found. Chuck later demanded Phillip to pay for the cost of hay that his cattle consumed, despite the fact that the bales were a product of Phillip's labor. Chuck took over three times the market price of hay and deducted it from Phillip's check. Phillip was lucky if he received a few dollars after Chuck had deducted all his charges. Later, after Chuck and Phillip dissolved their partnership, Chuck begged Bert to return to Minnesota to help him. Bert admitted that he baled hay in the same manner, all by himself.

During this time, Phillip considered himself a junior partner in the farm venture. He was working for Chuck and enjoyed the life of a farm laborer. Chuck married Mildred and had their first child; a year later, a second child followed. Chuck's disposition changed for the worse around this time. Phillip was often asked to take care of Chuck's children, usually three to four times per week. Chuck and Mildred began to frequent the bars; they both were known locally as partiers and philanderers. Phillip noticed Chuck and Mildred having marital problems, and Chuck was increasingly difficult to be around. Phillip worked extra hard covering for Chuck by making sure all the chores were done while Chuck was out. Phillip mentioned there were many instances that he made up excuses to prevent his dad from becoming angry at Chuck. One day, Phillip was picking up rocks in the cornfields across from Huntington Golf Course. Rocks were routinely removed prior to planting the corn crop to prevent equipment damage during planting and harvesting. Chuck told Phillip he was going to the bar to meet his friend and that he would meet up with him later. Phillip finished working in the fields, leaving to milk the cows; Bertrand stopped him as he was leaving the field. Phillip said, "Chuck is finishing up his work in the field." Phillip lied, covering for Chuck because getting his dad involved in his chores meant doing chores the hard way or the impossible way. Phillip said it was always much easier to get things done without his dad's help because he chose to do tasks with difficulty and angst.

The last time Kate telephoned Chuck—to wish him a happy

birthday—was on his fiftieth. Chuck complained to her about Mildred's interest in younger men. He said to Kate that he hadn't expected to live past fifty years. At the time, Kate thought his comment was odd, but with time, Kate understood that Chuck lived recklessly, without concern for financial and health consequences that could develop from his destructive habits which included gluttony, excessive alcohol consumption, illegal drug use, and lack of exercise. Bert mentioned Chuck often complained about Mildred taking vacations with other men. Bert said, "That is not right."

Chuck said to him, "I've done it too."

Phillip told Kate that Mildred grew tired of Chuck's shenanigans and negativity and occupied herself with boyfriends. Kate asked Phillip why they remained married. Phillip said, "Clearly, they decided to join forces at some point to take all of our parents' remaining land and property."

Often, Bertrand returned home from work and asked Phillip, "Where's Chuck?" Phillip worked twice as hard covering for him. Phillip knew where Chuck was. Most evenings, Chuck could be found at the local bar. By this time, they had a dairy operation. Dairy cows had to be milked on schedule. Often, Chuck was absent, but he could be found at the local bar. On occasion, Chuck showed up at the barn screaming angrily at Phillip for not doing the jobs that Chuck demanded. Phillip was a young boy when he began working for Chuck and now a young teenager. Phillip was expected to work as if he was an experienced adult.

Phillip worked with Chuck on the farm from a young age through junior high and high school. Phillip took some of the same classes Kate had taken in high school, excelling at math, accumulating enough credits to graduate a year early. Years later, Phillip said that college was not something that had ever been offered to him nor had he considered it, stating, "If I had attended college, it would have been to accomplish my desire to become a rocket scientist."

Early one morning, Phillip was milking dairy cows while Chuck was using vulgar language toward him. Phillip said to Chuck, "Do not talk to me using your coarse language. I am not going to tolerate it anymore." He saw rage engulf Chuck from two cow stalls away. Phillip immediately dashed as fast as he could out of the barn to a nearby barn, quickly scrambling up the high rafters, hearing Chuck jump into his truck, and pealing out of the driveway, gravel flying. Phillip started to descend the barn ladder from the rafters when he again heard Chuck's truck. Chuck thought Phillip had run down the road and raced to find him to beat him up. Phillip remained perched on the rafters, listening as Chuck charged about, trying to find him. Barn doors slammed, Chuck's profanity-laced screaming was audible. Chuck started his engine and again raced down the road. Phillip climbed down the ladder and ran as fast as he could into a nearby field where he thought he was safe. For some time, he quietly remained hidden in the field. Tired, he returned home and went to his room to lie down. Eventually, he awoke to Chuck stomping through the front door, yelling at Gloriette, "Where is he?" He busted into Phillip's room. By this time, Phillip was standing. Chuck grabbed him by his neck and threw him against the wall, lifting him off the floor by two feet. Phillip's face was blue, his eyes bulging; he was choking, and Gloriette begged Chuck to stop. "Stop, Chuck, you are going to kill him. Stop please, please!" she cried. After that incident, Phillip no longer worked for or with Chuck. This event marked the end of his joint-farming venture with Chuck and the dissolution of their farm partnership. Phillip was devastated and did not speak to Chuck for almost seven years. Eventually communicating with Phillip, Chuck asked him for money, a loan for his boat property and new pontoon boat. By this time, Phillip had developed a successful landscaping business and loaned Chuck the money. Later, Phillip sadly realized it was not a loan but a gift to Chuck because Chuck did not pay back loans.

Interestingly, this transaction showed up before the second judge mandated mediation. Kate spoke to Phillip the day after he received another large stack of legal documents from Cheetham, Steele and Morse LLP. He had received an accounting of Bertrand's trust which stated that Phillip owed over forty thousand dollars to the Bertrand trust. He said, "I don't owe anything. I paid off my loan immediately." Chuck had approached Phillip approximately sixteen years before Bertrand's death with an offer to go in fifty-fifty with him to buy property on the Muddy Boat Club Property. Phillip said, "I only have twenty thousand dollars in my checking account."

Chuck said, "No problem, Dad will loan you the remaining fifteen thousand." Chuck arranged the loan. Phillip paid thirty-five thousand for a partnership in lake property with Chuck. Phillip missed two months of payments, and Chuck foreclosed on Phillip's percentage of his property, keeping Phillip's 50 percent of the property for himself. Chuck said, "You lost your interest. I'm selling the property." He sold half of the property and said to Phillip, Bert, and Dad, "Phillip, your fifteen-thousand-dollar loan to Dad has been paid off, and you lost your twenty thousand dollars. Too bad for you."

Phillip realized that Chuck was a thief and not a business partner, brushing the incident off while saying to himself, "I will never loan Chuck money again."

Sixteen years later, his loan to Chuck showed up on the Bertrand trust accounting list. Phillip owed the Bertrand trust over forty thousand dollars for his original six-month fifteen-thousand-dollar loan. Chuck figured Phillip owed the amount, compounded at 7 percent interest for sixteen years. Initially, Phillip was upset. After thinking about the incident, he laughed and said to Kate, "Poor Chuck, he is pathetic, isn't he?" Phillip instructed Kate to change the title of this loan to "Chuck's Muddy Boat Club Loan."

After Kate's college graduation, she moved to California. During the late seventies, it was difficult to secure a professional job as a new college graduate because Minnesota was suffering a serious recession. Kate returned the following Christmas to spend time with her parents. Phillip talked her into cross-country skiing under the moonlight, her first experience cross-country skiing. The snow was deep, and the moon was bright, swooshing through the woods alongside the snow-covered road and through the hills of their neighbors, the Wilders, laughing and occasionally falling into the deep fluffy snow. It remained one of her favorite memories throughout her life, enjoying the camaraderie of her youngest brother.

Kate left her career as a sales representative in 1982 and joined MLPF and S as a registered representative. Kate traveled to New York City, living one month in the city to apprentice at MLPF and S headquarters. Her apprentice class stayed at a hotel in Midtown Manhattan, and Kate became accustomed to riding the subway to Lower Manhattan and Wall Street daily during her four weeks of training. While in New York City, her parents and Phillip came to Manhattan and vacationed ten days in the city. During their visit, they went to Broadway shows, museums, and took pictures atop of the World Trade Center. Kate still thought of him as her little brother, although in retrospect, he had become a young man. They visited the Marble Collegiate Church, the oldest Dutch Reformed Church in North America. Kate was baptized in the Dutch Reformed Church and was raised going to church twice on Sunday as well as weekly Wednesday night catechism classes. They were fortunate to hear one of Norman Vincent Peale's last sermons that he preached from his pulpit. Dr. Peale was well into his eighties at this time. Phillip mentioned Dr. Peale's books were a source of inspiration and positive thinking throughout his life. Dr. Peale wrote *The Power of Positive Thinking*. His book became an international best seller during the fifties and remained a best-selling book for decades.

Phillip took care of Bertrand when he had extra time. He lived with him during the years 2006 to 2007. It was during this time that Chuck sensed Phillip was getting too close to his dad. Chuck actively worked to turn his dad against Phillip. Phillip told Kate, "Dad did not want me when I was born. He wasn't around when I was growing up. He was tired of raising children by the time I was born. When I lived with Dad, we started to become close. He told me things about himself that he had never shared with me before."

During the time Phillip lived with his dad, Kate heard about the "blender incident," approximately in 2006. Kate heard about this incident numerous times over the ten years that followed, told to her by Ann. Ann repeated the story to Kate after their dad's death. She had no trouble retelling the tale, although ten years had passed since the incident. Kate typically didn't pay much attention to her stories, although she sensed something was afoul by the number of times the story was repeated. Ann said, "Phillip was intoxicated and ran the blender in the kitchen. Leonard and I worked over ten hours to scrape the food off the ceiling of the house."

Kate's gut told her the story was fabricated, so she asked Bert about the "blender incident." Bert said, "I scraped some of it off too. It looked like the blender was held up toward the ceiling, and it was done purposefully. There is no way for any substance to splatter as high as a cathedral ceiling. I would like to do a chemical evaluation because it seemed like it was a plastic substance. I believe that Chuck did this to turn Dad against Phillip." It was after this incident that Bertrand accused Phillip of plotting to kill him for his money. Phillip left his house and stayed away for a year. He knew that Chuck was threatened by their improving relationship. Phillip knew there was nothing he could do to stop Chuck's slanderous attacks toward him.

Ann removed her dad from Maybrook assisted home in the latter part of 2014, keeping her plan a secret from her brothers. She told Kate that her dad phoned her, begging her to take him out of Maybrook, repeatedly telling others that he did not like it there and wanted to leave. Kate reviewed years of medical records which revealed he was unable to use his telephone. Phillip worked in close proximity to Maybrook in Indian Falls, visiting after his local landscaping work. By this time, Bertrand spoke very little. He told Phillip and his friend the day before Ann removed him that he did not want to go to Arkansas, but he had to go because Ann told him that he had to leave Maybrook.

The last year of his life, Bertrand lived in Arkansas. Phillip drove to Arkansas to visit him when he was able to take time off work. During his visits, Bertrand often asked Phillip what he thought of all Ann had: her farms, her new barn, her land, and her extensive home remodels. Phillip didn't know what to say and remained silent. Bertrand said, "It's all mine. I paid for it all. It has taken me many years to realize the greed of both Chuck and Ann. I am disappointed in both of them." Phillip spent the last week of his life with him at his bedside, and he was comforted having his youngest son at his side as he was dying.

After his funeral, Phillip was told that Chuck was given Gloriette's home. Chuck lived and owned the 12100 Valley Egypt stone house property and claimed that he had paid for it. Chuck told Phillip that he owned the last 160 acres of the farm which Phillip had farmed for the first two and half decades of his life. Their parents' personal property was already taken by Ann and Chuck. Bertrand owned a few Paul Collins paintings. Phillip asked Ann for one of his paintings because he had known Paul for many years and had arranged for him to meet his dad previously. Ann said, "You're not getting it; Mildred is."

Phillip called Chuck's house to talk to Mildred about getting one of his paintings. Mildred answered the phone. She said, "You know Chuck deserves everything because he was the one who did all the work on the farm. He stayed, and everyone else left."

Phillip reminded her of all the times he took care of their children when they were out partying. He said to her, "You know the years I worked sunup to sundown and the work I did to cover for him. If Chuck wasn't so fat, I would pick him up by the neck like he did to me when I quit the farm."

Mildred hung up the phone, screaming to others, "Phillip threatened me! Phillip threatened to hurt me!" Cybil was in the room with Mildred and noisily told others that she heard Phillip threaten Mildred. Phillip shook his head in disbelief, telling Kate about the conversation he had with Mildred.

Kate told Phillip that she was going to question Chuck's actions as trustee of the Gloriette trust and the many discrepancies in his handling the assets of the trusts. Phillip stated that he was grateful that she was going to challenge Chuck's handling of their estate. However, the year following her dad's death, Kate was completely shut out of the accounting process for the Gloriette trust. The false records provided by Chuck were presented as fact, and she was not allowed to question any of it.

Bertrand's death and the events following his funeral were stressful, especially for Phillip. He handled the distractions by working especially hard, typically sunup to sundown. Reflecting on his years working the family farm, he had few fond memories accompanied by many painful thoughts and feelings. He remembered his childhood years when the farm was known as the 4B Ranch, which represented three brothers and Bertrand. He pondered what had happened to the 4B Ranch; perhaps it should have been called PC Ranch or Polo Chuck's Ranch, he thought.

EXPONENTIAL

During Kate's investigation, she reviewed twenty years of trust brokerage statements recording deposits, withdrawals, and checks. She reviewed the investments each trust held the month before her November mediation. She knew her parents' joint account did spectacularly well during the eighties and nineties. After Gloriette's death, the assets were divided to their respective trusts and continued to do exceptionally well during the 2000 to 2003 bear market. A bear market is a prolonged period in which investment prices fall accompanied by widespread pessimism. This particular bear market lasted three years and resulted in declines of over 90 percent for some securities. After her dad's death, she recognized the stockholdings recommended by Gordon and her; many of the holdings were acquired during the late nineties.

There were three stock positions she did not recognize, which were purchased after the accounts were transferred during March of 2007. Their new broker, Fred Schafte, worked for a small boutique investment shop in Minnesota. He purchased three stocks just prior to the financial collapse of 2008, all bank stocks. Kate carefully reviewed each monthly statement from the date the accounts were transferred away from Gordon as broker. Fred Schafte initially bought a twenty-five-thousand-dollar bank stock for the Bertrand trust; one year later, his recommended stock was worth less than one thousand dollars. Kate recalled the market conditions in the spring of 2007. Gordon and Kate did not own or recommend bank or financial stocks because they exhibited terrible relative strength; this was a technical indicator which alerted a knowledgeable investor to potential downside risk, essentially a high probability of losing money.

The trusts did well during the 2000 to 2003 market decline because the trusts did not own technology stocks; the sector lost on average of 70 to 99 percent of their market value during those years. The trusts were invested in utilities and consumer staple stocks, remaining stable, not losing value during the three years the overall stock market lost over 50 percent of its market value.

The bear market of 2007 to 2008 was disastrous for financial-related holding, such as banks and brokerages. It became clear that Fred Schafte was not a student of the stock market and was not stock savvy. Furthermore, the stocks recommended by both Gordon and Kate during the prior twenty-three-year period greatly benefited the trusts, increasing in value several fold in addition to the annual increasing dividends. They had accumulated high quality equities using sophisticated option strategies; their strategy sold a contract for money while agreeing to purchase the underlying stock at a particular price. If the price declined. The seller of the option collects option premium as income. The objective was either to collect income or potentially acquire quality stocks at below market prices. During the ten years Fred was broker for the trusts, he purchased three stocks, all bank securities, and none acquired using the option approach used in the previous twenty years. Each purchase was done just prior to the 2008 financial collapse. Bertrand never executed another put option to accumulate securities as he had the prior twenty-three years because Mr. Schafte was not licensed to execute put-option transactions. Kate had assumed her dad had a qualified person who was knowledgeable in the strategies they had employed successfully for so many years when he transferred the accounts. In hindsight, few brokers were licensed to execute these strategies because it required specific knowledge; Gordon and Kate were two of three in their office of over forty brokers for a span of almost twenty years. Kate spoke to Schafte's partner, Mr. Young, following her dad's death. Mr. Young stated, "Fred Schafte is a bond broker," explaining the liquidation of high-quality dividend growth securities after Chuck took control of the trusts. Fred Schafte reinvested the proceeds into long-term thinly traded bonds. Schafte told Mr. Young, "The transfer of these two trust accounts was under the strangest circumstances of my career." Kate asked Mr. Young what he meant by that statement. Mr. Young stated Schafte said it many times and did not explain what he meant by his repeated reference to her parents' trust accounts.

After Schafte's disastrous purchase of three bank stocks, Bertrand did not transact business with him again. Over a period of three years, few transactions occurred after the accounts were transferred. A number of companies Kate and Gordon purchased for the trusts were bought by other companies for cash, resulting in large cash deposits to the respective trusts. Fred Schafte invested the cash proceeds into long-maturity term bonds, high-commission bonds. Kate believed that her dad eventually realized that Schafte was not good at stock selection and was unable to accumulate securities as he had in the past. Ann and Chuck were vocal, stating, "Gordon and Kate didn't do anything with the accounts. That's why Dad transferred them." However, Kate never heard them say, "Fred Schafte didn't do anything with the accounts." The next transactions occurred after Bertrand relinquished control of his brokerage and bank accounts to Chuck. After Chuck took control of the trust transactions in the latter part of 2011, many long-held blue chip securities with substantial embedded capital gains were sold to invest in illiquid fixed income bonds. Upon Chuck's control of the accounts, liquidation of quality holdings, churning, and egregious commissions were routinely charged to the trusts. Ann and Chuck were happy with Fred Schafte because he had nothing to say about security liquidations necessary to make cash withdrawals from her parents' trusts.

Bertrand's first investment account and subsequent portfolio was started with Kate in May 1983. To her knowledge, he never purchased a bond during his previous sixty years of life. They had many conversations about the risks of bonds, understanding that any increase in interest rates corresponded to a decline in principal value. Interest rate risk was understood by knowledgeable fixed income investors. At the time Schafte was buying forty-to-fifty-year bonds for the trusts, Kate recognized that Schafte was paid the highest commission allowed by brokerage firms while interest rates were at historical low levels. Fred Schafte's strategy guaranteed the portfolios would experience significant losses when interest rates eventually rose to higher levels. After December of 2011, stock positions were aggressively liquidated causing substantial capital gains and commission charges, churning the positions into a number of illiquid bonds. His partner Mr. Young stated, "Most of the bonds held in the Bertrand trust haven't traded in over a year." This meant there were no buyers, and if you wanted to sell the bonds, you were not able to because there was no market for them.

During the early two thousands, Kate became a chartered market technician. This was an elite designation which demonstrated a competence of a large body of knowledge concerning stock market investing. The objective was to reduce portfolio risk while potentially achieving higher returns. The trusts did well during the two major bear markets, during 2000 to 2003 and 2007 to 2008, demonstrating that Gordon and Kate were good at stock selection as well as reducing market risk. The accounts were transferred to Schafte during March of 2007; the trusts did not hold any financial, banks, or brokerage securities. At that time, the sector of the market was exhibiting the weakest technical attributes and warned of a statistical probability of significant decline. Regardless, Fred Schafte proceeded to recommend purchase of bank stocks for the trusts which were treacherously high risk at this time.

Bertrand received employee commission rates for the years Gordon and Kate were brokers, a length of time that spanned twenty-three years; the rates they charged Bertrand were equivalent to deeply discounted institutional commission rates. Fred charged retail commission rates, the highest rates allowed in the industry. Kate confirmed the rates that were charged during her review of the ten years of statements from his firm. For example, the trust accumulated twenty-five thousand dollars of Occidental Petroleum stock during the nineties by selling a put option on Kate's recommendation. Kate and Gordon's commission on that specific transaction was one hundred twenty-five dollars of which they received fifty dollars after their employer took their percentage. The Occidental position increased in value over tenfold, excluding the annual dividends it paid. Therefore, this twenty-five-thousand-dollar investment grew to well over two hundred fifty thousand dollars. Schafte gradually sold this position in the last five years of her dad's life, generating a large tax liability for the Gloriette trust. He reinvested the proceeds into his expensive long-term bonds at commission rates as high as 5 percent of the bond's face value.

Schafte churned the trust accounts in this manner for the five years prior to Bertrand's passing, destroying the trust's increasing dividend income and greatly reducing the investment return. After the trusts were transferred, a number of stocks Gordon and Kate recommended were bought out for cash. The resulting cash deposits were credited to each respective trust. The buyouts included Heinz, Kraft, and Motorola Mobility, to name a few. The holdings they recommended and purchased for the trusts during the late nineties included Altria, Philip Morris, Texas Instruments, DuPont, PepsiCo, ConocoPhillips, and Union Pacific. These positions increased exponentially and fueled the increased wealth for the trusts until they were ordered liquidated by Chuck. Fred Schafte allocated all proceeds into his "bond of the week," thinly traded, commission-padded twenty-to-forty-year bonds.

After Bertrand's second hip surgery, Chuck took full control of working with Fred. During October of 2011, Chuck ordered the first distribution from her mother's trust. At that time, Kate sent her dad the following letter:

Dear Dad:

[Several paragraphs of news on family, etc.]

I was surprised to receive the check from Mom's trust. It's always nice to get a check; however, I am somewhat "perplexed" as to why we would receive a distribution at this time. I know Mom wanted her assets to go equally to each of six children. Hopefully, the house, the mortgage debt owed by Chuck, and her stock account have done okay to allow for the legacy that was meant for us equally. Although you believe Chuck "walks on water," he is the reason the communication was ceased between us. Chuck wants control (and he has done a good job of achieving it) over everything. All the backbiting that he has done against me for so many years resulted in our severed relationship. If I do not talk to you or have anything to do with you or Mom's investment account, he has run out of criticism against me after so many years. I would think maybe not. It's best that you not even mention that I have written you, or he will come up with more "vitriol" against me. I do hope Mom's trust is maintained as she would want for fair eventual distribution.

Love,

Kate

Kate had completely forgotten that she had written this letter on December 15, 2011. She had no idea that he was not able read. Evidently, Chuck read her letter because the following month, January 12, 2012, several legal documents were executed for both trusts, and the Gloriette's 12200 Valley Egypt home and property was sold to Chuck and Mildred for no money and no appraisal. Chuck's 1992 land contract was rewritten erasing hundreds and thousands of dollars of interest and principal due to her trust for the trust beneficiaries who were her children. The last remaining parcel of land across from Huntington Golf Course was transferred to Chuck, as stated within the newly executed trust amendment. At the time Kate wrote the letter, she did not know her dad did not read and that he hadn't read anything in years. This letter was discussed by Mr. Morse during Kate's November 24 deposition. Regardless, it did not matter because the legal documents were executed while Bertrand was alive and there was nothing she could do about it. Kate believed that Finn Nash and Chuck perpetrated fraud on the beneficiaries of the Gloriette trust by self-dealing changes as stated by the new trust amendments which benefited Chuck as trustee of the trusts.

Kate had forgotten about the excellent stock recommendations she and Gordon had made to her dad; their recommendations were responsible for all his wealth accumulation during the nineties, two thousands, and up to the time of his passing. The positions that remained from their time as his brokers had gone up exponentially and was the sole reason there were funds left in the estate. Bertrand and Chuck had a fiduciary obligation to put the interest of the trust beneficiaries over their own. The two years prior to their transfer from Gordon, both trusts appreciated in excess of 30 percent. Gloriette's trust increased over one hundred thousand dollars the year prior to his transfer to Broker Schafte. Gloriette's trust was left with less than two hundred thousand dollars the year following her passing. From that time until Bertrand's death, her trust holdings increased in value to over nine hundred thousand dollars. This was 100 percent due to the appreciation of the stocks Gloriette's trust held. Chuck did not make payments to the Gloriette trust, and Gloriette's house was removed as a trust holding. The Gloriette trust paid all taxes, renovations, legal charges, insurance, etc., for nineteen years. Therefore, Gloriette's trust was a fraction of what it was supposed to be. It did well, however, due to the research recommendations by Kate and Gordon. She asked others if the transfer of the trusts to Frank Schafte was due to performance issues, cost considerations, or if they acted in the best interest of the trust beneficiaries. Her gut response was no, emphatically no. It was Kate's opinion that this was Chuck's effort to gain control of the trust money. According to the statements she reviewed, she was certain that Chuck accomplished what he set out to do.

Chuck, Ann, and Cybil each submitted affidavits prior to the November mediation. They noisily stated, "Dad was mentally sharp and alert and able to make all his decisions. He did not suffer any mental decline up until his passing in January of 2016."

Fred stated, "Bertrand made all of his financial decisions, and he never witnessed Chuck had undue influence over him."

Schafte said, "Bertrand called me specifically to buy bonds and stated he wanted to sell his appreciated stock because he no longer wanted dividend income." Apparently, Schafte did not understand the tax laws which gave preferential tax treatment to dividend income. He said, "Bertrand researched the bonds and called him to purchase specific bonds." Kate looked at the dates that the bonds were purchased, recognizing the dates coincided with the time he was either at home crying or living at the retirement home and was unable to use the phone or his television remote.

Fred Schafte's affidavit stated, "Bertrand transferred the accounts away from his daughter because he didn't like her service. Bertrand stated Kate pawned off the accounts to her husband Gordon, and Gordon never returned his calls." Gordon worked with her dad for twelve years along with herself, another hurtful statement which was added to their list of slanderous lies. His affidavit further stated, "Bertrand didn't care about the performance of the accounts and wanted to sell trust stocks and put the money into bonds which he knew wouldn't make money." Schafte's reasoning was flawed because many of the positions were sold after the financial collapse; thereafter, the positions continued to appreciate substantially each year to her dad's death, increasing the annual dividends the companies paid. Additionally, Schafte's liquidations caused tax liabilities because the long-held positions sold were at substantial capital gains despite being temporarily hammered during the bear market of 2008 to 2009. The positions that were sold had paid dividends well in excess of the interest paid by the thinly traded risky bonds Fred Schafte purchased. Schafte's logic sounded fine to a financially illiterate person; however, it was not factual. Schafte sold conservative dividend-producing stocks with embedded capital gains during a depressed time, following the 2008 financial collapse, investing the proceeds into illiquid risky bonds with increased interest rate risk, meaning risk of loss of principal. A long-term bond of twenty-five years will decline in value at approximately 25 percent for each 1 percent increase in interest rates. Schafte and Chuck were fortunate because interest rates remained depressed through 2015. Gordon and Kate had been in the investment business for over three decades; an important part of their business was talking to people, and their long-term successful careers contradicted his legal affidavit. Incontrovertibly, Kate and Gordon did return clients' telephone calls.

The Monday following her dad's funeral, Chuck called Mr. Young and ordered liquidation of the remaining stock positions held by the Bertrand trust. In other words, he sold the securities owned by his trust. He did not ask the beneficiaries if they wanted to receive what remained of their distribution in stock. A few of the holdings sold were bought during the eighties. Bertrand's trust still owned the first stock Kate had purchased for her parents when she became a fully licensed registered representative during May 1983. This particular utility company common stock was purchased for two thousand dollars and appreciated exponentially and was worth in excess of thirty thousand dollars. Furthermore, the annual dividends paid by this holding exceeded the cost of the position thirty-three years before, paying three thousand dollars in annual dividends. The remaining positions were sold during the lowest point of the 2016 correction. The positions held would have added over 30 percent in appreciation to the beneficiaries the following year excluding the dividends that would have been credited to the trusts. Chuck disrespected her parents' legacy by his rapid liquidation of the Bertrand trust.

Kate had witnessed wealth transfers of several generations during her thirty-five years as an investment professional. She came to the realization that an inheritance was a legacy; securities, property, and land were legacies and should be treated with the respect due to the lifetime they took to accumulate.

Kate found it interesting that her sisters had so much confidence in Chuck's financial market savvy because his greatest talent, or lack thereof, was destroying their parents' wealth and his active self-dealing of her mother's trust assets. Affidavits were taken from Nurse Foe, Finn Nash, Fred Schafte, and Dick Crumbly, CPA, prior to the November mediation. They were "respected" opinions whereas Chuck's brothers were not questioned by Mr. Morse. Morse used Nash, Foe, Schafte, and Crumbly's affidavits extensively for Morse's court hearing motion to dismiss the undue influence charges against Chuck. Mr. Morse said Chuck's two brothers, Bert and Phillip, were disinterested parties. Kate spoke to Dick Crumbly following her dad's funeral. Crumbly had been her dad's accountant for over thirty years. Kate previously spoke to him annually, during tax season, during the decades of the eighties, nineties, and part of the two thousands. Kate asked Mr. Crumbly for copies of the most recent tax returns for the trusts. Kate asked him if he knew why her dad transferred the trusts from Gordon as she found it surprising to see the only quality holdings held at his death were positions they had originally purchased for their trusts.

Mr. Crumbly said, "Your dad said you are a b—, and he didn't want to work with you anymore."

Kate was taken aback by his statement. She replied, "Are you aware the remaining assets in the estate—our parents' land and houses—were transferred to Chuck?"

He said to her, "No, I don't know anything about that." Kate called him a month later and asked if he was going to send her the tax returns. He said he had just received a package from Cheetham, Steele and Morse LLP, and he would send her the returns when he had time. The package he received from Chuck's attorney instructed him to add schedules to the tax return which showed land contract payments. Prior to 2015, he had never prepared these schedules. Regardless, he added seven years of data showing exact monthly payments for both land contracts. Kate had reviewed monthly trust statements for ten years; no monthly payments were made, and two lump sum payments in 2014 and 2015 were from Bertrand's checking account. None of the payments matched the schedules he attached to Bertrand's 2015 tax return. Mr. Crumbly collected his billings for his audit of the trusts; however, he did not use the trust statements to conduct his audit, and he used Chuck's handwritten scribbled notes listing his fake payments. He stated during the litigation process, "Fred Schafte is a wonderful broker." Kate did not know if there was an ongoing relationship between Fred Schafte and Dick Crumbly or if they were cooperators to wash over any wrongdoing they had done under Chuck's direction.

Mr. Morse's reams of paper in response to Kate's June 16 petitions were dismissive of each statement of factual evidence she submitted. He continued to state, "Kate accepted the 2011 check from the Gloriette trust which confirmed she believed her dad was of sound mind." The problem was that the check was written by Chuck, and she did question the distribution; her December 15, 2011, letter was factual evidence.

Ann's affidavit stated, "Dad never lost his ability to make choices or manage his own affairs. He was very sharp and mentally alert right up to the end of his life." Cybil made similar statements as well as slanderous statements against Kate in her affidavit.

Each of Kate's factually backed petition charges was dismissed by Mr. Morse as inadmissible, hearsay, or subject to the five-year "statute of limitations" clause. Mr. Morse wrote, "Kate is illogical and not trustworthy. Her sisters state the basis of her claims are conversations she has had with her parents' spirits." Kate didn't know why they made these statements or why they were in the court transcripts. It seemed to her that many illogical statements were made to discredit her. Kate assumed Chuck was behind the slander, and these were just a few of the numerous statements made to discredit her. Kate had not spoken to her sisters in a year. The slanderous statements against her intensified leading up to a multigenerational reunion on her mother's side. Coincidentally, she was removed from receiving e-mail notifications about her mother's family reunion around this time. She did not respond to their statements and sincerely hoped the facts eventually would reveal the truth. Mr. Morse's court-filed document stated, "Kate believes the settlement should be one million dollars per beneficiary. She is unwilling to reach a reasonable compromise."

Kate found the written statements in the court documents attributed to her disturbing. She heard the statements repeated by others to her. She believed that Chuck, Ann, Cybil, and Mildred repeatedly made these statements in an effort to characterize her as a greedy, eccentric, crazy person living in California. Kate recalled visiting her parents after she had moved to California. She overheard Chuck disparaging people who lived in California as he categorized California residents as being flaky and strange. Kate thought his statements were patently absurd and did not participate in his conversation. Knowing that he made the statements intending to demean and insult her, she did not engage and left the room. Reflecting and thinking about this incident, she realized that he had probably disparaged people who lived in California for decades, which explained why the statements were written in court documents to purposely discredit her professionally and personally.

Kate filed petitions stating the facts she uncovered from twenty years of trust statements; her petitions asked relevant questions regarding significant changes in the trust holdings incongruent with her parents' estate plan. Chuck's attorney's response was to ignore her questions and counter with statements intended to discredit her. She had reviewed Chuck's credit history from the time they transferred the trust accounts away from Gordon. His credit history showed he held numerous revolving credit cards with significant balances. Compound interest was an incredibly powerful wealth accumulation tool. Alternatively, high interest rates charged by credit cards caused wealth destruction. Kate had copies of what remained from her parents' trust accounts and had a reasonable idea of the value of the remaining land. Chuck's credit history as well as his refusal to answer questions and reach an agreement indicated to her that he did not have savings or an ability to pay what he owed the trusts. Furthermore, it was clear to Kate that he had lived on her dad's bank account. Kate recognized payments made to cover his credit card balances from both the trust account as well as from her dad's checking account. Chuck did not have his own financial resources, and he exhibited characteristics of being heavily in debt. "Why would I request one million dollars per beneficiary if the funds did not exist?" Kate asked Bert. Chuck's actions immediately following his dad's death, his avoidance of answering pertinent questions, and his aggressive legal response toward Kate personally confirmed her belief that Chuck had no intention of repaying the trusts money he legally owed each trust.

Mr. Morse's slanderous statements documented in court filings started following the filing of Kate's June 2016 petitions and did not stop. Kate hadn't had a conversation with either sister about the case after the petitions were filed. At the time of their affidavits, months had passed since she had spoken to them. Cybil and Ann worked tirelessly to slander and discredit her while supporting Chuck's position that "everything was as Dad wanted it." She heard about their repetitious rants from others. It was her belief that the slanderous statements were concocted by Ann and Chuck in a concerted effort to discredit her. Mr. Morse's court filings were written to disparage and dismiss her as the named successor trustee of the Gloriette trust and erase her history as her parents' financial advisor for twenty-three years. The statements were intended to dismiss her as her parents' daughter. "Was this what Dad intended when he removed me and appointed Chuck as sole representative for his estate?" Kate asked Gordon.

Kate had assumed or hoped Bertrand would find a competent replacement for Gordon. He did not. Fred was self-serving bond salesman, and the statements proved that he had no interest in making sure the wealth was maintained for the beneficiaries because his actions destroyed annual dividend growth. Following Bertrand's death, each bond held in both trusts were worth less than what they were purchased for. Since the bonds did not trade at bids, sales price, valuations were less than what was listed on the statements. Furthermore, the cost to liquidate the bonds was egregiously expensive. Fred, Chuck's friend, did well churning out tens of thousands of commission dollars to line his pockets from her parents' trust portfolios.

In summary, the growth and appreciation of the Gloriette trust was due solely to the quality stock recommendations Gordon and Kate gave during the eighties, nineties, and early two thousands. The trusts remained stable and appreciated during two significant bear markets. Liquidation of high-quality dividend-paying stocks for purchase of illiquid, expensive, long-term bonds dramatically increased the risk of loss. "Why was it okay for Chuck to ignore his fiduciary responsibilities?" Kate asked. "What were the reasons for the transfer of the trust accounts?" Kate asked repeatedly to deaf ears. "Did Chuck fulfill his fiduciary duty to the beneficiaries of the trusts with his insistence and aggressive tactics he used to pressure Dad to transfer the accounts to an unknown bond broker?"

Prior to Kate's November deposition and mediation 2 ordered by the judge, Mr. Morse questioned Kate's credibility, stating she was dishonest. Mr. Morse's written statements within the court documents discredited Kate as a professional and were filed with the court. Kate was a certified financial planner in excellent standing since 1989. As a certified financial planner professional, she upheld Certified Financial Planner Board of Standards of Professional Conduct which provided the highest level of ethical competence. The organizations she belonged to adhered to the highest levels of integrity, objective advice, competence, fair treatment, privacy, diligence, and professionalism. Mr. Schafte wasn't a member and never had been an eligible member in any of the top financial advisory organizations that Kate belonged and was in good standing for three decades. It would not be possible for Kate to be a member of excellent standing of her prestigious organizations if Mr. Morse's allegations had merit.

During their second mediation, mediation 2, Bert, Jack Napp, Joseph Stone, and Kate were in their separate rooms. Joseph Stone mentioned he was a member of a church where Fred Schafte previously attended. Joseph Stone said, "Many members of the congregation sought investment advice from Schafte. Their investment results were devastating, and Schafte was forced to change churches." Schafte transferred to a new church, finding his next victims, including her dad. Coincidentally, Fred Schafte, Finn Nash, and Chuck all attended the same church.

Kate commented to Bert, "Perhaps their church should be called Thieves Church." Fred was a shyster who mascaraed as a bond broker, not a credible financial advisor. He didn't understand the objective of a successful stock investor—buy stocks low when they are out of favor and sell them when they are expensive and popular. Maybe someone should have told him, "Buy low, sell high." Then again, he was a salesman, and he only knew how to make wealth for himself, churning his client's accounts.[14]

---

14   Statements referencing positions and transactions found in "References."

SISTERS II

Chuck did not telephone Kate after her dad's death, following her dad's funeral, or during the fifteen-month legal process. After Kate told Ann she was going to file petitions with the court regarding Chuck's actions as trustee, both Ann and Cybil shunned her. Kate was disinvited to Ann's daughter's bridal shower that Kate had agreed to pay for and host. Ann and Cybil made a point to walk away and avoid Kate during Ann's daughter's wedding and festivities. She received a letter from each sister following the filing of the petitions with the court. She subsequently learned a small percentage of estate cases are ever questioned by family members. She understood why the process required a brave and strong person to endure the personal attacks from those with a different perspective.

Kate instinctively knew her sisters' letters were critical and harsh, opting not to read their letters. The legal process was emotionally painful and difficult for Kate. In response to Kate's petitions, Chuck and Mr. Morse filed numerous motions in an effort to discourage Kate from continuing the legal process. Kate's two sixteen-page petitions covered each trust. Chuck's attorney's response to each petition was to file legal paperwork countering Kate's statements with denials and statute of limitation defense. The statute of limitation defense was predominately used by Mr. Morse throughout the case. His defense stated that too much time had passed for Kate's charges to be relevant. They did not respond to her detailed evidence of wrongdoing. Instead, Mr. Morse cited other legal cases and filed numerous motions to dismiss Kate's petitions. Morse attacked Kate's character in his written responses and court filings. Kate realized these were typical tactics of some big-name, expensive law firms. It was evident that Mr. Morse and Chuck's goal was to bury her in paper and legal expense.

She forwarded their correspondence to Bert, asking him to read the letters for her. Several months passed until it was week of mediation and her deposition. Bert gave her the letters or what he referred to as "hate mail." Just before her November mediation, Kate read her letter.

Cybil wrote to Kate, stating that Bertrand was devastated that Kate removed him from her desert home and he wanted to take Kate off his finances because of her hatred toward him. Cybil wrote that she believed Kate was preparing a case against Chuck at Bertrand's funeral, and she believed that Kate's questioning of the estate settlement process was unwarranted as she had no right to have any opinion regarding the process because Chuck had done an outstanding job and took such good care of their father.

Kate was relieved that she had not read her letter months earlier because she interpreted the letter as spiteful, and she believed she tried to do what was morally right. Kate wondered why she had never given her any information until her dad had died. Cybil often visited the desert and spent time with her family, visiting their dad. Cybil knew Kate was designated to oversee their trusts because she explained this to her after her mother's death. She was aware that Gordon and Kate professionally positioned their assets for them to live comfortably the remainder of their lives because she explained it to her after her mother's death. The later part of the two thousands, Kate hosted a bridal shower for her daughter, traveling to San Diego to attend Cybil's daughter's wedding. Kate questioned why Cybil did not say anything about her dad's statements at any time during the last years of his life.

Cybil knew Kate had a close relationship with her mother as well as of their parents' travel and holiday time spent with Kate's family because they often visited her family during those years.

Kate was slightly consoled her letters showed she had been brainwashed by Chuck. Cybil stated that Kate had removed Bertrand from her desert home. This was not a true and factual statement, and Kate believed this was all in Chuck's plan to turn others against her. Kate was told by others that Cybil had financial problems and was facing home foreclosure. She was told that Chuck promised that she would get her inheritance within weeks of her dad's death. As a financial professional, Kate had been involved with many estate settlements; none of which settled so quickly. Chuck's promises to his sister positioned Kate as an obstacle to her receiving badly needed funds.

Cybil's letter emotionally stung her because Kate had helped her financially when Cybil moved to the West Coast as a teenager. Cybil lived at her home until she was able to afford her own apartment, and Kate had given Cybil the deposit for her first apartment. Kate spent many weekends taking care of Cybil's daughters during her twin daughters' first five years of life, driving several hours to their home for monthly weekend visits. As Kate's nieces celebrated the twin's sixth birthday, Cybil told Kate that they had become emotionally too close to Kate, and she did not want her to visit her children. She told Kate to have her own children because she did not want her girls to have a close relationship with Kate. Kate saw Cybil on rare occasions following her dictate.

One day before Kate's sixtieth birthday, she received a letter from Ann. She did not receive a birthday card; however, she received a letter which Kate interpreted as follows: Ann stated that Bertrand and Kate's relationship resembled his hatred toward his stepmother. Ann charged Kate with bowing out of her relationship with her dad and not working to repair the damage caused by his statements and actions. She stated that Kate was destroying generations of relationships by her actions. As she read her letter, her written words emotionally stung her and hurt her deeply.

Ann's letter revealed her resentment toward Kate, explaining why Kate did not receive any of Gloriette's possessions. Fortunately, Gloriette had handed her treasured ring on her deathbed; otherwise, Ann would have confiscated that too. Kate spent the last week of her mother's life at her bedside along with Ann. Ann's letter confirmed that Ann was Chuck's partner in their scheme to remove her dad from Kate's life. Ann and Chuck convinced her dad that Kate wanted nothing to do with him. Ann was diligent, making sure their relationship wasn't repaired the years following Chuck's brainwashing efforts and Ann's manipulation.

Both Ann and Cybil mentioned that Kate had a lifetime of unresolved bitterness, anger, and resentment toward Chuck. The truth was, when Kate figured out Chuck's negativity and backbiting against everyone, she ignored him. She did not engage in conversations with him because she did not call him. There was no evidence any of their accusations had merit. Kate did not change her parents' legal documents, and she did not participate in brainwashing her parents against Chuck. Kate did not have an agenda to turn her parents against Chuck during her lifetime. They had zero evidence to support their repeated vitriolic charges against Kate.

Ann's letter was written the day before Kate's sixtieth birthday and was followed by additional letters and e-mails, all demanding she stop the petition process. She told relatives and family friends that Kate was suing Chuck. She said repeatedly to others that Kate was wrong to sue Chuck. Kate had explained to her following the funeral that she had a legal and fiduciary obligation as successor trustee of the Gloriette trust. Ann knew she was required to do an accounting of the trust assets because she carefully explained it to her prior to and following her dad's funeral.

Chuck's refusal to cooperate by supplying requested documents to Kate's lawyer was a bold tactic to prevent transparency regarding his past actions as trustee. Kate didn't understand why she wasn't represented by the law firm that was settling her parents' estate, and Kate did not understand why she had been removed as her dad's successor trustee without any notification. Kate was taken aback by the active campaign against her by both the law firm and Kate's siblings during the months and years following her dad's death.

Ann knew Kate was unable and rarely spoke to her dad during the two years prior to her dad's transfer of the trust accounts. Kate had asked Ann many times why did Bertrand did what he did. Ann remained silent. After her dad's death, Ann repeatedly said to Kate that she did not do her job. Gordon was her dad's financial advisor. Gordon had conversations with her dad. Gordon did his job, and the trust statements proved Gordon did an outstanding job. Kate asked Ann directly, "Why had my oversight of our parents' finances been taken from me without any questioning from either you or Cybil? Did you ask about the credentials of Dad's new broker? What were Fred Schafte's credentials compared to Gordon's expertise and experience? Did you know Dad did not have a working relationship with Schafte? Why weren't we ever given any explanation?" Ann and Leonard ignored Kate's questions. Kate realized this was the result of having been slandered for a decade behind her back. Their slander was not backed by facts, facts which the statements proved.

Ann stated in her letter to let Chuck pay what he has committed to. Unfortunately, Chuck did not commit to pay anything. He fought against disclosure. Chuck refused to acknowledge the debt he owed the Gloriette trust. Chuck would not explain why he owned Gloriette's home without paying anything for it. Chuck was battling Kate using the largest legal firm in the state with her parents' trust assets. Kate believed Ann was fervently sticking up for Chuck because she knew any admission of wrongdoing implicated herself. They worked closely together manipulating her dad, particularly in the last decade of his life.

The only sliver of truth in Ann's statement was that there was a divide between Kate and Bertrand at the end of his life. He did not telephone or respond to the cards and letters Kate wrote to him the last years of his life. Two years following her dad's termination of her professional connection, Kate continued to be deeply hurt and angry by what her dad did. She had no choice but to disengage emotionally from the hurt. It was too painful to think about. Kate shut down that part of herself emotionally; his termination of their relationship both personally and professionally after so many years and so much effort was a crushing blow. It was their way of connecting. Her dad was unable to speak about feelings and emotions; but they had become close discussing companies, investments, and finances. This had been her position in their family. It was where and how she fit in. Kate's position was removed, and she was ostracized. No one seemed concerned or questioned what happened, which deeply disturbed her. Kate had been stripped of her station in life. By questioning all that had transpired, following her role as successor trustee, she was accused of breaking up their family. Ann sent mean-spirited letters to Bert and Phillip, claiming that Bert caused shame to his name. They were upset by her accusations because they were not participants during the legal process that Kate had initiated. Although they wanted the truth disclosed, they were not willing to take sides and told Kate that was their position. They told Kate they appreciated her efforts to uncover the truth. Ann and Cybil were vicious toward Bert and Phillip, sending hurtful e-mails and letters because their brothers did not sanction what Chuck had done or what he stated. Kate would have filed petitions regardless of Bert's and Phillip's feelings toward Chuck. Ann and Cybil worked to get Phillip on their side, determining if Phillip supported Chuck's position; the odds would favor four siblings against Bert and Kate. Ann and Cybil desperately wanted whatever money was there, and they wanted it sooner than later. Phillip did not support Chuck's position because he knew it wasn't the truth. Bert was never on either side. He was an objective observer. He wanted the truth to come out. However, he did not help Kate. Phillip recalled Chuck telling him about his scheme to take over the remaining land from his siblings. At that time, Phillip wanted no part of Chuck's plan, walked away, and forgot about Chuck's scheme. Phillip recalled the conversation and told Kate that Chuck told him of his plan approximately sixteen years before his dad's death.

Ann sent Phillip a letter prior to their first mediation on November 22, 2016. Phillip told Kate that she wrote that she was embarrassed she ever questioned Chuck's bookkeeping records of his payments. Kate thought her written statement was laughable because Chuck routinely had stacks of important paper scattered about his vehicles. Chuck's office was the main floor bedroom in the stone house; papers were always strewn all over the room and on his desk. Kate recalled her dad having to write a forty-thousand-dollar check to the Internal Revenue Service because Chuck had not filed his income tax return for several years during the eighties. Gloriette complained to her, saying, "We told him many times to file his income tax returns. Now he faces jail if we don't write this check for him." During a weekend visit from college, Kate recalled being a passenger in one of Bertrand's newly purchased farm trucks and recognized dirty signature paperwork strewn over the floor while Chuck grinded the manual gears and pumped the clutch recklessly. His operation of the farm vehicle was characteristic of how he operated facets of his life.

Kate received another letter from Cybil days before the judge ordered mediation 2. The letter that accused Kate of holding up her inheritance and that, because of Kate, Cybil's money was just sitting there. Cybil stated that Kate should have sorted out her differences with Chuck after the settling of the estate. Kate questioned what she would have done had Bertrand lived many years longer. What if there wasn't a stock portfolio that left the last of their remaining wealth? Was she waiting for her dad to die to get his money? Kate asked Bert what she ever did to Cybil. Bert said, "It's all about the money with Cybil. Don't take her comments seriously."

Kate sent Ann and Cybil copies of trust checks that were written by Chuck and cashed just prior to, during, and after mediation 2 in March of 2017. Kate received the following letter from Cybil accusing Kate of ignoring the facts and making up charges out of thin air. Cybil believed that Kate did not have any basis for her petitions and that Chuck had done everything right and had complied with all the requests for documents. She believed that Chuck supported their dad the last years of his life, and she stated that she believed Chuck had saved the estate over three hundred thousand dollars.

In Cybil's letter, she wrote that Kate promised to pay for all the investigation, but now Kate was using the trust money to pay for it. When Kate filed the petitions, she had twenty years of trust statements records. The legal petitions were based on what the statement records factually showed. Kate had assumed Chuck would admit his wrongdoing and immediately reach a settlement with the trust beneficiaries. Kate assumed her personal expense would be less than twenty thousand dollars, not realizing that the litigation would extend over fifteen months. She hadn't considered that Ann and Cybil would fervently support Chuck's position that he didn't owe anyone an explanation for any the numerous changes, discrepancies, and outright transfer of their wealth since their mother's death. Kate sent Ann and Cybil copies of her personal checks which paid her monthly legal expenses. Kate had no authority to withdraw funds from the Gloriette trust. She had authority to receive copies of the statements and bring up the accounts online and was able to print copies of cleared trust checks written to Cheetham, Steele and Morse LLP by Chuck to pay for his legal defense team. After several months, Kate was able to terminate his ability to write checks on the Gloriette trust; however, she had no authority over what Chuck did with the Bertrand trust assets. Kate did not understand why Cybil made the statements because she was given copies of Kate's personal payments and cleared copies of checks Chuck wrote from the trust accounts.

It became apparent to Kate that Cybil was manipulated and conned by Chuck. Cybil posted videos of Chuck and her on an instant message site in November 2016 riding Chuck's John Deer tractor, a combine purchased with the Bertrand trust funds. Additionally, she posted a social media video of Mildred, Chuck, and her cruising the Indian Falls river sitting on Chuck's boat bought with Phillip's money years before. During mediation 2, a document was produced showing Cybil's diligent payments to Bertrand's checking account for her fifty-thousand-dollar loan. Bert and Kate knew Cybil was always having financial problems. The organization and presentation of the document appeared to have been put together by Chuck's daughter, Flo. The document was not plausible because Cybil never had money and was always in debt, asking her brothers for money. A month following the final mediation agreement, Cybil posted another social media video drinking champagne while happily exclaiming that she bought Chuck a brand-new Cadillac car. She thanked Chuck for taking care of her dad the past forty-two years. According to Cybil's statement, Chuck took care of her dad from the time he was forty-seven years old, a practicing surgeon, and Chuck was twenty-eight years old. Cybil believed that Kate was the villain. Kate knew she would always be the villain because they refused to consider the facts and be objective. Cybil was Chuck's brainwashed puppet.

Ann's and Cybil's letters showed emotions that reminded Kate of her dad's belligerence to her during the years Chuck was having coffee with him and brainwashing him against her. Ann and Cybil wanted what Chuck promised— money. Kate was depriving them of the money they had spent many times over.

Phillip, Bert and Cybil Standing on the steps of the stone house.

Bert

Phillip

SOLIDARITY

ate's deposition was taken the day before Thanksgiving. Chuck's lawyer, Mr. Morse, e-mailed and telephoned Stone and Napp several times indicating he was anxious to settle. After Kate's deposition, his actions indicated that he believed Kate was credible and her claims were backed by facts and Chuck was in a losing position. Jack Napp told Kate Mr. Morse anxiously telephoned him expressing his desire to reach a settlement. Mr. Morse had told Chuck he needed to put together a reasonable offer and immediately work toward a settlement with Kate. He stated emphatically to Jack Napp that he would have an offer to present to Kate by middle of January.

Immediately after the November 2016 mediation and Kate's deposition, Mr. Morse canceled numerous court objections to her petition claims with the exception of one motion, "the motion for partial summary disposition of the mental incapacity and undue influence," claims against both trusts. He kept this court date despite the fact that he was adamant that Chuck would have a settlement offer in January. The court date was set for February 16, 2017, two days after Gloriette's birth date and one year and one week following her dad's funeral. Mr. Morse received updated and expanded affidavits from Nurse Foe and Broker Schafte. By the end of January, it became evident that Chuck was not going to offer any settlement to Kate. Mr. Morse proceeded to have his motion heard in court by the judge; his intent was to have Kate's claims dismissed, stating, "Bertrand was of excellent mind and was not influenced by Chuck."

Finn Nash's affidavit was submitted during January 2017. Nash had made significant changes to Bertrand's trust in November 2006 in addition to removing the provision against trustee self-dealing that had been part of the Bertrand trust since it was established over a decade before. These facts had been established by the newer trust amendments. Although Kate had been her parents' financial advisor and successor trustee for over twenty-three years, Mr. Nash had no problem changing the terms of the trusts which triggered the events causing Kate and her dad's estrangement for the remaining ten years of his life. Furthermore, none of the changes was disclosed to Kate or any of the other four siblings until after his death. Four years following the initial new amendments, in January 2012, Finn Nash rewrote the land contract owned by the Gloriette trust erasing hundreds of thousands of dollars of principal and interest owed by Chuck. He added an amendment transferring her parents' remaining farmland to Chuck. He orchestrated the transfer of Gloriette's home to Chuck and Mildred through a legal document. None of the five siblings who were equal beneficiaries of the Gloriette trust was informed. All changes were implemented by Chuck as trustee and Finn Nash as his attorney. Finn Nash's affidavit stated, "I represented Bertrand in drafting the new amendments to his trust, and he had the ability to understand what he was doing. I knew Bertrand as a member of my church and as a client of Cheetham, Steele and Morse LLP, after the move of Ken Powler, his previous estate planner." He additionally stated, "I know Chuck and Mildred as attendees of my church and as clients of my law firm for their estate planning and legal proceedings." As Kate read his affidavit, she was struck with the most powerful point he made: "I attended the same church as Chuck and Bertrand."

"Was his statement "attendee of the same church" meant to *wash over* and erase the irreparable damage he did to their parents' estate?" Kate asked Bert. As beneficiary of her parents' trusts and a financial professional, she knew the changes he made were unethical and immoral. His legal work benefited one beneficiary who happened to be the trustee of both trusts. The changes were not disclosed to the trust beneficiaries.

Kate questioned whether Finn Nash earned a bonus or commission for the money his legal work generated for his law firm during Kate's fifteen-month legal ordeal. The revenue they received was a result of Nash's legal advice and actions for Chuck's benefit. "Where was the ethical oversight? Why was Nash allowed to make major trust alterations without any of the beneficiaries being notified?" Kate asked Jack Napp.

Attorneys Stone and Napp were confident Mr. Morse's motion would be denied. Prior to the court date, Bert, Phillip, and Kate prepared their affidavits. Kate's November 24 eight-hour deposition transcript was not requested by Mr. Morse. She traveled to Minnesota, spent an entire day being interrogated by Morse, and was recorded by an official court reporter, during which she gave substantial evidence against Chuck's actions as trustee, irrefutable evidence that he committed fraud and breached his fiduciary duties to the trust. Kate substantiated each allegation she made and backed it with documented evidence. Yet no transcript of her testimony was requested for disclosure or for a future court testimony. "Why?" Kate asked Jack Napp. Jack Napp said that they would have to pay for the court reporter transcript to be printed, and they did not want a written record of her deposition.

Chuck stated in his affidavit, "I exerted no undue influence on Dad, and he was mentally sharp." Stone and Napp agreed with Kate that Bert's and Phillip's affidavits were needed to counter the defenders of Chuck's affidavits. His younger brothers had witnessed Chuck's shenanigans over their lifetime. Their affidavits were recorded with the court and submitted along with the Wright, Coolidge and Stone PC's brief requesting Mr. Morse's motion be denied.

For the first time in over a year, Kate experienced a feeling of satisfaction because her brothers were finally being recognized as her parents' children. Bert and Phillip lived close to her dad, worked on the farm for decades, yet were never personally contacted or questioned by Cheetham, Steele and Morse LLP. An entire year had passed since her dad's death, Bert and Phillip had been completely ignored by the law firm representing their parents' estate. Bert, Phillip, and Kate repeatedly asked why. They had been ignored during the entire legal process.

Cheetham, Steele and Morse LLP was paid to represent their parents' trust and six beneficiaries. Three of the six beneficiaries were treated as adversaries. The year following the filing of Kate's court petitions, neither Bert or Phillip was questioned about their backgrounds or their knowledge of Chuck's handling of their dad's finances. Finn Nash, Mabel Snatt, and Mr. Morse charged significant legal fees against her parents' trusts defending Chuck, making no attempt to obtain information from the two brothers who lived within miles, cared for him, and worked on the farm during their childhood and teenage years. Mr. Morse requested that their affidavits be dismissed as irrelevant. He gave tremendous time and attention to Nurse Foe and Broker Schafte affidavits yet demanded Bertrand's son's statements be thrown out. Bert's and Phillip's affidavits stated that Chuck was not trustworthy or honest, using Bertrand's checkbook for personal expenses and his lavish lifestyle. Bert and Phillip witnessed Chuck's manipulative dealings with others throughout their lifetimes. Between them was the equivalent of over a half century of experience.

Chuck's lawyers refused to respond to legitimate questions asked by the successor trustee, Kate. Mr. Morse, Chuck's attorney, denied, delayed, and claimed statute of limitation defenses. Mr. Morse filed numerous court motions to block supplying requested documents. Nurse Foe's testimony was used extensively. Although Nurse Foe was around the last several years of her dad's life, she did not know all the children and was paid periodically by Chuck the years that she visited Bertrand at his home, approximately from 2008 to 2014. The bond broker, Schafte, took all his direction from Chuck after Bertrand's second hip surgery in the fall of 2011. Furthermore, Nurse Foe's affidavit was a duplicate of Ann's affidavit. Kate believed it was an attempt to hide the true facts. The affidavits of Nurse Foe, Broker Schafte, Finn Nash, Ann, and Cybil contained numerous false statements and lies.

One year following Kate's dad's death, the two youngest sons, Bert and Phillip, were asked about their lifetime of experience with Chuck and Bertrand during their court-ordered affidavits in January 2017. Bert's affidavit was different than Phillip's, and they were both different from Kate's. Each was independent but supported the other's facts: Chuck controlled her dad's actions, was verbally abusive, and used Bertrand's checkbook and credit cards for Chuck's personal expenditures. Bert and Phillip both witnessed a lifetime of Chuck's excessive and reckless spending of Bertrand's money. Bert's and Phillip's affidavits were based on recalled personal stories, whereas Kate's affidavit was based on provided documents, checks written, and brokerage statement records. The brothers each had varied stories of Chuck bad-mouthing his sisters, particularly Kate.

Bert arrived at the courtroom early Thursday morning. He walked up several flights of stairs to the fourth floor of the courthouse. As he was walking down the hall corridor, he saw Leonard, Ann's husband, staring out of a large glass window. Bert wondered if he was contemplating the difference between right and wrong. Bert walked into the courtroom and was surprised to see so many people sitting on the left side of the courtroom with Mr. Morse. Chuck, Mildred, Ann, Leonard, Cybil, and Chuck's children, Brenda, Flo, and Bart were gathered together. Conspicuously missing was Chuck's eldest son, Theodore. Kate was told by others and those who had witnessed Theodore being beaten by Chuck throughout his childhood. Chuck, Mildred, Ann, Leonard, Cybil, Brenda, Bart, and Flo, having used Bertrand for their financial gain, sat together, showing solidarity. Chuck was now the patriarch of the family.

Mr. Morse hoped to prove Bertrand was of sound mind when he signed the legal documents and trust amendments four years prior to his death. He relied on the affidavits of Nurse Foe and Broker Schafte to make his case. Broker Schafte purchased forty- and fifty-year maturity bonds at high commission rates, earning thousands of dollars for each trade he executed. Broker transactions occurred when Chuck ordered highly appreciated stock sold to withdraw funds for his large trust withdrawals. The broker's affidavit stated, "Bertrand did all his own research and called him with the purchase and sale requests." The bonds owned at her dad's death were thinly traded, locally issued paper. Many purchases were made while he was living at Maybrook. Chuck and Schafte wanted everyone to believe that although Bertrand was not able to read or use his telephone, Bertrand was able to research nonlisted forty-year maturity bonds, calling Schafte to demand purchase while selling his long-held profitable holdings.

According to Chuck, Ann, and Cybil, their dad was mentally capable of performing surgery at the age of eighty-six. While Kate personally knew individuals mentally competent to make legal decisions at his age, her dad was not one of them. His medical history included a serious stroke and many ministrokes during the twenty years prior to his death. He hadn't driven a car in years, did not cook, had his meals prepared and delivered, and was incontinent, having worn diapers for a decade. Chuck, Ann, and Cybil affirmed he was competent to take assets out of the Gloriette trust and assign them over to Chuck and Mildred. Morse stated, "Bertrand was competent to sign over the last parcel of land worth millions to one beneficiary who happened to be the trustee of his trust." Morse vigorously defended Chuck and tried to convince the judge that he was competent to forgive Chuck's debt to the Gloriette trust, thousands of dollars, interest, and principal due from the land contracts he had signed twenty years before, harming beneficiaries of the Gloriette trust.

Extensively quoted throughout the brief was Nurse Foe. She stated, "He told me over five times he wanted Chuck to get everything. He wasn't concerned about his other children. He told me that they would just have to accept it." She continued, "He had very long elaborate conversations telling long tales. He told me about his finances all the time. Chuck and Mildred paid for everything, including his food and personal items."

Kate had questioned many cash withdrawals and checks written to Chuck and signed by her dad over the years. When she reviewed copies of canceled checks and questioned the withdrawals, Chuck said, "The cash withdrawals were for Dad's expenses." Yet Morse stated Chuck paid for Bertrand's expenses with Chuck's personal money, again contradicting the evidence.

Mr. Morse hoped to prove that Bertrand had full mental faculties signing checks for Gloriette's trust distributions. Gloriette's trust appreciated dramatically because of the select stockholdings purchased during the nineties and early two thousands by Gordon and Kate. Chuck arranged for annual gifting out of the Gloriette trust to the beneficiaries. Chuck bragged about his success in persuading him to gift Gloriette's trust funds to Bert, Phillip, and Ann. Chuck complained to Bert and Phillip that he would not get credit for the distributions. Chuck bragged to his brothers, "I did it. It's because of me!"

Mr. Morse made the argument: "The distribution checks from the Gloriette trust was evidence Bertrand was of sound mind. Bertrand was able to write checks; he was of sound mind." The problem with Morse's reasoning was Bertrand was not the one writing the checks. It was either Chuck, Ann, or another person who wrote the checks, their signatures legible.

The judge said, "Do you have a handwriting expert to testify?" Kate recognized their handwriting and characteristic signatures; she recognized their distinct individual signatures. Mr. Morse made the argument that Bertrand wrote hundreds of checks, which proved Bertrand was mentally competent.

Kate questioned why her dad was writing so many checks. Bertrand had Chuck's friend coming to the house to occasionally clean for very little money each month. "Why was Bertrand writing so many checks each month?" Kate asked Bert. Bert sat with him for hours most Sunday afternoons. Bert remembered staring at his dad's bruised arms and wrists.

Bert wondered what caused the bruises the last year his dad lived at his home. Now, Bert was disgusted at his naiveté and trust in Chuck's care.

During court, Jack Napp argued the case, "Bertrand suffered from declining mental health and Chuck's undue influence." Napp mentioned the exhaustive medical records stating the following complaints listed year after year: "depression, loneliness, memory impairment, memory loss, frequent crying spells, sadness, tearfulness, and severe depression." The medical records listed the medical complaints for consecutive years. Jack brought up information from Bert's and Phillip's affidavits which mentioned their dad's inability to use the phone or television remote. Bertrand confused the remote and phone regularly as Bertrand's fine motor skills had declined with age. The legal process had little to do with common sense and much to do with redistribution of wealth.

Mr. Napp called attention to Bert's and Phillip's statements which stated, "Chuck was abusive and continually bad-mouthed and spoke poorly of his sisters, particularly Kate." Both brothers stated, "Chuck hated Kate." Bert stated, "Chuck is not an honest person. He took advantage of Dad's lack of mental capacity for his own personal gain." Jack Napp and Joe Stone did a brilliant job defeating Mr. Morse's motions; they countered Chuck's weak case with facts.

Mr. Morse argued that Kate bought her brothers off and stood to benefit greatly if the motion was not granted. "How do I benefit?" Kate later asked Bert. Chuck had absconded with a fortune since her mother's death. Ann took substantial money in the form of gifts, loans, and payments for what she billed for her services. Chuck transferred most of the assets out of the Bertrand trust and removed Kate as beneficiary for the insurance policies he pressured him into purchasing. The trust assets were transferred to Chuck and Mildred; most of the money was now gone. Kate's hope was for disclosure and the truth.

Bert told Kate that a significant part of the court case was based on the statements "Kate is a b—" and "Kate is a b—, the rich b—"

repeatedly stated by Mr. Morse. Bert occasionally glanced to the other side of the courtroom. Cybil, his sister, glared at him with hate-filled eyes. Chuck, Mildred, Ann, Leonard, and Chuck's children sat on the opposite side of the courtroom; and all ignored Bert as if he wasn't there. Bert said that he was lonely sitting on one side of the courtroom. Bert said to Kate that he felt good knowing the truth and that he was on the right side. Glancing across the aisle, Bert saw Chuck's three children, each owning a home bought by the Bertrand trust. Bert looked across the room at Cybil. Bert knew that Cybil had a big loan she expected to be forgiven if Chuck prevailed with the elaborate scheme. Both Ann and Chuck owed the Bertrand trust significant personal loans they knew would disappear if they succeeded. After Gloriette's death, Chuck and Ann became skilled at asking, "Dad, can I borrow some money?" Bertrand let them use his checkbook, and the check copies showed different handwriting for the names and sums with most checks signed by either Bertrand or Chuck. Chuck, Ann, and Mildred believed that no one would know and that they would never have to pay back a cent.

Mr. Morse stated repeatedly that Kate would benefit if this motion was denied. Kate was the petitioner against Chuck as trustee of her parents' trusts. As petitioner, Kate represented all beneficiaries: Bert, Phillip, Cybil, Chuck, Ann, and herself. Any right action benefitted everyone. "What did I do other than make our parents wealthy with my investment advice?" Kate asked Bert. Gordon and Kate were generous to her dad over many years. Cybil screamed at Kate after her dad's funeral, "Dad knew you hated him." The only reason Bertrand repeated this statement to others was because Chuck told him this over and over. After her dad's death, Kate was called names by those who supported Chuck in his efforts to ignore her requests for disclosure and transparency of the estate settlement process. Mildred stated repeatedly to others, "Kate is a b——, Kate is a b——." She heard of her rants following the funeral.

"I suppose it was because I got up and read a tribute to Dad. What did I do to those people?" Kate asked Bert.

Bert said, "Mildred tried to sway us. She repeatedly stated to others, 'Kate is a b—.'

Following her dad's funeral, Ann stated, "Mildred says you verbally attacked her following Mom's burial."

Kate was shocked at Ann's statement. Kate responded, "Why did she say that? You were there. You knew what happened." Ann shrugged her shoulders and walked away.

Following Gloriette's burial in June 1997, a reception was planned. When Kate arrived at her house, no food or preparations had been made. She walked over to Mildred's house as she was driving out the driveway. Kate asked her, "Where is the food?"

Mildred screeched, shouting out of her car window, "Who are you, Kate? You think you are the only person who is affected by her death? You are so inconsiderate! You only think of yourself!" She proceeded to shout at Kate a litany of reasons of why she did not like Kate. After she ran out of her explicative, she peeled out of her driveway. Kate was numb from her rant and thereafter avoided Mildred. Kate had spent the last week of her mom's life at her bedside. The week following Gloriette's death, Kate planned her funeral service and took care of Bertrand and her two-year-old daughter. At the time of her mother's death, Kate was seven months pregnant with her son. Mildred had accurately stated that Kate did not think about other's grief because Kate's grief was deep, real, and it was Kate's. The death of one's mother is significant to each individual and inevitably deeply personal. Mildred's job was to order the food for the reception. Kate simply asked her, "Mildred, where is the food?" Nineteen years later, Mildred stated, "Kate is a b—because she viciously verbally attacked me following Mom's funeral," which was repeated to Kate by Ann. Kate realized they had to have their narrative about Kate whether it was true or not. Ann went along with it and repeated it despite knowing it was not the truth. At the time of the incident, Ann knew Kate was shaken by Mildred's rant. Kate remained away from others at the reception, extremely upset about Mildred's verbal lashing. Ann instructed Kate to not tell Chuck what Mildred said because he would be very angry at Mildred for treating her badly. Kate recalled this incident that occurred nineteen years before that was nevertheless repetitiously repeated to disparage and demean her. Bert had signed a land contract on his property during November of 2006.

Bert made his monthly payments religiously. His payments went into the joint bank account that was used to support Chuck. Bert did not know this fact until Kate explained it to him, after researching years of trust and bank statements. Bert's land contract was a legally executed document. Chuck, Ann, and Cybil expected Bert to pay his loan back. Whereas Chuck, Ann, and Cybil's personal loans were not legal documents and were buried in the bank records, in addition to Chuck's hundreds of thousands of dollars of personal loans which would never be paid back because the records disappeared. Chuck wrote down the principal and interest of his land contract on three occasions, thereby cheating the Gloriette trust beneficiaries of monies owed. The legal documents Chuck held had been fraudulently changed and discounted. The amount stated was considerably less than the actual amount Chuck owed the Gloriette trust because Chuck and his lawyer amended his land contract payments as if the payments were made, when they were not. Fifteen years before, Chuck said to Bert and Phillip independently and on separate occasions, "I have spent all of my inheritance." Kate remembered a notebook that her dad recorded of personal loans that were made to both Chuck and Ann. She assumed the notebook was destroyed by Chuck and/or Ann.

Following the presentation of Kate's extensive research and each person's affidavits, the judge denied Mr. Morse's motion and ordered all beneficiaries to mediation called mediation 2. The first mediation was held on November 22, 2016. Chuck had stormed out after Kate recommended her younger brothers, Bert and Phillip, receive half of the last parcel of their parents' farmland. The mediator explained to Kate that

Chuck threw the mediation papers down on the table shouting, "They will not get any of my land!"

Bert called later that day to give Kate the news while attorneys Stone and Napp both e-mailed her claiming victory in defeating Morse's motion. The judge agreed that Chuck exerted undue influence over Bertrand. Kate did not want to go to mediation again; it had been exhausting, unproductive, and expensive. She called Jack Napp and asked, "We already went through mediation at a great expense. Why will the outcome change?"

He said, "The judge ordered you to go."

Kate replied, "Does he have any idea of the amount of money spent to get to the truth?" The month of November included their first mediation and her deposition. Kate was billed over forty thousand dollars that month. Kate was personally spending more money with no resolution in sight; perhaps it was time for her to simply give up and be done with their demands, and she asked herself. Kate was required to cancel her obligations and expend more of her time and money, returning to Minnesota for mediation 2. "Where is Chuck getting his money for this continued litigation?" she asked Phillip. Phillip mentioned that perhaps Ann gave him some money or perhaps Mildred's father, who was expecting to live in Gloriette's prior home. Kate noticed a gambler's mentality of going for broke and realized that this was his modus operandi; he had no regard for the value of money. Kate recognized that Chuck's directive to his attorney's was to "take her out" at any cost. After the February court date, Kate continued to receive new motions from Chuck's attorney and new "statute of limitations" defenses along with numerous documents to increase the litigation expense at the urging of Chuck. Chuck wanted Kate to give up and walk away, reversing Mr. Morse's actions after Kate's November deposition when Morse cancelled the numerous motions he filed previously.

Kate told Jack Napp that Chuck needed to divide the remaining land equally. Ann and Cybil might allocate their percentage to Chuck, and the remaining 50 percent would go to Bert and Phillip. Chuck immediately stormed out of the November mediation when the proposal was made by the mediator. "Chuck doesn't want his brothers to have it." Jack Napp said to her, "The property is the problem, and he is not going to let it go."

Napp said to Kate, "Joe and I talked about it, and we suggest filing a legal action in which Chuck is declared in default of his land contracts. Chuck has already admitted he is."

Kate agreed and stated, "Absolutely, this should have been done before." Later, this strategy was dismissed as explained to her by Jack Napp because it might have compromised other legal points.

One year passed since Kate started the uncovering of the deceit and manipulation perpetrated by Chuck, Ann, and Mildred. Mr. Morse took over the estate file from Mabel Snatt in June when Chuck's legal representative realized Kate filed petitions against Chuck. However, Mabel Snatt stayed on the case as administrative attorney. Snatt wrote a letter about once a month to all the beneficiaries of the trusts; this allowed Snatt to charge the Bertrand and Gloriette trusts additional legal administrative expenses.

After Bertrand's funeral, each of the children were given the packet of legal documents prepared by Cheetham, Steele and Morse LLP, which included a form stating each child had received one-sixth of their parents' property, which they were each required to sign. Kate asked Ann for one of the antique rocking chairs and an antique clock. Ann replied that Chuck had taken it and she was taking everything else. Ann ignored individual requests for any of their parents' possessions. Bert, Phillip, and Kate did not sign the form. Months later, Mabel Snatt mailed a letter stating, "Since we haven't heard from you, we assume you received one-sixth of your parents' property." Essentially, whether you received it or not, it doesn't matter. Ms. Snatt received monthly legal billings from their parents' trust while working on Chuck's behalf.

Early during the petition process, Kate compiled a list of their parents' personal property. Most of the items had already been taken by Chuck and Ann. Kate sent the list to Ann and asked for confirmation of the inventory; however, Ann refused to admit she had taken most of the property out of their parents' home over the many years following Gloriette's death. Bert, Phillip, and Kate no longer had any interest in receiving any of their parents' possessions; however, they each wanted a written disclosure of the disposition of their possessions.

The letters Ms. Snatt wrote each month were often targeted against one beneficiary, Kate. She wrote, "Kate is suing your parents' trusts."

Kate asked Mr. Napp, "How do you sue paper documents?" Kate filed petitions against the trustee Chuck, asking questions; none of which had been answered one year later. Mabel Snatt's letters were hostile toward the three beneficiaries who refused to sanction Chuck's actions—Bert, Phillip, and Kate. Gloriette and Bertrand established the trusts for the equal distribution of their estate. Kate knew they did not imagine any law firm handling their estate would deliberately take the side of one beneficiary over all beneficiaries while charging egregious legal fees, dissipating their trust's assets.

Kate remembered back to the November mediation. She had asked Jack Napp about Morse's motivation. Napp said, "I've seen Mr. Morse take many estates down to nothing. I don't know if he is in it to win or for the money. I know he has no regard for the estates or beneficiaries." Kate bought a plane ticket and made plans to take time off from work for mediation 2. Each sibling received additional packages of legal documents. Mr. Morse secured a second court date in March to disallow Kate's claims under a new statute of limitation defense.

She received Chuck's required accounting of the two trusts from her dad's date of death to the following year. As co-trustee for the Gloriette trust, Kate was not consulted or allowed input to the accounting for the Gloriette trust. Kate reviewed trust balance sheet information as confirmed by Chuck as co-trustee. The accounting for the Gloriette trust was verified accurate from either Chuck's bank records or the joint checking account he held with Bertrand. In other words, they did an accounting of the Gloriette trust without using her trust statements. The principal amount owed stated the falsified amount from the 2012 amendments which had erased thirteen years of principal and interest owed to the Gloriette trust by Chuck. (Chuck's land contract was amended and rewritten in 2012 by Finn Nash.)

Kate had copies of the annual Bertrand trust statements from 1997 to the present. She also had copies of trust checks which specifically listed loans Bertrand made to both Chuck and Ann. Prior to her dad losing his memory, he wrote "loan" in the memo section of his checks to either Chuck or Ann. The checks and the notations during these years were in his handwriting. Chuck's and Ann's past loans disappeared during Chuck's accounting process. There were, however, two debts listed: Kate's 1996 loan, now purporting to owe over one hundred and forty thousand dollars and a debt owed by Phillip to Bertrand's trust of approximately forty thousand dollars.

Kate found it interesting that Chuck refused to provide any supporting deposit documentation over the history of his loans. He emphatically stated, "You have no right to the information as it exceeds the five-year statute of limitations." Yet Chuck listed what he referred to as Kate's debt to the Bertrand trust, which was over twenty years old, Phillip's loan from 2000, and Bert's ten-year land contract, all at 7 percent compounded interest.

Chuck's twenty-four-year land contract payment history, including three amendments wiping out principal and interest, was acceptable to the estate attorneys because they refused to respond to the petition claims and factual documentation submitted through the court process, ignoring the documentation because it wouldn't support their defense of Chuck. Mr. Morse vigorously fought to disallow transparency of trustee dealings, claiming a statute of limitation defense. Trust documents from the five years prior to her dad's passing were difficult for Kate to receive, requiring months of legal procedures and court orders to receive.

According to Chuck's interrogatory filings, Cybil owed the Bertrand trust fifty thousand dollars. This particular loan was not listed in his trust accounting. Bert, Phillip, and Kate realized that if you were on Chuck's team, your loans were forgiven. However, Kate, Bert, and Phillip owed significant sums compounded at 7 percent over many years, even if this was not accurate.

Throughout the fifteen months of litigation, Kate's intent was to make sure Bert and Phillip were represented. Kate was overwhelmed by Chuck's legal maneuverers and complicated scheme meant to hurt and discourage her from her role of successor trustee. During this time, Kate realized her younger brothers were subjected to a lifetime of Chuck's devious schemes and manipulation.

Bert and Phillip each had suffered financial setbacks and hardships at various times during their life. Individually, they told her of their older brother's glee and smiles during the times they had experienced a particular failure. A thought struck her like a thunderbolt as she realized Chuck manipulated Bertrand against his younger sons their entire life. Kate recalled Bertrand's cruelty toward Bert and Phillip, his youngest sons. Bert and Phillip were a threat to Chuck who did not want to share the farm or any property with his brothers. Chuck used Bert and Phillip for their hard work ethic over many years under Chuck's tyrannical direction. Chuck was physically and verbally abusive to his younger brothers; she had witnessed it, and the stories she heard over the years confirmed it. After using Bert and Phillip for their work, Chuck wanted them to go away, to disappear; Chuck pretended they did not exist. The law firm representing their parents' trust pretended Bert and Phillip did not exist, and Ann and Cybil pretended their younger brothers did not exist. However, Bert was mentioned only to pay back his legally executed promissory note on his land. Other than Bert's loan, Kate's younger brothers were not mentioned. Chuck stated throughout, "They left. I stayed, and I deserve everything." Bert's land contract payments went into Bertrand's joint checking account. Chuck used Bert's deposits to pay for Chuck's personal expenses. Chuck was always calling Bert to ask him to do errands and help with Bertrand's daily care. It had become clear to Kate that Chuck resented Bert and Phillip since their birth. Chuck was threatened by them and was overcome with envy at their success. Chuck did not understand how they lived their life expecting nothing in return for good deeds and fair treatment of others.

QUE SERÁ, SERÁ

"Que será, será (whatever will be, will be) was a line used in the movie Barefoot Contessa, starring Humphrey Bogart and Ava Gardner, a movie premiering during 1954. The line was used again a couple of years later in a song from the Alfred Hitchcock film starring Doris Day and James Stewart. Kate and her dad shared a common fondness for classic black-and-white movies. She kept thinking of this phrase after months of researching facts to support her legal petition process. She was deeply disturbed to realize the part Ann played in causing an estrangement with her dad. During the months following her dad's death, Kate often asked her husband, "Why?" Gordon's response was "Accept the truth. It is what it is." Kate woke in the middle of many nights asking the same question, "Why?"

One weekend in November of 2004, after Bertrand arrived at the desert home for the winter, Kate was visiting her dad. He began haranguing Kate about what a rotten child she had been. Kate was now forty-eight years old, successful in business, and enjoying a happy family life. Her dad's angry rhetoric stung. Kate had telephoned her dad on a regular basis, once or twice a week since college graduation. After her dad's rant, Kate was upset and hoped he would cool off and come to his senses. Kate did not telephone her dad any longer. In hindsight, she realized her mistake. The cessation of the normal telephone communication made Bertrand increasingly upset. When Kate eventually called her dad, he was angry at her and she was angry at him, both angry for the same reason. It was during this time that Bertrand started calling his daughter Kate by ugly names. He would call Kate a "b—" and hang up the telephone when she called. Their relationship went rapidly from good to bad. At the time, Kate did not know the reason her dad's behavior toward her had become so hostile. In time, she realized Chuck was working aggressively to turn their dad against her. Kate believed Chuck repeated stories about Kate being a terrible child and called her names; eventually, Bertrand repeated Chuck's repetitious slander as if he was a parrot. These occurrences coincided with the time Ken Powler, their parents' estate attorney, moved to another law firm.

Bert and Phillip remembered Chuck constantly complaining about Kate's loan, telling their dad that Kate owed money and Kate wasn't repaying her loan to Bertrand. Chuck would say, "Kate is ungrateful." Chuck continually referred to Kate as "rich b—" as Kate was later told by her siblings and cousins. Kate was dumbfounded that they routinely called her a "rich b—," ungrateful, and that she hated her dad. Kate gradually came to understand her dad was manipulated by repetition, over and over, until ugly statements became truth to him. Bert and Phillip individually told Kate that Chuck repeatedly said she was not doing a good job of handling the trusts during those years. Chuck would say, "Kate is ungrateful."

Kate asked Bert why Chuck would say Kate was ungrateful. Bert said, "It's because Dad bought you a car, and you were ungrateful."

Kate responded, "What car? I don't know of a car Dad bought me?"

Bert said, "Yeah, you never saw the car or knew he bought it because he returned it immediately." The phantom car purchase was during her high school years when Kate was working a total of four part-time jobs in addition to her high school honors classes. She did not know that he bought a car for her nor did anyone tell her that he bought a car. Kate didn't think he actually bought a car. She believed this was another story that was concocted by Chuck.

During the November 2016 deposition, Kate learned Ann's role in her sibling's scheme to turn her dad against her. Ann told Bertrand and

Chuck that Kate purposefully did not visit her dad when she was in town for her high school reunion.

Kate and her dad had not talked for several months. Ann suggested to Kate that she write a letter to him because he would not speak to her. After Ann's urging, Kate wrote a letter attempting to defend herself as a girl, teenager, and finally an adult. She attempted to explain that he did not have a basis for his derogatory claims. Kate gave the letter to Ann to read and asked her opinion if it would help her dad thaw his anger toward her. Ann said to Kate, "It's a good letter. Mail it to him." Despite receiving her letter, her dad would not take her calls. Kate did not realize that this letter would be used as weapon against her for the rest of her life. Her intention had been to defend herself and help him understand her better. After her dad's death, Ann said, "Your mean letter sat on the kitchen table for three years." Ann said, "You ruined your relationship with Dad by the letter you sent."

Kate replied, "You read the letter, and you said it was good."

She responded, "It wouldn't have mattered what was in it. Chuck ranted about how much you hated him by sending him the letter." Her statement proved that she knew he was unable to read. She knew the letter was used against her for years, saying nothing to Kate.

After their dad's death, Phillip told Kate, "Chuck carried on about the letter at each opportunity he had, usually during their morning coffee time. Chuck said, 'Kate is a b——, and she hates you, Dad.'" Philip and Bert both heard Chuck's rants about Kate's letter for years; neither one of them read it, and they ignored Chuck's rants. Chuck had negative and critical statements to say about most people he knew. They witnessed Chuck's negative statements about relatives, neighbors, sisters, and, most often, Kate. Kate was dumbfounded; nine years had passed before she heard Chuck's passionate rhetoric about a letter she had written to repair her differences with her dad.

Kate was exiled for years because of a letter; the contents of which she thought was innocent. She was falsely accused—reminding her of Edmond Dantè's exile to the harsh island prison Chateau d'If off the coast of Marseille, France. Edmond suffered under solitary confinement for fourteen years because of a letter. A letter he delivered innocently, unaware of its contents. He did not know his crime, why he was imprisoned, or who his accuser was. Ten years passed when he realized he was falsely accused by his best friend, Fernand Mondego. Fernand wanted him out of sight because of his intense lifelong jealousies and his desire for Edmond's fiancée, Mercedes Herrera. The Count of Monte Cristo was written long ago in 1844 by Alexandre Dumas. Kate related to his exile; she was unaware the letter would cause hatred and estrangement. Interestingly, Chuck gave her his copy of the book decades ago. "You must read this book," he said as he handed Kate the thick paperback book.

Ann knew her dad refused to talk to Kate. She knew she wrote the letter hoping to repair and help him understand her. Ann listened as Kate lamented about her unfair treatment. Ann and Kate had the same conversation many times over the years, yet she remained silent. After his death, Kate learned what they said about her—she's a "b—," and she is not doing a good job, and she's difficult to work with. Yet she wasn't her dad's broker at the time; Gordon was. The accounts did extremely well during the years Gordon and her dad worked together. The statements showed the truth. Ann and Chuck's claims were not based on facts; instead, they were purposeful lies.

After her mother died, Kate gave Ann money each Christmas for her to buy gifts for her children as her mother had done previously. Kate wrote checks to her for her missionary travel and volunteer work. Kate wrote checks for Ann's children's college tuition. Ann's family stayed at Kate's home on occasion, and Kate traveled to Ann's home numerous times, yet Ann never said one word when Kate asked why her dad was upset. Ann traveled to Minnesota often. During the legal process, Kate came to understand that Ann did this to get her dad's money and her parents' property. She often drove her dad long distances to see his siblings. All those times together and she did not ask her dad, "Dad, why have you been so unfair to Kate? Why do you call her names and not talk to her? You know, she has been upset by the things you have said to her. The letter she wrote was only to defend herself against all your name-calling. Dad, let's figure this out and repair it. She needs to be a part of your life. Kate and Gordon have been good to you. This is what you and Mom planned and expected." Ann never mentioned to Kate about her dad's unhappiness about the estrangement or Kate's deep hurt she suffered from her dad's actions. Yet Ann was active in her dad's life and regularly spoke to Kate. According to Bertrand, Chuck, Ann, Cybil, and Mildred, Kate was the bad person, the villain. Bert and Phillip had been told for years that Kate was a bad person during discussions at their dad's kitchen table. They did not participate in the conversations because they rarely saw Kate after their mother's death and did not relate to what they were saying about her. Ann and Leonard were two people who could have put an end to the estrangement; she could have been the bridge builder. Instead, she promoted the estrangement as it served her purpose. Ann chose to manipulate her dad to her benefit and did it because she didn't want Kate asking questions or preventing her extraction of trust assets. After Bertrand's death, Kate recognized that the extensive home remodels, barn renovations, second farm purchase, decks, trips, vehicles, and expensive musical instruments were all purchased by her dad's trust. Ann took her dad to Arkansas during his last year of life to justify all she had taken. It was her objective to convince others they were selflessly taking care of her dad. The truth was really financial motivation. Slowly, Kate realized Ann cared only about her dad's money. Kate listed the checks written to Ann for nineteen years from the trust, the nineteen years following Gloriette's passing. Kate recognized there were many checks written by Chuck, signed by Chuck, and noted in the memo section of the check as "gift." Ann and Leonard collected monthly payments which equaled the amount Maybrook was being paid for their dad's twenty-four-seven care. After two months caring for her dad after Ann had moved Bertrand to Arkansas, Ann told Kate that she couldn't handle taking care of her dad. Bertrand's care was turned over to her husband, Leonard. At the end of Bertrand's life, Kate was told that Ann and Leonard checked Bertrand into a low-end nursing home. Phillip was told by the nursing home staff that Bertrand escaped from the home one cold winter night, wearing few clothes and no shoes, after which Bertrand developed pneumonia. Bert, Phillip, and Kate were convinced their dad would have been better off staying at Maybrook in Minnesota.

Kate was never given any indication her dad cared for her at all by anyone, her brothers, her sisters, or Bertrand's close relatives. Ann knew what had transpired; she knew Chuck brainwashed their dad, and Ann knew about the lies because Ann told Kate she knew. Kate confronted Ann about what had been learned after her dad's death. Ann had eleven children.

"What if she had one child who manipulated her against another child during her aging years?" Kate asked Gordon. Kate had always assumed Ann and her dad had a close relationship because Bertrand was financially generous to Ann that had been evident. Kate recognized her dad always gave Ann whatever she asked for. Kate realized that Ann was an expert manipulator. Ann's manipulation started as a child, and her mastery improved as she became an adult and her dad's senility increased. Kate realized that Ann did not care for her dad because if she had, she would not have treated him as she did and used him openly for financial gain.

Kate understood why Chuck did what he did; however, she did not understand Ann's motivation until she read about sibling envy. She researched sibling envy psychology after her dad's death, realizing Ann was envious of Kate's relationship with her dad. Ann was envious of Kate's family, home, lifestyle; and most of all, she was envious of Kate's relationship with their mother. Ann made disparaging remarks about Kate and Kate's family behind her back, which were eventually repeated to Kate. Ann made sure Kate did not receive one thing from her mother's kitchen. Gloriette was an excellent cook and baker; and her love toward her children was reflected in her cooking, baking, and the meals she planned. Ann gave her children Gloriette's possessions. Kate asked her many times for one of her cookbooks. Ann ignored Kate's requests, turning sibling rivalry into adult envy.

Ann ensured that the relationship between her dad and Kate was never repaired because she withheld information. Eventually, Ann appeared instrumental in an arranged meeting. Four years had passed and her dad's senility was entrenched. By this time, her dad had forgotten the reason for the estrangement. They were cordial; however, the relationship would never be the same. Ann was the one person to confront her dad about his verbal abuse and transfer of the trust accounts when it happened because she knew that Chuck was behind her dad's actions. Ann admitted this fact to Kate after their dad's death and after Kate confronted Ann about the timeline of events. Ann was integral to the entire scheme as Kate explained the events which were twisted by Chuck and Ann. Ann could have told their dad the letter was an effort to defend herself. She could have acted as Kate's advocate. Kate was ignorant and naive for ten years, thinking Ann would act in both of their interests. Ann had one agenda, and it was her own.

Phillip visited his dad as often as possible in the last year of his life in Arkansas. Phillip drove nonstop to spend the last week of his dad's life with him. Arriving at the hospital room, Ann confronted him, "What are you doing here? You are going to ruin all I have done the past year!"

Phillip replied gently, "How could I take away any time you have spent with our dad?"

Ann was angry she brusquely shouted at him, "I do not want anyone else here!" She stormed out of the room and did not return for an entire day. She harshly said to Phillip, "I do not want you to say anything to any of our brothers and sisters about Dad's condition. I do not want anyone else here."

During his last days, Bertrand repeatedly asked Phillip, "Where is Chuck? Is Chuck coming to see me?" Although Phillip was instructed not to tell his siblings of his condition, he called Chuck.

Chuck said, "I'm not coming. I am done with him."

Ann sent group texts informing all siblings that their dad had pneumonia. Her texts stated that she thought he would recover and improve. She did not admit their dad was passing until the last days of his life. During this time, Kate said to her, "I am envious of you for being at Dad's bedside. You are fortunate to spend time with Dad as his soul passes on. We both know how special the time was when Mom passed, gently and peacefully. It was a beautiful experience." Ann was silent and hung up the phone.

Phillip was with his dad at the end of his life. He confirmed that he was sad his children were not with him. Phillip and Kate agreed that most would want their children with them at the end. He asked for his children, each one. He said he loved his children; he named each child. The only reason Kate knew this was because of the time Phillip spent with him. Fortunately, this son wanted nothing but his love. Bertrand saw Phillip's pure love and unselfishness toward the end of his life. For the first time, her dad was able to express the love he had for his children because of the unconditional love Phillip expressed toward him.

During Phillip's visits to Arkansas, his dad stated to him that he was disappointed with Chuck and Ann. Bertrand said, "I have seen their greed and finally realize they wanted my money." Phillip told Kate that their dad realized Chuck and Ann manipulated him to gain control of his assets, finally realizing they tricked him into changing his trust, transferring assets to themselves, and eliminating mention of his other children. He told Phillip they told him to do what they said because they were the only ones taking care of him. He apologized to Phillip for the financial mess he was leaving. At the time, Phillip did not know what he was talking about.

Following their dad's death and the months of research that followed, Kate no longer believed her dad was properly cared for during the last years of his life. Just prior to the first mediation, she received hundreds of pages of medical records detailing the last seven years. She asked, "Why wasn't he admitted to Maybrook many years earlier? He would have had a better opportunity to get acclimated and have the social interaction he did not have at home." Chuck took him out periodically and drove him to church to make his appearance as a dutiful son; and afterward, Bertrand returned home and sat alone.

Kate was told her dad had caretakers look after him; however, after she reviewed his bank records for the last five years of his life, she was alarmed to see the small expenditures for his care. There was one person, Polly Nest, who received consistent checks for small amounts. Kate asked Bert about her. Bert said, "Polly is a barmaid Chuck befriended, and she cleaned the house."

Kate asked Bert, "Who took care of Dad's personal hygiene?" Bert said, "I think Dad did."

Kate knew her dad's expenses were minimal at home because she studied the Lloyd's Bank statements. The medical records stated he suffered from intense loneliness and depression and had frequent crying bouts and that he was not ambulatory. The other children assumed Chuck and Ann had their dad's best interest and they cared for him; after all, they assured each of their siblings they were giving him the best care available. One year following his death and months of bank and brokerage statement research, medical records, and conversations, Kate was convinced Chuck and Ann acted only for their own financial interests. They were more interested in appearances than their dad's well-being. Kate asked herself what would motivate a child to turn his parent against his other children. Bert, Phillip, and Kate realized that Ann and Chuck did this throughout their lives, earnestly trying to create a divide between their dad and each of his children by telling repeated negative stories to their dad. Ann stated in her affidavit, "Most people thought Dad had only two children, myself and Chuck." Chuck and Ann successfully convinced all to believe just what they wanted them to believe. To her revelation, Kate said, "Que será, será."

CORN, COWS, AND MANURE

During the early seventies, Bertrand and Gloriette purchased 640 acres of land across from Huntington Golf Course. The 640-acre parcel was equivalent to one square mile of land. At that time, their parcel was considered inexpensive to comparable farmland. Kate remembered thinking it was quite a distance to drive tractors and combines for crop harvesting, being about seven miles from their family farm. The parcel was part of the one thousand five hundred acres owned at the height of the farming operation during the late seventies. During mid to late eighties, the farmland was sold to pay off debts as the operation was liquidated. Just before her mother's death, there were two parcels of farmland remaining. There was a thirty-eight-acre parcel separated from the 160 acres. The remaining parcel was wooded with rolling hills and small lakes.

Forty years after the original purchase, the land had become very valuable as the surrounding area had been residentially developed, as professionals bought acreage and built large homes following the 2008 financial panic. Additionally, small upscale housing developments were constructed, using previous farming acreage. During 1999, Chuck explained to Kate why the farm acreage had greatly appreciated, explaining to Kate that the county's school district was one of the best in the state. Hunter County was the county where Huntington Golf Course was located, across the street from her parents' remaining farmland. At that time, Bertrand agreed to construct access entrances for the eventual development of the property after his death; and after the division of the property, each inheriting one-sixth of the property, the farmland enhancement expenditures were paid for by his trust.

Her parents' trust documents clearly stated, "The two remaining parcels of farmland are to be divided equally between six children at the death of the second parent." Gloriette talked to Aunt Faye, her sister, about her concerns and said, "I'm afraid Chuck will do something with the property and steal it from his siblings." Gloriette and Faye were two of three triplets. Faye was Gloriette's confidante, discussing their deep personal thoughts between each other. Kate became close to her aunt Faye after Kate moved to California in June of 1978. Aunt Faye died two weeks following Bertrand's death. Kate visited her aunt on an almost-daily basis the last weeks of her life as she lived close to Kate's home. A few days before Aunt Faye's death, Aunt Faye told Kate about her conversation with Gloriette, just before Gloriette died, about the farmland. Kate's parents' estate attorney, Ken Powler, suggested the property be titled and entered into an LLC or limited liability company to ensure its legal protection for the benefit of the six beneficiaries. Kate supplied his documentation during the discovery phase of her petition process. She gave the extensive detailed asset list and instructions to Ann and Leonard immediately following her dad's funeral. The list and directions were detailed prior to Gloriette's death and again extensively reconfirmed during the separation of her assets into the Gloriette trust.

Within three years of Gloriette's death, Chuck sold the thirty-eight-acre parcel. During the discovery phase of the case, Kate was given bank documentation for this particular land sale that had been orchestrated by Chuck. The proceeds from the sale were deposited to a new joint account between Chuck and Bertrand, one more example of Chuck's influence to transfer assets out of the trusts and into Chuck's personal possession.

After her dad's death, Kate heard about Chuck's corn-growing scheme. She called it a scheme right away, although it seemed most people bought Chuck's story that her dad wanted Chuck to farm again.

Their family farm had ceased operation for twenty-four years, yet Chuck said, "Dad gave me the remaining 160 acres so I could start farming again."

Phillip was disappointed because he had planned on building a home on his one-sixth of the property and knew exactly where his dream cabin was to be built. Bert lived down the street and thought his one-sixth as potential pastureland for his expanding shorthorn cattle herd.

Kate had assumed Chuck would offer to buy each of their one-sixth parcel after her dad's death because she knew the value of Bertrand's portfolio holdings would allow Chuck to buy everyone out. Chuck had other plans as he decided no sibling would inherit any of the land he coveted, planning to clear part of the land and grow corn. Chuck convinced neighbors and long-term acquaintances of Bertrand that Bertrand wanted Chuck to have it all as Chuck began a new farming operation. Most commercial farmers grew thousands of acres of corn either at a profit or loss. Chuck told others that he was going to make money on his small-time corn operation.

Bertrand finally entered Maybrook retirement home during 2014. Shortly thereafter, Chuck hired excavators and cleared hundreds of trees. After the farm operation was closed down during the late eighties, Gloriette and Bertrand planted hundreds of seedlings to return the property to its natural state. Chuck bought over twenty thousand dollars of seed corn, fertilizer, a combine, and John Deere tractor as well as the other equipment he needed for his new venture. He paid laborers to implement his corn-growing scheme. Kate reconciled the checks written from her dad's checking account against Chuck's farming purchases, confirming all the monies came from Bertrand's trust account and were transferred into his joint checking account with Chuck. After months of legal expense, she received copies of specific checks she had requested. Kate questioned Chuck through the legal process about his corn-scheme checks. He said, "They are all gifts from Dad. He wanted me to farm the land."

Chuck planted a parcel of corn on 160 acres of development property, his effort to demonstrate to others he was going to return to farming. "Dad wants me to farm again," adamantly Chuck claimed to relatives, neighbors, sisters, and his younger brothers.

His final trust amendment signed four years before her dad's death transferred this valuable land to Chuck, upon his death. Prior to that time, he was to pay for his annual use of the land. Kate asked Chuck the following question through her petition claims on the behalf of the trust beneficiaries: "Chuck did not pay the trust for the use of the land, and we did not receive proceeds from the crop and timber taken from the land. Where are the proceeds owed to the trust?"

Chuck responded through the legal process and his attorney, "I don't make money growing corn." He submitted his tax return schedule showing that in the first corn-growing year he lost sixty thousand dollars and that the second year losses were over fifty thousand dollars. "I don't need to pay the trust for the use of the land because it is unprofitable, and I don't make money." Bert, Phillip, and Kate shook their heads in disbelief.

Chuck lived on the original family farm property, which included two Harvestore silos, several barns as well as nice cattle-feeding area. He was given twenty acres of pastureland surrounding the stone house, barn, and farm buildings included in his 1992 land contract. Around the time of Chuck's return to farming, Bert asked Chuck why he did not take advantage of raising some cows since he had the perfect setup for cattle. Chuck became red in the face and stormed off swearing and muttering to himself as he was waving his arms wildly.

During the late eighties, Chuck failed to empty the moist corn crop from the Harvestore silo. Within a period of time, the stored moist corn turned to what looked like manure. Bert often mentioned to Kate that Chuck had substantial environmental cleanup expense because the silos were no longer useable, having stored rotten silage inside for years.

Phillip returned to the old family barn occasionally after his farming partnership with Chuck had dissolved. He vividly remembered seeing dead calves lying around the lower barn feeding area. Phillip realized the dead calves suffered an early death at the cruel hands of Chuck, realizing Chuck beat the calves to death to vent his anger and rage on the helpless animals. During the years he was a farm partner, he witnessed Chuck pick up sick calves, screaming at them with spit and drool flowing out of his mouth, and Chuck cursed at the animals with his rage-filled eyes.

Kate asked Bert about Chuck's treatment of his animals. Bert replied, "Chuck does not have good animal husbandry skills. His dog doesn't like him."

Kate responded, "Bert, why do you make such a statement? A dog is man's most faithful friend."

Bert stated, "I have seen Chuck beat his dogs on many occasions. Do you remember Daisy?" Kate recalled her dad's fondness toward Daisy. Bert mentioned that Mildred drove her car over young Daisy as she backed out of their driveway. Bert said, "Mildred has driven over several dogs. She doesn't bother to check behind her car."

Daisy ran into the woods while Bert and Chuck chased after her as she was bleeding from her mouth. Chuck said, "She's a goner."

Bert carried her to the water pump and washed her mouth out. Bert took her to his barn and nursed her back to life. Kate said to Bert, "I guess that's why her teeth stuck out of her mouth."

Bert replied, "Yes, of course." Bert gave Daisy to her dad when he temporarily moved back to Nebraska.

Kate asked, "What happened to Chuck's little shepherd?"

Bert replied, "Mildred drove over that dog and killed him. Chuck often beat the little dog. Shep was skittish around Chuck and often shook from fear." Bert stated, "Chuck sped out of my driveway one time and ran over one of my favorite dogs. Chuck often jumped into his truck and sped away without any concern for animals that may be lying next to his vehicle."

Following mediation 2, Chuck's John Deere tractor sat in his driveway with a "for sale" sign. New, this particular tractor cost over two hundred thousand dollars. The barn door with the 4B sign was covered with a piece of brown cardboard. Kate assumed Chuck was getting prepared to develop his valuable acreage across from the golf course. Chuck's corn-growing scheme turned out to be quite an elaborate long-range plan to trick his siblings out of the land they were to inherit. Chuck fooled most people, but he did not fool Kate.

THE EPIPHANY

On March 16, 2017, the mediation agreement was signed by all siblings. The agreement stated that there was a forty-five-day period of time to complete and perform what was stated within the agreement, requirements which required Chuck's sole execution. Bert and Phillip were skeptical that Chuck would comply with the agreed-upon terms while Kate was relieved and hopeful the ordeal was close to ending.

While reviewing the brokerage statements for each trust just before mediation 2, Kate noticed that Chuck wrote a large check from Bertrand's trust account. The check he wrote appeared to pay for his January litigation expense. Kate e-mailed Jack Napp while recognizing a check was also written in March which appeared to cover his February court expense. Kate telephoned Jack Napp and stated that Chuck was violating their mediation agreement because it had been agreed that all litigation expenses was the responsibility of both Chuck and Kate. The response from Chuck's attorneys, Ms. Snatt and Mr. Morse, was the immediate elimination of Kate's ability to receive any and all statements on the accounts. They rescinded her ability to view the account activity and statements online. By eliminating her ability to monitor the accounts online, she was unable to monitor his checks made payable to Cheetham, Steele and Morse LLP.

Mr. Morse stated to Jack Napp, "Kate has no right to receive copies of the trust statements." Previously, Kate had received the statements from the date of her dad's death to March 2017. Kate already had copies of all the checks Chuck had written during this time.

Kate sent copies of the cleared checks Chuck had written during February and March 2017 to Ann and Cybil. Cybil immediate mailed a letter to Kate, in essence stating that Kate had no right to accuse Chuck of spending their parents' trust money. According to Cybil, the tangible property expense, the legal expenditures, and the estate settlement delays were entirely Kate's fault as she stated in her note to Kate.

Cybil's claim was unfounded because Kate had nothing to do with Mabel Snatt's letters, the tangible property list, or the related attorney expense. Bert told Kate that Ann and Leonard returned some of their parents' personal property from Arkansas to Minnesota several months earlier, property they had previously taken. Bert was told Cybil spent time doing an inventory of the items prior to mediation 2. One of Chuck's attorneys, Ms. Snatt, sent out the inventory list with a caustically worded letter. Kate set Mabel Snatt's letters aside and did not response to Ms. Snatt because Kate had spent the past year carefully reviewing brokerage and bank statements, medical records, and the endless legal documents drafted by Cheetham, Steele and Morse LLP. After her dad's funeral, Kate had asked Ann if she could have one antique rocker and a register clock. Ann said they were taken. Additionally, Kate mentioned to Ann that she would like Mrs. Fredericka's side table and a particular painting. The following day, Bert told Ann that he wanted the same painting that Kate had requested. Kate telephoned Bert and told Bert that he could take it and perhaps share the painting. Ann handed the painting to Bert on that day, February 6, 2016.

Following mediation 2 in April 2017, Mabel Snatt sent a letter to each sibling regarding their parents' tangible property. She wrote, "Bert, Phillip, and Kate did not respond to my previous letter; therefore, all remaining items are to go to Ann, Chuck, and Cybil. And the painting that was given to Bert will to be picked up by Cybil." Bert, Phillip, and Kate realized that the one item handed over by Ann was to be seized.

Ms. Snatt classified her monthly letters to the trust beneficiaries as "administrative expense." The inventory list Ms. Snatt prepared assigned a value to their parents' tangible items of one dollar. Kate did not understand how she arrived at her valuation; it was the amount she determined was the valuation of her parents' household possessions. Mabel Snatt called Bert eighty-one days after the second mediation agreement was signed. She said to Bert, "You are to drop the painting off at my house."

Bert said, "This seems unusual. I thought you had stated that Cybil was going to pick it up from our home."

She stated, "No, you are holding up the distribution of the estate. There is to be one more meeting before the distribution."

Bert said, "Our agreement stated everything was done as of the mediation date. Is this normal?"

Ms. Snatt replied, "Kate sued Chuck, causing your fifteen-month delay. Nash did everything correctly according to your dad's stated wishes. Kate is responsible for this delay."

After Bert relayed their conversation to Kate, she telephoned Jack Napp. Kate stated, "I do not want any tangible property. Chuck, Cybil, and Ann can keep it all. Why can't Bert have one painting?"

He replied, "If you want me to challenge this, it will cost several thousand dollars." Kate questioned why Ms. Snatt blamed her for causing the delay of the estate settlement. Jack Napp replied, "She was wrong to say what she did."

Kate replied to Jack Napp, "She is either totally corrupt and/or unqualified to practice law."

Mabel Snatt charged administrative expenses for her one-sided representation of Chuck. Cybil continued to tell others that the legal costs were Kate's fault and that she caused the delay of the estate settlement and the legal expenses. The problem with Snatt's accusation was that Kate had not had one conversation with Ms. Snatt since her dad's funeral. Why wasn't Kate allowed to ask questions of the estate settlement process? Why was Kate removed as successor trustee? Why was Gloriette's house sold for no money and no appraisal? Kate was the villain and treated as such by the attorneys charging egregious sums of money under the guise of settling her parents' estate. Kate sent two letters which questioned Mabel Snatt's dictate that all tangible property was to be given to Chuck, Ann, and Cybil. Jack Napp sent an e-mail questioning Snatt's changing tangible property distribution procedure. Mabel Snatt ignored Jack Napp's questions and corresponded in an increasingly vicious manner. Joseph Stone mentioned to Kate during mediation 2 that he found Ms. Snatt's e-mails purposefully inflammatory, antagonistic, and detrimental to reaching a compromise.

In the second week of May 2017, two months following mediation 2, Bert saw Chuck's truck drive past him down the gravel road; he bird-dogged Chuck, following him right into his driveway. Bert immediately jumped out of his truck to confront him, looking directly into his darting, shifty eyes, loudly stating, "Chuck, you are a crook and a liar, and you better repent!"

Chuck glared past him, yelling, "I'm not getting into an altercation with you!" Continuing to stammer on, he added, "I have done everything right. I have made every single payment. I stayed after you all left, and I deserve everything!" Chuck was defiant, and although his rage was contained, he waved his arms as if he was shoving his brother away and stomped off to the front door of the stone house. Bert climbed back into the cab of his truck and backed out of Chuck's vehicle-crowded driveway.

Later that day, Bert called Kate, asking her why Chuck stated emphatically that he made his land contract payments. Kate carefully explained to Bert that she had irrefutable proof he never made necessary payments to the trust; furthermore, the statements clearly showed the sporadic deposits made to their joint account were immediately transferred back to Chuck and Mildred's personal accounts. Kate said, "Chuck is a liar."

Bert replied, "Of course, he is a liar. I've been witness to a lifetime of his lies and shenanigans."

Kate was shocked by the statements Cybil made following their day in court and mediation 2. Kate did not understand why Cybil made the statements that Cybil did because she was present, heard the evidence, and had to have recognized the judge ruled against Chuck's motion. Chuck lost. Cybil was ignorant regarding Chuck's extensive long-term manipulative scheme, defrauding their parents' trust, her dad, and her siblings. Kate did not understand why Chuck continued to state that he made his required payments when it was proven he did not. The attorneys representing both sides, the judge, and the mediator all recognized Chuck had breached his fiduciary duty with the multitude of self-dealing transactions, explaining the lawyer's eagerness in reaching a settlement during mediation 2.

The court case had proven that Chuck exerted undue influence over her dad. The judge definitively denied Mr. Morse's motion that Chuck did not exert influence on Bertrand. Yet according to Chuck and Cybil, he was completely innocent, and Kate had an unjustified vendetta against Chuck.

Kate's friend, Sunny Smart, said to her, "Chuck is a psychopath." Sunny Smart had been Kate's close personal friend for over thirty years, having been friends since the day they met. Kate considered Sunny a friend she could discuss deeply personal confidences with. Sunny's childhood was turbulent, caring for her mother's young children because her alcoholic and abusive mother depended on Sunny to care for her siblings. Sunny appreciated Kate's experience because it helped her understand her own childhood.

Interestingly, Sunny's mother died the year before Kate's dad. Sunny was the oldest child of six children and had been the named successor trustee of her parents' trust for three decades. She was told by her younger brother that her mother's trust was changed while she was in intensive care, one month before her death. Her brother told her that she was no longer successor trustee and was removed as a beneficiary of her trust. At that time, he told her that she had no rights to get a copy of her mother's revised trust because she lived in a different county. She later realized that his statement was against California state law, and she should have been allowed to receive a copy of her trust document. Her brother and sisters' malicious actions following her mother's death including their attempt to exclude her from her funeral service were a crushing blow to her. Sunny chose to walk away from the entire situation because it was emotionally too painful. Because of her experience, Sunny was interested and supportive of Kate's pursuit of truth regarding her parents' trusts. Kate had heard the term "psychopath"; however, she didn't understand what it meant. She began researching the term on the Internet. An article appeared, "Profile of a Sociopath."

The following summarizes sociopath behavior according to numerous psychological sources. A sociopath is a pathological liar. He has no problem lying coolly and easily, and it is almost impossible for him to be truthful. A sociopath can create and/or get caught up in a complex belief about his own powers and abilities. He is extremely convincing. A sociopath feels entitled to certain things as "his right." He has a lack of shame, guilt, or remorse and has a deep-seated rage, which is split off and repressed. He does not see others as people, only targets and opportunities. The end always justifies the means, and he lets nothing stand in their way.

Sociopaths have a need for stimulation; they live on the edge. Verbal outbursts and physical punishments are normal, and promiscuity and gambling are common traits. They have poor behavior controls and an impulsive nature. They express rage and abuse, alternating with small expressions of approval producing an addictive cycle for the abuser and abused. They believe they are all-powerful, all-knowing, entitled to every wish, have no sense of personal boundaries, and have no concern for their impact on others.

Sociopaths are not concerned about wrecking other's lives and dreams; they are oblivious and indifferent to the devastation they cause. They do not accept blame themselves but blame others, even for acts they committed. They tend to be parasites, exploiting others. Additionally, they are authoritarian, secretive, paranoid, and unable to feel remorse or guilt and have extreme narcissism and grandiose opinion of themselves.[15]

During the previous fifteen months, Kate came to realize that Chuck suffered from some sort of mental illness. She considered her dad might have had a bipolar disorder as he often displayed the characteristics of that disease. Kate was not a psychologist; however, she reached her conclusion from all that she had read about the mental disorder. She had asked herself the question why repeatedly over the past year. Now she instantaneously realized that he likely had an undiagnosed mental illness, explaining why he would not admit he was wrong and why he was entitled to her parents' entire estate. The factual evidence proved he was a pathological liar; the idea hit her like a thunderbolt.

Chuck was an expert manipulator. Mr. Morse was aware of the factual evidence and had admitted to Kate's attorneys that Chuck must reach a settlement seven months before, yet Mr. Morse, Chuck's attorney, continued to argue on Chuck's behalf as if Chuck was innocent of every petition charge. Mabel Snatt and Cybill unequivocally supported Chuck.

Following mediation 2, Kate briefly spoke to Joseph Stone, "Chuck has not cooperated once during the entire process. I do not believe he is going to abide by the mediation agreement." Joseph Stone agreed, mentioning to her that the courts were pressing for a conclusion to their case. Kate was relieved; however, she had realized that Cheetham, Steele and Morse LLP would continue to drag out the process until all her parents' trust money was transferred into their corporate coffers because their firm was building a new high-rise in Indian Falls. Their aggressive

---

15   This website, https://www.mcafee.cc/Bin/sb.html, summarizes some of the common features and descriptions of the referenced psychological profile.

legal tactics indicated to her that they would do everything possible to egregiously bill legal expenses for as long as possible.

Kate prepared a two-phase distribution plan, meeting the terms of the mediation agreement, aware that Chuck wasn't going to let his brothers and sisters get anything. Chuck sincerely believed he deserved it all; after all, he had stayed. For some reason, the epiphany of his mental illness helped Kate understand why Chuck refused to cooperate and settle with her.

Kate experienced a sense of relief and calm because she finally had an explanation of Chuck's irrational and unexplainable behavior since her dad's death. She realized Ann knew of Chuck's illness because she and Chuck worked closely together during the last ten years of her dad's life, knowing Chuck was abusive and used his dad. A parasite, Chuck had lived on her parents' money his entire life. He sincerely believed he was entitled to everything because he incessantly repeated the statement. The person responsible for her dad's care in the last ten years of his life had been cold, calculating, and ruthless. Chuck's superficial charm, manipulation, and cunning allowed him to get away with siphoning her parents' trust assets, imprisoning her dad in his home, and changing the terms of her parents' trusts. Kate realized that her fifteen months of litigation and investigation were futile because Chuck was going to defend his position and take every last dime of the trust. Chuck's refusal to cooperate and his direction to Mr. Morse to file numerous motions against Kate showed that he only cared about himself.

Kate saw a viciousness in people she had never seen before. Ann and Cybil were vicious. Cybil demanded to receive Bert's painting although she wanted nothing to do with any possessions following her dad's funeral. Cybil stated to all, "I want the money. I do not want anything else." Mabel Snatt forwarded Jack Napp an e-mail Cybil had sent her. Cybil stated, "I authorize Mabel Snatt to get my painting. I will never step foot on Bert's property in my life, and I will never return to Minnesota."

Bert asked Kate, "What did I do?" Bert had loaned Cybil money periodically at different times during her life. Cybil often suffered financial troubles, including bankruptcy. Cybil had no interest in the painting. Importantly, the artist had lived next door to Bert, and Cybil had no knowledge of the artist. Cybil knew Bert took care of her dad for many years without any thought of receiving money. Cybil cared about Bert paying off his land contract and her share of Bert's money. Bert was deeply hurt by Cybil's cruel statements made to others. Cybil knew Bert had admired the painting of Coram, as Kate did because Ann told her both Bert and Kate wanted the painting. Cybil planned to take it from Bert because Mabel Snatt said she should get it. Ann continued her viciousness throughout the legal process, supporting Chuck and slandering Kate. Kate realized people became vicious if they are backed into a corner and have something to hide.

Kate received a bill from her attorney on September 12, three months following the final settlement of her parents' estate. Her bill reflected correspondence between Mabel Snatt and Jack Napp regarding Bert's Coram painting. Kate told Bert to keep the painting and didn't believe Mabel Snatt had authority over her parents' tangible property. Ms. Snatt drove over to Bert's house and demanded the painting from Bert's wife, Diana, two weeks before. Neither Bert nor Kate received the painting they asked for following her dad's burial; however, Kate received a bill for one thousand six hundred twenty-five dollars, representing correspondence between Jack Napp and Ms. Snatt regarding the painting. It didn't matter what was right or proper; Ms. Snatt took the painting, ignoring the tangible property procedure that had been agreed upon. Kate believed that Ms. Snatt's e-mails and letters toward Bert, Phillip, and Kate expressed disdain toward them. Kate believed Ms. Snatt gave the painting to Chuck, following his instructions. Chuck disposed of it because he wasn't going to allow Bert or Kate to receive or enjoy any of their parents' possessions.

Kate told Joseph Stone and Jack Napp they needed to go directly to the judge. "Chuck is not going to cooperate." Each month, she made the same statement. Fifteen months passed, almost two months following the second court-ordered mediation, Chuck hadn't complied with the terms of the signed mediation agreement nor did he give any indication that he intended to. Chuck continued to write checks for his expenditures from the trusts. Contrary to what Ann and Cybil claimed after the funeral, Chuck still hadn't come up with the deeply discounted amount he owed the estate, what was agreed to by all during mediation 2.

During the first mediation in November 2016, Kate asked Jack Napp his opinion of this case. He said, "This is one of the more difficult estate cases I have been involved with." She wanted to ask his opinion of the case after another seven months passed because she had a feeling their case may have risen to rank 1 in difficulty. Although it was impossible to reconstruct and repair the damage to her trust, Kate believed her attorneys did what they could to make Chuck accountable through the mediation agreement they structured with Chuck's attorney, Mr. Morse. The attorneys on both sides and the mediator agreed that Chuck was difficult to reason with. "You must let Chuck have the last say in this agreement; otherwise, he will not agree to it." They agreed that Chuck had to have the last say in any agreement because he was a misogynist. This was a descriptive noun for someone who loathes, dislikes, mistrusts, and/or mistreats women.

Jacob Broader, the mediator, said to Kate, "Unless you agree to Chuck's final terms, there would be no agreement."

Ann and Chuck repeated to relatives and family acquaintances, "Kate took everything. The lawyers took all the money, and nothing was left." However, the truth was that Chuck was required to reimburse the trust for an amount of money. Jack Napp structured the amount that Chuck was required to reimburse, a minimal attempt to honor Gloriette's trust. Ann's statement "The lawyers got all the money" was incorrect, although Chuck got away with the multiyear complicated scheme because the altered trusts remained as such. It was not accurate that the lawyers got it all because Kate's efforts exposed his fraudulent schemes and made him defend his actions over fifteen months.

Chuck continued to state, "I did everything right." However, the professionals involved knew that he had not. Kate came to believe that Mr. Morse vigorously defended Chuck through his numerous legal actions to cover up the wrong action of his fellow attorney, Finn Nash. After the ordeal was over, Kate was assured she did the right thing by filing her petitions against Chuck. She did what she was financially and emotionally capable of. Kate was deeply disappointed in the legal process because she had incorrectly assumed by submitting facts and proof, a settlement would occur. Regardless, the process dragged on for over fifteen months while Chuck continued to state, "I did everything right!"

TWO

Her legal name was Katharine. Her parents and siblings called her Kate. She was their second child, the eldest daughter of Gloriette and Bertrand. Phillip told her that her dad stated the following as he was dying, "Tell Kate I am sorry. I am so sorry." He repeatedly muttered, "I'm sorry, I'm sorry to Kate." Phillip's presence during his final days, sharing his experience, opened her heart to the great sadness her dad experienced the last years of his life. At the time, Phillip's kind words hit her hard. Fifteen months following her dad's funeral, she did not know whether he actually made those statements or if Phillip said the words because he knew it was what she wanted to hear.

She wrote a tribute to her dad for his funeral service. She had visited her dad's minister before the service and asked to give his eulogy. He said to her, "Chuck gave me instructions that you are not to say anything. You will ruin Bertrand's service. Chuck was adamant that you are not allowed to speak during the funeral service." Kate handed the minister her written eulogy, saying, "Read it. You will see it will be a positive addition." He briefly glanced at the paper and looked away as Kate said, "I will take any blame for speaking." Kate later realized that Chuck's narrative about her could not be challenged. Chuck had to ensure his lies were believed by relatives and friends of Bertrand. Chuck convinced others that Kate did not love her dad or care for him the years before his death. The tribute she wrote proved that his statements had been patently false.

Years passed since she thought of their relationship, questioning whether she had ever consciously thought about her lifelong relationship with her dad from childhood to adulthood. Writing her dad's tribute forced her to examine both the positives and negatives. She did not remember kindness from her dad during her childhood or teenage years. In fact, she couldn't think of one nice thing he said to her during her first twenty years of life. It had been evident he thought a great deal of Chuck, but not so much of her because she was treated differently. Reflecting upon her childhood years, she worked diligently to please her parents. She maintained a low profile in hopes of not doing anything that might provoke her dad's anger. Kate often felt like she was walking on eggshells around her dad, his mood instantly changing from a happy disposition into an angry, volatile, tempered individual who usually spewed hurtful criticisms toward her.

During her early teenage years, her dad said to her and others, "You will never amount to anything." Kate overheard him make similar statements to Chuck when they were sitting at the kitchen table while she was playing the piano in the next room. He said, "Kate is not going to amount to anything." He was verbally abusive to her while at home, away from the confines of his medical practice. In retrospect, she realized that for some reason he was always abusive to her when Chuck and Ann were around, intending to create rivalry among his children throughout his life by his words and actions.

Kate went to work at his office when she was twelve years old, initially learning basic receptionist skills from his secretary, assistant, and office manager, Virginia, who oversaw his daily schedule and office administration for over thirty years. His office was run efficiently as Kate typed professional letters on an IBM typewriter, flawless letters visually and grammatically. Often, he made corrections and asked Kate to retype his letters until they were without imperfections. Her dad taught her writing and presentation skills that were old-school proper because that was how he learned to write and followed the textbook illustration for formal letter formatting. Kate learned basic bookkeeping and billing skills from Virginia, recording the billing for his patient visits as well as any supplemental insurance payments. At that time, he charged eight dollars for an office visit. Kate found it interesting the number of people who did not pay their outstanding medical bills, carrying forward the accrued amounts from ledger to ledger. Additionally, Kate recognized he was ethical in his business dealings working in his office until she permanently moved from Indian Falls to attend college.

During her office tenure, she assisted him with routine office surgeries, learning some nursing skills. During a particular office procedure, while her dad was excising a small growth from a patient's face, dizziness caused her to collapse to the floor, unconscious. Although she was a premedical student through college, she realized that her calling was not going to be a surgeon because of her negative reaction to the cutting of human flesh and the resulting blood and puss that was part of surgical procedures. While working in her dad's office using a Dictaphone, she typed patient histories that had been recorded following office procedures and examinations and follow-up visits after major hospital operations. Kate learned about medical terminology, diagnoses, and specific surgical procedures routinely performed by general surgeons. Other than farm life, this was the occupation she had been exposed to. Naturally, applying to college, she intended to eventually go to medical school to become a doctor, following her dad's career path.

While working in his office, she and her dad existed peacefully, often driving to and from his office, routinely having lunch at his favorite local restaurants. Kate thought he was respectful to her as his employee and developed an admiration and respect for his surgical skills, recognizing his positive patient relationships. Later, she realized she possibly hoped to receive both acceptance and praise from her father while learning skills necessary to work more closely to the man so highly regarded by the medical community.

Kate worked several jobs during junior and high school; she was one of their church janitors, cleaning every Saturday. She held this position for five years, to her, a coveted job, appreciating the twenty dollars she earned monthly to pay for her new clothes. Her mother was a Depression era child, a scrimper and saver, shopping department store basements for bargains. Kate wore hand-me-downs or sewed dresses and skirts on her grandmother's Singer sewing machine using Simplicity or Butterick clothing patterns. Additionally, Kate worked at a local factory after school and Saturdays and assisted in her dad's office as she was needed until she was nineteen years old. During high school, she took honors classes and graduated with academic honors at the top 5 percent of her class.

At the age of thirteen, she began working for Mr. Brin. Most days, she got off the school bus and walked to the small factory located at the corner of Crest and Valley Egypt roads. This business was close to their family farm, allowing her to walk to or from her workplace to home. Brin's factory provided electrical wiring for boat and automobile panels. His employees were typically high school dropouts with alcohol and substance abuse issues. Kate's hourly wage at that time was one dollar and sixty-five cents, working long shifts on Saturday, typically ten to twelve hours, many times without breaks. Mr. Brin often brought Kate blueprints of wiring jobs and asked her to put together prototypes of specified products by his manufacturing customers. Additionally, she spent a tremendous amount of time soldering wires and developed an acute case of teenage pimples and acne from the soldering smoke. While working in her dad's office, she asked if she could see the dermatologist upstairs under the standard professional courtesy agreement between doctors. Her dad flew into a rage and said, "Absolutely not, you are not going to take advantage of that agreement." Without his knowledge, Virginia, his office manager, arranged for Kate to see the skin doctor. He prescribed little pink pills, tetracycline. Kate's face immediately cleared; thereafter, Virginia and Kate held the secret of clear skin.

Kate was berated and embarrassed by her dad during her early childhood throughout her teenage years both at home and in front of others, often calling her derogatory Dutch names, such as "you lummox." A lummox was a clumsy and stupid person. He said, "You are a dummkopf." A dummkopf was a dumb person. Kate was required to play a musical instrument in school and repeatedly pleaded, "Please can I play the flute?" Her dad said, "No, you are not talented. You are to play the extra coronet we have." Kate played the coronet for her six years of school because her dad did not believe she was worthy of having a musical instrument of her choice, saying she had no musical talent. Although there was nothing wrong with the coronet, to her, it was an embarrassment because she thought it was a masculine instrument, and she was excessively self-conscious and humiliated playing the coronet. With daily disdain, she carried the bulky instrument case to and from school.

Toward the end of her eighth grade, when she was thirteen years old, her band director, Mr. Strange, stated that all girls were to wear navy blue skirts, white shirt, and nylons for the year-end concert. Kate considered Mr. Strange an angry, mean, and unhappy man because he was critical and harshly complained about his band students. Kate begged her dad to allow her to wear nylons for their last concert, fervently pleading and crying, asking him repeatedly to allow her to adhere to the concert dress code. He said to her, "No, you will wear white knee socks."

The night of the concert, in front of 120 seventh and eighth grade students, Mr. Strange announced, "Kate is the only student that did not adhere to the dress code, and Kate has ruined the concert for our entire junior high band." Kate was deeply humiliated by his public statement, wanting to disappear and shrink out of sight. After this traumatic incident, Kate retreated to her inner self, becoming a good listener and rarely participating in conversations with others.

Kate wore glasses since she was five years old, being farsighted in one eye. Although she required eyeglasses when reading, her dad demanded that she wear eyeglasses at all times, without exception. Eventually, the frames broke between her eyes; she was in seventh grade, approximately eleven years of age. Afraid to tell her dad that the frames were broken, each morning, for almost two years, she carefully taped her glass frame together at the bridge of the nose so her dad would not know that they were broken. She was embarrassed to be seen in the ugly broken glasses; one side of the glasses occasionally flew across the classroom because she accidentally nicked her frame as she pulled back her hair, a repeated personal horror. If Kate wasn't wearing the ghastly spectacles, her dad tersely yelled, "Go put on your glasses!"

As a young girl, Kate was teased by her classmates about wearing the same clothes to school each day, having two outfits for school and a good dress for Sunday. She complained to her dad and mom about her blue blouse and the spinach-colored skirt she wore each day. He said, "Why are you complaining? You have a blouse that matches the sky and a skirt that matches the green grass. Be happy."

Because of the barrage of family criticisms, Kate had a low self-esteem. She enrolled in college as an insecure person, having great difficulty talking in front of others and participating in class discussions. She preferred a lower grade than speaking up in front of fellow classmates and professors, which was a problem since her grade often depended on participation. During college, she had a quiet demeanor and a debilitating inferiority complex. Although she talked little around others, she was an avid listener and developed an attitude of perseverance, focusing on her primary goal—to obtain a college degree and live a life far different than what she had experienced during her childhood. She believed a college degree would give her credibility and an opportunity to work in a job that did not require manual labor, farm, or factory labor. Kate wanted to receive compensation by using her God-given brain.

She dreamed of attending Hills College during her high school years. Her dad said, "No, you go to Corinth College." She enrolled at Corinth because her dad told her to go there while complaining bitterly about the cost of her college tuition. While attending Corinth, the farm was expanding at a fast pace; two Harvestores were built, and hundreds of acres of land and farm equipment were purchased. Farm loans were extended to construct and purchase two Harvestore silos using borrowed money. A tractor costing the equivalent of twenty years of private tuition at Corinth College was proudly purchased by her dad for Chuck's farming venture. He repeatedly complained to Kate that he had no interest in paying for her college tuition. Kate worked full-time jobs throughout her undergraduate years, paying for her semester tuition bills by working food service, waitressing at the local steak restaurant, and doing the billing for a local ambulance company during her senior year of college. After four years, she received her bachelor's degree, no longer having the desire and passion necessary to attend medical school, exhausted from full-time work while cramming for difficult science subjects. She bought a small car and headed to the West Coast, immediately securing a job with a biological testing company.

Within months of arriving in California, she was hired for her first professional job as a pharmaceutical sales representative. Kate became the first woman salesperson in the West Coast territory for a pharmaceutical division of a major company. At that time, the pharmaceutical sales industry was all men, referred to as "detail men." She realized her interest was business and desired a job with unlimited upside and no constraints other than her ambition and desire to learn. During these years, she developed a respectful relationship with her dad; he appreciated her initiative and admired her work ethic, and he related to her new career in the medical industry. During these years, she thought they finally developed a normal father-daughter relationship because their conversations were civil and covered many topics: business, music, and literature. Her parents often visited her on the West Coast and enjoyed spending time with her and, later, her family.

Once she realized her career goal was to become a stockbroker, she chose to forgo her comfortable salary, stock options, and company car, in turn for not having a guaranteed paycheck for a low starting salary. At this time, she was paid nine hundred fifty dollars per month starting salary, with the knowledge that if she did not make required performance standards, termination followed. Years later, she learned newly hired men were paid several hundred dollars more per month whether they had sales experience or not. At that time, her branch manager said to her, "You will never make it in this business. I have to hire you because of your high test scores and your broker simulation evaluation." She thought his statement sounded familiar: "You will not be successful." He could have said, "You will not amount to anything." Kate committed the time to develop her sales ability and became a lifelong student of market history and technical analysis. She attended graduate school to improve her business knowledge during the early eighties. She telephoned her dad regularly during these years. He had little life exposure to the business world; he was a medical doctor and farmer but became interested in learning about stocks and starting his own investment portfolio. During these years, their relationship developed into a friendship, enjoying their conversations discussing stocks, the economy, and politics.

She realized, early in her career, that to acquire wealth, one must have extensive knowledge and expertise as a stock picker; stock-picking expertise became her goal. She realized that she would not acquire wealth as a salesperson because her investment style was a long-term acquirer of quality, undervalued holdings. At the time, commissions earned were less than one-half of 1 percent of which her employer took 60 percent of the revenue that she generated. Unless a broker was a "churner" or bought high markup holdings, such as Chuck's broker friend, Fred Schafte, it was not possible to acquire wealth buying undervalued, high quality holdings for clients.

Her dad mentioned that Chuck complained about her success and was envious of what she accomplished on her own. Her parents began spending their winters at their desert home, enjoying the California climate during the winter months. They took up playing golf, her mother regretful that she had not taken it up years before; sadly, she died after her sixty-eighth birthday, eighteen and one-half years before her dad's death.

At the time, Kate did not realize the intense envy that was raging within Chuck. Chuck didn't like that Bertrand boasted to others about her success and did not appreciate him giving her referrals of his friends. Chuck stoked her dad's anger toward her by the statements he made to him, repeatedly saying, "Kate is ungrateful and hates you so much." Kate knew about his statements because they were repeated to her by different people after her father's death. She did not make the statements that were repeatedly attributed to her. Bert and Phillip both mentioned that Chuck spoke often of Kate's ungrateful attitude. Interesting, since he was given all his dad could provide for him, yet it was never enough.

In April of 2005, Kate founded White Point Capital. By this time, she achieved the following designations: chartered market technician, certified financial planner, and certified investment management analyst. Each designation required a level of proficiency in the subject matter determined by passing a series of exams, additionally work history, and colleague recommendations were required. Annual continuing education and ethics standards were required to maintain her designations, acquiring her distinguished designations over a fourteen-year period of time.

During the years 2004 to 2007, her dad became increasingly angry toward her. Kate was reminded of his cruel treatment to her as a child and teenager. Following her father's death, she learned Chuck was behind Bertrand's change in behavior. Prior to that time, she did not realize that Chuck harbored intense envy toward her; however, it became clear with the numerous legal documents executed against her, which had been previously concealed from her. Chuck transferred assets to guarantee Kate would not inherit any of her parents' money. In reality, she was far more interested in being part of her dad's life as his daughter than receiving any money. Sadly, Kate and her dad both ended up losers in the end.

Kate thought back to the years she worked in her dad's medical office and realized the skills she learned from him were skills she had used throughout her career. She fondly recalled the lunches they had at his favorite German and Chinese restaurants. His office was in downtown Indian Falls, so they had spent walking downtown during lunch hour, stopping at Herpolsheimer's department store for fresh sugar donuts from their street-side bakery or stopping at a local pizzeria on their way home from work. Kate had a keen sense of smell and appreciated the aroma of fresh Italian dishes. Many of her positive memories involved food because it was one of the ways her parents showed their love. Kate developed a lifelong fondness for food because it represented an expression of love to her.

Herpolsheimer's and Steketee's were the two major department stores located in the downtown city during her childhood and teenage years. Herpolsheimer's had a nice restaurant on the second floor. Her dad, mom, Chuck, and she attended the Symphony series held at the large Civic Auditorium, located at the edge of the river. They often had dinner at the fancy department store restaurant just before the concert. Kate learned to appreciate classical music during this time. At Christmastime, her dad gave each child one dollar to buy gifts. She typically bought a little box of Whitman candies for twenty cents apiece, presents within her budget. The Christmas shopping excursions were a fond memory, ridding the elevator up and down the eight floors of the department store. In those days, an adult worked operating the elevator, opening and closing the metal gate closure, announcing each floor as they entered or departed, making the elevator ride an exciting journey in itself. Her dad seemed to have as much fun as the children, discussing how to spend their Christmas dollar.

Bertrand had a distinguished reputation in Indian Falls as a surgeon. Kate met many of his longtime patients, such as Willie, a man who received multiple gunshot wounds, requiring regular medical visits for the remainder of his life, and Barbara, a longtime cancer patient whose husband left her when she was diagnosed with breast cancer. Bertrand was known locally as an excellent surgeon with a good bedside manner. Patients, nurses, and fellow physicians stated this fact to Kate during the years she worked in his office. She was sad when her dad retired because she believed it was the end of a life chapter during which he truly used his God-given talents. As a young father, he recited the Heidelberg Catechism. Kate recalled him reciting "The Confession of Faith" from the Heidelberg Catechism question-and-answer book. He repeated by memory:

Q: What is your only comfort in life and death?

A: That I am not my own, but belong—body and soul, in life and in death—to my faithful Savior, Jesus Christ… Because I belong to him, Christ, by his Holy Spirit, assures me of eternal life and makes me wholeheartedly willing and ready from now on to live for him.

He recited certain Bible verses, especially Matthew 6:26, NKJ: "Look at the birds of the air, for they neither sow nor reap nor gather into barns; yet your heavenly Father feeds them. Are you not of more value than they?" His professional, educated side was admirable and enjoyable to be around. Kate regretted not understanding her dad during his life as she came to understand him after he had passed. As a young girl, she admired his recitation of Bible verses from memory.

She remembered him stitching her cracked head, gashed leg, and gashed mouth, three occasions his surgical talents were put to use on her.

Together, they enjoyed classic black-and-white movies and novels, such as *Of Human Bondage.* Her dad related to her the story of the orphan facing bleak options who questioned the meaning and purpose of life. They shared a love of classical music and great composers, especially Ludwig van Beethoven. Her dad was touched by Beethoven's deafness caused by his father's cruelty, reminding him of his own father.

Kate recalled her dad being critical of successful women who had careers. He was critical of Gloriette's sister, Aunt Faye, an independent and successful businesswoman. He had philosophical discussions with others about why women should not hold important positions in the church or in government. Kate overheard his debates with Reverend Dan Canfield, his favorite nephew, about these topics. She did not participate in their conversations, having no interest in discussing sexual discrimination, and would leave the room. For some reason, Kate thought she was exempt from his disdain of successful career women because she was his daughter.

Although her dad was dismissive to her as a young girl, she believed their relationship developed to one of mutual respect as she became an adult. His belligerent attitude toward her during the three years before he transferred the trust accounts to Broker Schafte did not make sense to her. Her dad's new behavior reminded her of his treatment toward her as a child, that she was not worthy of equal treatment, treatment Chuck and Ann always received from him. Ann repeatedly told Kate that he said, "Kate is not doing anything." He may well have said, "Kate will not amount to anything." It was a familiar statement she heard as a child; however, it was no longer accurate or relevant.

Cybil told Kate after their dad's death that he was sad that Kate hated him. She repeated to her that he didn't want to take her off his finances; however, since she hated him so much, he had to do it. Kate was stunned by Cybil's statements because no one thought enough of her to let her know what he was saying and thinking. Kate did not understand a person who works with someone weekly for decades, consults them for financial advice, vacations together, and lives in that person's home for part of the year to thinking that the person hates you. Kate asked Cybil, "Who told Dad that I hated him?" She did not respond to her; no one did. It was okay for her relationship with her dad to be terminated without one word said by Chuck, Ann, or Cybil. However, it was not okay for Kate to question Chuck's dealings with her parents' trusts without getting verbally attacked and slandered by her siblings. It was okay for Ann to give court affidavits dismissing Kate's relationship with her dad during her entire lifetime. Ann's affidavit stated, "Kate was mean to Dad, and they did not have a good relationship during his lifetime. He transferred the trust accounts because she didn't do anything." Ann and Chuck continually told lies over the years to manipulate and take assets and possessions from their dad.

Chuck used to repeat the phrase "No good deed goes unpunished." Which means that if you do something for another, it will not be appreciated and eventually will be used against you. Bert mentioned that this phrase was another one of Chuck's colloquialisms. Chuck repeated the phrase with contempt. Kate came to understand the meaning of this phrase after the passing of her dad.

Kate knew her dad had emotional highs and lows, easily changing his happy disposition to being angry and tyrannical. She witnessed his professional side when he was both honest and ethical; he behaved normally at his office and the hospital. At home, however, he became another person: critical, angry, and abusive.

Kate was surprised that he transferred the trusts. She firmly told him, "Your actions are unethical." She thought she knew his professional side; he was ethical. She did not recognize his alternate personality. They had an agreement that they would be compensated for their years of work and advice when trust securities were eventually sold. He broke their agreement without justification or explanation. Kate had not been exposed to his unethical behavior until this incident which severed their professional relationship. Phillip confirmed their dad had two personalities. He was a completely different person at work than he was at home. At that moment, she realized Phillip was perceptive and an excellent closet psychologist.

Kate realized the relationship she had with her dad was his business and professional personality. The years she worked in his office, the years she worked in the medical industry, and the years she was her parents' financial advisor were good years. His alternate personality was cruel, tyrannical, critical, judgmental, and dismissive. His alternate personality was brought out by Chuck and Ann; their negativity and criticisms intensified his insecurities. Chuck easily manipulated her dad during his aging years as his senility increased. Ann helped Chuck accomplish their mental manipulation to serve her purpose of getting her parents' money and possessions for herself and her family.

Her dad had little regard for Kate other than what she could do to benefit him. He used her both professionally and personally, with purposeful intent to punish her. He punished Kate for not playing his manipulative games; he punished her as a child, and he punished her as an adult. Sadly, his actions backfired when he became senile and Kate was no longer in his life. At the end of his life, he was at the mercy of Ann and Chuck, having to follow their bidding. Kate finally understood why Chuck and Ann were treated differently from her as children. They were good at manipulating their dad, and they manipulated each other. Kate finally understood why she had always been the outsider, seeking to gain her dad's approval throughout her life. However, she was never able to gain his love or acceptance.

Kate grew up in a home in which there were no boundaries. Boundaries, structure, and discipline were demonstrations of love. A strong family was one with boundaries and structure. Discipline without love was another word for abuse. A psychologist and friend told Kate that her dad did not understand emotional love. To him, expressing a need was close to an expression of love. Ann and Chuck were always needing something or asking for money, whereas Phillip, Bert, and she did not ask for anything from him, further explaining their poor treatment.

Kate was blessed to have an inner drive and passion which pushed her to be the person she became; for this, she credited her dad for saying, "You will never amount to anything." Although she often longed for a biological father who cherished her and loved her for who she was, she did not understand why she deserved a dad who was cruel and dismissive. After his death, she came to realize she was special, despite and because of her father.

THE LAST CHAPTER

Six months had passed since Bertrand's funeral, Kate wondered if her cousin had additional information on her dad's condition before his death. She telephoned Dan Canfield, a retired protestant minister, her dad's favorite nephew. Dan had known her dad his entire life because his mother and Bertrand were sister and brother and shared similar personalities.

Bertrand's siblings did not talk about their childhood. Their father, Richard Charles II (Dick), was legendary. Throughout Kate's childhood, this grandparent was described to Kate as tyrannical. Kate believed her dad had a similar personality to his father Dick. Dick was the youngest boy of twelve children, named after his father, Richard Charles Sr., having immigrated to Nebraska from the Netherlands with his young bride, Rosella. Richard Sr. settled in Orange, Nebraska, opening a furniture store, eventually constructing and selling caskets in his store. As Richard Sr.'s business prospered, he expanded its success by becoming a funeral director to service his casket buyers. Richard Sr.'s timing was fortunate because he capitalized on the growth years of the late nineteenth century, which was known as the railroad era. Richard Sr. retired shortly after the turn of the century at a young age of fifty-three, giving his estate to his oldest sons, Nick and Will. Unfortunately, Richard Sr.'s youngest son, Dick, was not part of the new thriving business, having seven sisters and two brothers. Richard Sr. adored his daughters and oldest sons Nick and Will because his sons were entrepreneurial and successful, learning from him. Nick and Will established a lucrative, reputable, funeral home and mortuary in the booming town of Orange with the money and expertise their father gave them. Their business was not affected by the economic cycle, and customers remained loyal and predictable. One hundred years later, the sixth-generation family ran the enterprise. Richard Sr.'s affections were devoted to his seven daughters and two oldest sons, not having the time or interest for his youngest son Dick. Dick was a low-paid farm laborer, working rented farms during his life, manual labor to support his family of five children, never owning his own land and struggling to pay his family bills. Because of his father's disinterest, Dick was considered a loser and black sheep by his siblings and had a difficult time finding his niche. Richard Sr. was seventy-six years old when he died. His obituary stated, "He was respected by all and cherished by his widow and ten children." Originally, there were twelve children; however, two died during their childhoods.

His youngest son Dick had grown to develop a violent, autocratic temperament because he was the victim of physical abuse from a young age by his father. His father was well-liked by all, except the son named after him. Richard Sr. died under mysterious circumstances. At the time of his death, there was talk that young Dick was involved, and although the talk was hushed, Dick remained a family outcast. Dick married Pearl and had five living children, two having died shortly after birth. His young wife Pearl died the year following his father's death. Pearl became ill, and the next day, she was dead. The pain of losing the one person who loved him along with the unresolved deep hurt of his father's death was too much for Dick.

Shortly after his wife's sudden death, Dick moved his family far away from his wife's family and where he had farmed. At the time of Pearl's death, their infant baby had been born with a rare genetic disease and now motherless. Pearl's mother took care of the motherless baby and cared for the infant until the baby died a few months later. After twenty years of working for local farmers on rented land, Dick opened his own furniture store in a town a distance from where they had lived. His move separated Dick and his children from Pearl's family—loving aunts and uncles on his wife's side. In hindsight, this was a detrimental move for

Dick's children as they were sheltered from the love of their many aunts and uncles during their important formative childhood years.

Dick's older brothers ran the family mortuary twenty miles from his small town of Elkhorn, Nebraska. Dick supplemented his furniture sales by operating an ambulance and hearse service ferrying the wounded to the nearby hospital and the corpses to his brother's mortuary. Aunt Irma exclaimed, "I don't know how my dad went from farming all those years to selling furniture!" Aunt Irma was Dick's eldest daughter and Bertrand's close sister and lifelong confidante. She outlived all her siblings, with exception of one brother, living to one hundred years of age.

Dick took his anger out on his youngest son, Bertrand Alan, replicating his dad's anger toward him, a tragic transgenerational pattern of abuse. Bertrand was four years old when his mother died. Bertrand was beaten as a boy and teenager by his angry, tyrannical father. At the age of sixteen, his father Dick died of cancer. Dick died days before his forty-ninth Christmas, which was a few weeks following his cancer diagnosis. Dick's gravestone and his obituary read, "Richard Charles II, Father." No other adjectives were engraved. Kate recalled her dad's emotional tears when he described his tombstone which had deteriorated and was no longer upright. Kate asked Aunt Irma about her grandfather. Refusing to give her any information, she said, "I am not going to say anything bad about my father!"

Bertrand's family lived in a small white house with a well in the backyard, explaining to Gloriette that he was beaten by this well daily. He dreaded coming home from school as he knew he faced a whipping from his father. His mother Pearl died when he was four years old. Although his Dutch grandmother was alive during his childhood, she chose not to develop a relationship with her grandson because she had little affection for her son Dick. Unfortunately, Dick's children were too far away from their mother's mother, their loving grandmother, missing out on affection from relatives who may have made their childhood more pleasant.

Because of the stark, bleak conditions he suffered as a boy, Bertrand had a tough personality, carrying his emotional burden throughout his life, finding it difficult to be positive; however, he was skilled at being critical and negative, the traits he learned from his father. For almost ninety years, he carried the loss of his mother, a source of bitterness, believing that he was robbed of his mother's love. As a young child, he was punished by the relentless verbal and physical cruelty of his father. Kate gradually learned these facts throughout her lifetime from snippets of conversations he shared with her, although she did not truly understand the depth of the psychological damage until after his death.

The sudden and unexpected death of his mother resulted in a quick remarriage by his father after they had moved from the farm to the small town of Elkhorn. His father was thirty-seven years old with five children when he married his second wife, an older spinster who became their strict stepmother. Bertrand joined the United States Army the day he turned eighteen years old; his goal was to get as far away from his home town and his stepmother as possible. He was sent to Berchtesgaden, Germany, Hitler's vacation haven. Kate did not hear him speak of his years that he served in the army during World War II. She was aware of one remnant—a violin he brought back from Germany. Bert enjoyed learning to play his violin until Ann took it from him, claiming their father had given the violin to her.

After the war ended, Bertrand enrolled in college, taking advantage of the government Pell grant which allowed World War II veterans to attend college cost free. He attended a Dutch Reformed liberal arts college and graduated at the top of his class, awarded magna cum laude, a college degree received with great distinction. The sudden death of his mother from a bowel obstruction and the fast deterioration of his father from colon cancer combined with the medical atrocities he witnessed during World War II helped him direct his attention to a medical career. At the same time, his older brother was studying to become a minister while he desired to become a missionary. His outstanding grades in the area of math and science allowed him to seriously consider attending medical school, applying to the University Medical School. He was accepted, attended four years, and graduated as he applied to a missionary post. However, he needed additional specialization, continuing with a residency in surgery. Following ten years of medical school, an internship, recent marriage, and a new child, he decided to practice general surgery in the city of Indian Falls, Minnesota.

Bertrand became a medical doctor because of the helplessness he felt after the sudden death of his mother Pearl and the cancer which killed his father. He hoped to save others from the pain he endured with the loss of his parents during his formative years; perhaps in hopes that by saving others, he'd save himself. This sequence of events following World War II unfolded perfectly for him to become a surgeon. He did not realize his goal of missionary work until he retired from thirty-plus years as a medical doctor.

Bertrand's brothers and sisters visited annually throughout their working lives. Kate observed his siblings sitting around the kitchen table, with silence between them, little to talk about, never as much as reminiscing about their childhood. Their mother Pearl, a young woman, died suddenly; their father Dick remarried quickly. Their coldhearted stepmother was a wretched stepmother to them all while their father beat them periodically. The siblings did not talk about their family dynamics; they believed any discussion of their dad would be against God's commandment, "Thou shalt honor thy father and mother." Additionally, they adhered to the adage "Best not to speak of the dead."

The cycle of abuse continued to the next generation with his son, Chuck, named after his grandfather Dick and great-grandfather Richard Charles Sr. Their type of life and abuse perpetrated over generations are part of the reason the elder abuse and elder financial abuse occurred. This can be a warning sign for others with similar or less intense but equally combative sibling and family dynamics.

A medical doctor degree and the respect that came from a MD salutation, doctor, allowed him a high level of respect from people with whom he came in contact. As a respected surgeon, he was given a level of acceptance regardless of his behavior; his angry outbursts and tantrums were allowed without social repercussions. He had few long-term relationships, many simply moving away from a relationship with him after experiencing his gruff and critical personality. Bertrand's negative behavior was overlooked because he was a medical doctor; a prestigious degree was used as armor.

Bertrand and Gloriette were missionaries in Ethiopia during a turbulent civil war era. It was a traumatic time because there was an ongoing civil war raging within the country when they were stationed in a remote area of Ethiopia, unable to understand the native language. He had hoped to help the sick Ethiopian villagers with his surgery skills during his station there, however finding the conditions primitive and the medical facilities in poor condition. Kate sent them care packages and letters during the time they were assigned to the village, later telling her that they deeply appreciated the care packages and letters she had faithfully sent to them, telling others that her packages helped them get through the difficult time they had in that remote war-torn area of Africa. It was a stressful time, and it took a toll on their health, both losing a significant amount of weight during their stay. Kate recognized that they aged years during their time in Africa and happily returned home to enjoy their remaining retirement years.

Dan Canfield, his favorite nephew, visited his uncle during the decades following his college graduation. Dan graduated from a well-known college and seminary in Indian Falls. Kate recalled his visits during her childhood and teenage years. It was during this time that Dan and her dad developed their friendship. Dan told Kate that he found her family dynamics interesting because he found them similar to his. Although Dan's father was happy and gregarious, his mother was stern, critical, and mean, quite similar to Bertrand's demeanor and personality. Bertrand knew no other way of treatment than to carry on as he had been raised.

Bertrand graduated from college and medical school with honors and was a Phi Beta Kappa. The Phi Beta Kappa Society is the oldest academic honor society in the United States. Phi Beta Kappa aims to promote and advocate excellence in the arts and sciences and induct the most outstanding students at American colleges and universities. Bertrand was a medical doctor and worked at a prestigious Catholic hospital surrounded by priests and nuns. He worked daily with people who were trained to deal with mental and spiritual concerns. Kate did not understand why he never sought help for his unhappy mental and spiritual state either from the medical profession or clergy he spoke to on a first-name basis. Kate recalled conversations she had with her mother, questioning why he didn't seek help for his emotional turmoil. Later, she understood that doctors were known as terrible patients. He had confided to Bert that he had no control over his negative outbursts.

Bertrand usually responded to situations with sharp criticism and verbal sarcasm, emotionally scarred and unable to overcome his deep-seated inferiority complex, explaining why he was easily brainwashed and convinced something untrue was true. Chuck told him repeatedly, "Kate hates you." Chuck repeatedly told him lies about Kate. Chuck worked diligently to turn her dad and anyone else who would listen against her. Her dad was insecure, and he did not believe he deserved her love or anyone else's sincere caring.

During the summer following her dad's funeral, she telephoned Dan Canfield. Kate had documented proof of her dad's manipulation by Chuck and Ann. She realized what transpired years ago wasn't necessarily his fault; he had been brainwashed to believe she hated him. The timeline, now clear to her, allowed her to understand the depth of Ann's deception. Dan said simply, "Sibling relationships are very complicated." At the time, his statement did not give her comfort. Dan was a Bible scholar. She hoped for a relatable Bible story, offering comfort, perhaps a story about deceit and stolen inheritance, a parallel story that might have helped her understand what happened. She welcomed Dan's wisdom. Their conversation was cut short as Dan was called away for an emergency funeral. Kate eagerly awaited his response to her questions which she hoped would give her peace of mind.

Weeks passed until they spoke again. His advice was to take heart the following verse: "Rejoice in all things. Keep on praying. No matter what happens, always be thankful, for this is God's will for you who belong to Jesus Christ" (Thessalonians 5:16–18, KJV).

Kate thought of this Bible verse often during the weeks, months, and the year following their conversation, knowing there was a reason that she was going through her legal process. The petition process was difficult, emotionally trying, and expensive. In the months that followed, she felt contempt directed toward her from Ann, Cybil, and Chuck. She heard their hateful words toward her from her younger brothers and relatives. Ann repeatedly stated to others that Kate was bringing shame to their dad's memory and causing the breakup of their family and that Kate was financially ruining Chuck and Mildred and causing destruction to generations of their family.

Ann, Chuck, Mildred, and Cybil stated to others that Kate caused their financial hardships. Kate knew from what she was told that Chuck expected to rapidly liquidate the estate holdings and distribute what was left. Chuck expected to receive title to the remaining assets and receive the valuable land across from Huntington Country Club. Kate would be long gone, not to be seen or heard of again. Mildred lamented to others that she could not retire because of Kate's questions. Kate knew that Mildred had a high-paying job, and they didn't have the normal expenses of owning a house because they did not make house payments for over twenty years. Kate did not have sympathy for her because she had uncovered the facts that proved dishonesty regarding their land contract payments. They chose to manipulate Bertrand and change her parents' estate plan during his final years of life. They organized and put into motion a multiyear scheme. To the day Bertrand died, everything they did was to take advantage of him financially.

The statement repeated by Chuck, Ann, and Cybil was "How dare you, Kate, cause this trouble to our family? You weren't involved the last years of Dad's life. Who are you to question Chuck? Chuck did everything correctly. He stayed. You left, and he deserves it all. He's entitled. Dad wanted Chuck to have everything."

The problem with their statements was that this wasn't what her parents had wanted; Kate knew the truth. It was her burden to reveal the truth because it was the right thing to do. Kate believed a wrong could not be made right if it is simply swept under a rug, if the truth was not revealed. Bert often repeated this phrase, "The only way for evil to prevail is for good people to do nothing." This is a paraphrased quote by Edmund Burke, an eighteenth-century writer and philosopher.

Kate believed exposure of the facts was needed for her siblings and their children. Bertrand and Gloriette originally requested Kate to be their successor trustee. Because of their request, she believed that she had a moral, ethical, and professional obligation to fulfil her responsibility. Perhaps her story may be used for others to prevent anything like this happening to their families and loved ones, essentially to be used as a case study to improve expected outcomes of estate settlements.

Kate periodically read biographies of successful, happy people, admiring John Templeton as a great investor and philanthropist. He was born poor and died one of the wealthiest men in the world. He was interviewed later in his life and asked, "What is the single most important trait needed to be successful in life?" He responded, "You must be grateful—grateful for all that you have." The attributes of gratitude and joyfulness promote a positive attitude needed to live a successful and happy life.

As difficult as the legal process was, Kate was grateful for all that she had and appreciated that she had the inner resolve to see the process through to the finish. Bert repeatedly said to her, "It will never be over." Kate believed that the quote attributed to Louis L'Amour was appropriate: "There will come a time when you believe everything is finished. Yet that will be the beginning."

EPILOGUE

Following her dad's funeral, Kate wrote the following letter. Her letter was eventually rewritten by the Long Beach attorney she had retained and was sent to Mabel Snatt at Cheetham, Steele and Morse LLP. Kate wrote the following:

March 14, 2016

Mabel Snatt

Cheetham, Steele and Morse LLP 999 Dead End

Indian Falls, Minnesota Dear Ms. Snatt:

Your paperwork stated that Chuck and Mildred purchased 12200 Valley Egypt from our mother's irrevocable trust for a purchase price of $125,000 with monthly payments beginning February 1, 2012. You stated there was no appraisal done on the property, and a comparative market analysis was used to determine the market value of the property during 2008 to 2010, two years prior to this sale.

Bertrand and Chuck were trustees of the Gloriette irrevocable trust and had a duty first and foremost look after the interest of the trust beneficiaries. Furthermore, no monthly payments were made by Chuck or Mildred to the Gloriette trust during the two years following their "purchase." Two lump sum payments were made from Bertrand's checking account for two years prior to his death.

There is no evidence this transaction was not self-dealing on the part of the trustees. I request an appraisal as of December 2011. This is not an allowable transaction by the trustees of the Gloriette irrevocable trust, and remedies must be made to trust beneficiaries.

Sincerely,

Kate, successor trustee of the Gloriette trust

After sixteen months, Kate had not received a response to her letter prepared and mailed by her local attorney. Her court petitions listed and documented a history of self-dealing, fraud, and breach of fiduciary duty by Chuck as the trustee of both trusts.

Chuck's law firm responded to her petitions with citations of numerous court cases, statute of limitation defenses, and slanderous statements made about her. Mabel Snatt exhibited a vicious personality during her telephone calls as well as her letters to the three beneficiaries—Bert, Phillip, and Kate. Ms. Snatt's e-mails sent to Joseph Stone and Jack Napp were caustic and antagonistic. Joseph Stone told Kate that she made inflammatory, acrimonious statements about her within her e-mails.

After mediation 2, eighty-eight days had passed, Mabel Snatt telephoned Bert and told Bert that the case was Kate's fault. "Finn Nash did what your dad wanted, and Chuck did everything right." She stated that if Kate had not sued Chuck, they all would have their money.

Mabel Snatt sent Joseph Stone and Jack Napp scathing e-mails blaming Kate for the delay in the case's closure. There were three assets in the Gloriette trust: the 12200 Valley Egypt house, the 12100 Valley Egypt land contract, and the trust investment (stock) account. After twenty years, her trust investment (stock) account was the sole remaining asset. Numerous principal withdrawals were made from her trust: payments to Chuck's attorneys, 12200 Valley Egypt house expenses as well as questionable withdrawals not related to her trust holdings. Gloriette's land contracts had been written down to a fraction of their value, and the sporadic payments that should have been deposited to her trust were credited to Bertrand's checking account. Bertrand's checking account was used by Chuck for his personal expenditures or transferred back to his joint checking account with Mildred. Gloriette's 12200 Valley Egypt house was owned by Chuck and Mildred, disclosed only after Bertrand's death.

Mabel Snatt charged the trust's monthly administrative charges. Chuck liquidated the twenty-to-thirty-plus-year held quality stocks the day after her dad's funeral without explanation. There was no evidence of the fiduciary duty he owed to the trust beneficiaries. Kate carefully liquidated the long-term bonds held in the Gloriette trust during the six months following her dad's funeral, carefully securing at the best prices available for thinly traded bonds. This process required her to communicate with Mr. Young to ensure everything was executed properly. The liquidations of the Gloriette trust bonds were completed just prior to interest rate increases which occurred in July 2016. The interest rate increases would have significantly affected the liquidation value because of the poor liquidity and changing marketplace. However, two illiquid positions could not be sold. Mabel sent a caustic e-mail to Jack Napp stating that Kate was negligent in liquidating the illiquid positions. Kate did not understand what she hoped to gain from her nasty e-mails. Kate believed Mabel Snatt was operating under the direction and dictates of Chuck.

Ms. Snatt stated the trust accounting charges were fair. As successor trustee, Kate was excluded from the accounting process for the Gloriette trust. Ms. Snatt did not use trust statements, relying instead on Chuck's handwritten notes for outstanding loan balances which he listed in the final estate accounting. Loans listed were not found anywhere on the trust statements. Chuck's and Ann's numerous loans recorded on brokerage trust statements were omitted.

Kate requested information from Ms. Snatt regarding the two insurance policies bought with the trust money. The policies named Chuck, Ann, and Bert as beneficiaries. Kate was promised the policies would be part of the final accounting by Mr. Morse and Mr. Broader during mediations 1 and 2. They said, "Mabel will provide the accounting for the two policies bought with trust money." After mediation 2, Mabel said, "We don't know anything about promising to provide that information."

Bert lived down the road from Bertrand for eighteen years. Mabel called Bert once and eighty-plus days after mediation 2 demanding he deliver his painting that he had hanging in his house since the day of his dad's burial. Ms. Snatt told Bert that he was to personally deliver his painting to her home.

The last statement Kate heard from Mabel was "Bertrand ordered to buy the thirty-plus-year bonds and limited partnership when he was at Maybrook. Chuck had nothing to do with that, and it's Kate's fault they haven't been liquidated. Chuck has done everything right, and he deserves everything because that is what Bertrand stated to Finn Nash four years before his passing."

Kate replied to Jack Napp, "Illiquid means there are no buyers."

The final day of the estate distribution and settlement that had been agreed to during mediation 2 was June 16, 2017, twenty years to the day of Gloriette's death. Kate thought this was an interesting coincidence because she had nothing to do with the date of the final distribution. She thought it was significant because the entire legal process was an effort to honor her mother's legacy and do what she would have expected of her.

The painting Bert had asked for and received the day after her dad's funeral was picked up by Mabel Snatt on August 12 from his home. Ms.

Snatt went to his home and demanded possession of Bert's painting. It didn't matter what was just or right; she made sure she followed Chuck's instructions on what she was to do.

Wright, Coolidge and Stone PC's administrative assistant informed Kate by e-mail that all the documents related to this case would be destroyed. Kate told her she wanted all the legal documents to be preserved for future reference, if needed, to confirm the facts regarding this case. Bert picked up six boxes of files the end of July 2017. He assured Kate that he would store all the legal documents for her. It was her understanding that the case was closed because Joseph Stone told her it was closed as of July 2017. She had received a final billing statement in August 2017, paid the bill, and closed her file.

Kate received an invoice at the end of November 2017 and wrote the following note on the invoice: "I thought this case was closed. What is this invoice for?

Please tell Mr. Morse that I am done with this litigation." Jack Napp sent Kate an apologetic e-mail, stating that he had to meet with Mr. Morse regarding the final court filing of the case. He stated that for some reason the court procedure had been overlooked. The court date was set for December 20. Kate wrote a check on December 21 for what she hoped was the final billing. Attached to the e-mail invoice was the following court order: "The stipulated order approving mediation settlement agreement and trust accountings and resolving litigation. This court has reviewed and hereby approves the confidential mediation settlement agreement and trust accountings. This order resolves the last pending matter and closes the case."

Kate received another bill from Wright, Coolidge and Stone PC in February 2018, twenty-four months following her dad's funeral. They had forwarded an e-mail that had been sent to them by Mable Snatt.

Kate sent the following e-mail to Mable Snatt: "You do not have my permission to communicate with anyone on my behalf. You can e-mail me directly. This case was supposed to be closed last July. What is this billing for?"

Kate replied to Ms. Snatt by e-mail:

> It is my understanding the case is closed. I am no longer represented by Wright, Coolidge and Stone PC. Neither Phillip nor I have anything to do with Chuck's demands. Tell Chuck to deal directly with Bert who lives two miles from him. There should be no reason for you to ever contact me in the future. Thank you.
>
> — Kate.

Do members of state bar associations have ethics requirements to practice law? Does the state have ethics oversight for attorneys who practice estate law? Would you like this law firm to represent your family when you are gone?

Should states consider legislation against elderly people who are shut-ins against what Finn Nash and Chuck did to Kate's parents' long-standing estate plans and their raiding of Gloriette's irrevocable trust?

This case raises questions about the ethics of the law firm who was hired and paid to represent the Bertrand and Gloriette trust. After sixteen months, hundreds of thousands of dollars were paid to this law firm for their representation. The legal expense incurred was a result of representing Chuck, the trustee, as if they were criminal defense attorneys. Questions asked by certain beneficiaries were not answered.

PART 2

THE RESPONSE

SUCCESS: THE FIVE-POINT PLAN

As a financial professional, I find the story of *Valley Egypt* disturbing. I related this true story because of what transpired and the sequence of events that occurred contradicted common sense and ethical practices. Two parents had the foresight to set up legal documents which detailed the specific instructions regarding their estate distribution. The trusts were executed when they were both healthy and of sound mind. The initial response to this story is as follows: "Could the outcome have been prevented? Wasn't the Gloriette trust irrevocable?

If it was irrevocable, how was it changed? How can I ensure this doesn't happen to my trust or my estate when I become unable to oversee its administration?"

I have outlined a five-point implementation plan to accomplish proper distribution of your estate according to your wishes. This plan will ensure or greatly reduce the opportunity for someone to take advantage of you and your wealth.

For some, death and dying is a subject that is difficult to talk about. Each of us desire to live a long and healthy life. We do not know how many years we will live or what the quality of our end of life will be. We may ask ourselves, "Will I remain mentally alert and healthy, or will I develop a debilitating illness, dementia, or senility during my aged years? Did I carefully save my money and develop an estate to ensure I am not a burden to my children or relatives? Where do I want to spend the remaining years of my life if I am no longer able to care for myself? Do I want my accumulated wealth given to my children, or should my money be given to a particular charity or cause?" These are questions we each must ask and answer.

The first step of a successful estate process is called *plan*. Bertrand and Gloriette had an estate plan. It was legal, written, and thorough. Unfortunately, their plan was articulated to the two oldest children, Chuck and Kate. They trusted their two children to execute their trust documents as they had carefully structured and prepared. Their intent was for the two children to act as co-trustees at the end of both of their lives. Kate was their financial advisor and understood what they wanted to accomplish. Chuck had received the majority of the farm liquidation assets as well as a deeply discounted price of what had been the family farm by May 1992. It was understood between the parents and the two elder children that the remaining assets at the end of their lives would be distributed equally to six children.

Although Bertrand talked about eventually going to a senior home by the river most of his adult life, his desire was not included in their written plan. Additionally, their plan was well-documented; however, it was not shared with all the beneficiaries. I believe Gloriette or Bertrand did not imagine that one of their children would work diligently to discredit Kate and remove her from their plan. The younger children did not know the specifics of their estate plan; however, they knew Kate was one of the successor trustees. Her younger brothers always assumed she would make sure things were done properly as that is how she had conducted herself throughout her life.

A meeting following the trust plan document execution with all six children would have been beneficial. It is imperative for parents to discuss their intentions with all children and to have their intensions and plans honored. Particularly, if trust grantors become unexpectedly incapacitated prior to death. This is not an easy conversation; however, it is a conversation that needs to take place between children and their parents.

The second step is called *inform*. Gloriette developed cancer and died almost twenty years prior to her husband's death. The family story indicates that Gloriette was an integral part of the farm because she worked along with her sons and husband doing chores over the life of the farm. She was a partner in the purchase of all the farm assets and land along with her husband. She deserved to have her estate preserved and honored. The two trustees who took over her trust after her death aligned their interests above Gloriette's beneficiaries. By inserting language into her trust mandating that any changes to her legal documents must be disclosed to all beneficiaries may have prevented the wrongdoing that occurred. The "inform" requirement would have been an impediment against the potential for trustee self-dealing actions. Self-dealing between both trustees occurred systematically during the twenty years following her passing. If disclosure of trustee dealings had been required, questions may have arisen about Chuck's continued borrowing from her trust. Additionally, disclosure would have called attention to the fact that his land contract payments were not being made to her trust. Annual disclosure would have meant that the beneficiaries would have been aware of the excellent investment advice given by Gordon and Kate. The deeply discounted institutional commission rates also would have been disclosed to the beneficiaries. When the trusts were transferred, the transfer was not disclosed nor was the reasoning. This missing requirement allowed the trustees to take advantage of her assets. Although her trust was irrevocable, the trustees disregarded the legal language and their fiduciary duty to put the interests of the beneficiaries above their own. There was no oversight and no accountability once the accounts were transferred away from Gordon. An annual review of the accounts handled by Fred Schafte would have caused concern given the liquidation of highly appreciated securities that had substantial embedded capital gains. The capital gains increased the annual tax liabilities and the high commission charges that the uninterested, self-serving broker charged for the liquidation of long-held securities.

The medical report and history suggest that Bertrand did not have the mental capacity to act as a competent trustee for many years. This fact could be argued since the time of Gloriette's death. This is one of the most significant and important facts of this case. There are instances in which spouses are unable to mentally function competently after the death of their long-related spouse. In this case, Bertrand had a long history of health issues, particularly stroke, ministrokes, and not being ambulatory. An annual disclosure of trust assets and changes would have caused alarm among the trust beneficiaries. The beneficiaries may have questioned the wisdom of transferring the trusts from competent investment professionals who had aligned interests. Additionally, Gordon and Kate had worked to provide excellent advice at minimal expense. This information was provided by the annual statements during the many years they were the broker of record.

Mandatory disclosure by the trustees was not part of the Gloriette's legal trust document. Due to the confidential nature of investment accounts and extensive brokerage compliance requirements, Kate did not have the authority to inform the trust beneficiaries without Bertrand's consent.

In summary, changes to the trust custodian, investment holdings, investment professionals, and returns should be disclosed to beneficiaries at least once a year. Gloriette's trust was irrevocable, and her trust assets were to be divided equally among her six children. Unfortunately, because this important requirement was omitted from her trust document, the two trustees did not act as a fiduciary and there was no accountability. Upon Bertrand's death, Kate proved the history of self-dealing, theft, breach of fiduciary duty, and investment churning by the Minnesota broker; however, it was too late as the assets had been either removed or harmed.

The parents' long-term estate planning attorney was changed. No beneficiaries were informed of this change. Ken Powler had detailed knowledge from both Gloriette and Bertrand as to how their estates should be distributed. When the estate file was transferred from Ken Powler to Finn Nash, disclosure to all the beneficiaries would have alerted their internal thought process that something was wrong.

The story of *Valley Egypt* has to do with two parents and their children. Often, a spouse dies, and the remaining spouse remarries. The second marriage may result in destruction of the first spouse's estate. This an unfair and unfortunate occurrence for the children of the first spouse and their intended inheritance. Inserting language of disclosure is imperative to ensure proper estate plan execution. The beneficiaries must be informed at least annually of any changes to an irrevocable trust and its holdings.

Having over three decades of experience in the financial advisory industry, it's been my experience that the number 1 reason there are problems with settling of an estate is because the terms and wishes of the trustor are not discussed with the beneficiaries prior to their death. This step is of utmost importance if you desire your estate to be distributed without or with minimal legal entanglements.

The trusts were transferred away from competent professionals. There was no justifiable reason to transfer the investment accounts from Gordon. Gordon had an excellent reputation, track record, and furthermore was licensed to execute the trades that had been so successful since the accounts were established twenty-three years before. This story explains why the accounts were transferred and it was done under nefarious circumstances.

The third step of the estate plan process is *safeguard*. Who is the trustee of your estate? Who is your co-trustee? What are their qualifications? Do they understand the term "fiduciary duty"? Do they understand what self-dealing is? What if you become mentally or physically incapacitated?

Do you trust your trustee to act in your best interests? Who is providing additional oversight in the event you cannot continue to administer and monitor your assets? Safeguarding the estate involves asking and answering these questions. The answers should be officially documented for future reference and confirmation of intentions.

In this case, Chuck was able to remove Kate. The story explains that Kate's removal was necessary for Chuck to continue to transfer assets to himself and change Bertrand's trust the final years of his life. This could have been prevented had a few simple safeguard techniques been used. Primarily, what is the financial condition of the appointed trustee? A credit check should be a mandatory requirement to be a trustee. A credit check on Chuck would have disclosed someone heavily in debt and not a competent handler of finances. Additionally, what is your trustee's educational background? There are many self-educated individuals who are competent and trustworthy. In this case, Chuck was neither and became sole trustee of both trusts during the last years of Bertrand's life, eliminating his sister's role in their parents' financial estate. Bertrand was no longer mentally competent to make investment decisions. Additionally, this positioned Bertrand to be abused financially. He was dependent on Chuck and Ann and felt he had to do what they told him to do. In summary, to safeguard means to appoint the proper trustee(s) to act in your interest. Additionally, competent, ethical oversight is imperative. In this case, Bertrand could have appointed his long-term friend and experienced business professional, Adrian Van Stern, to act as an overseer of his financial interests. This would have allowed Kate to have an advocate to go to and discuss potential "foul play" and "self-dealing" by the trustees.

Kate made a mistake in confiding her concerns with Ann, not realizing that Ann was not trustworthy. Kate should have discussed her concerns with her younger brothers. Additionally, she could have called Ken Powler's office and discussed her concerns with him. If she had called him, she would have been informed of his change of law office and may have pieced together the sequence of events and the reasoning behind her dad's belligerence toward her. Additionally, she could have conducted a background check on Fred Schafte. Her dad's lifelong treatment of her, her new business, and her young family explains why she accepted his decision and disengaged herself emotionally. She had hoped for the best. Hoping is not a strategy for success. It is important to find a neutral and ethical person to discuss financial estate concerns with.

A professional in-state trustee should have been appointed to Bertrand's trust and Gloriette's irrevocable trust immediately following Gloriette's passing. A meeting with Ken Powler and a discussion of Bertrand's health issues may have promoted the importance of having an objective in-state professional handling the trust assets. The use of the local bank account should have been discouraged, anticipating potential abuse by self-interested individuals. In this case, Bertrand had minimal living expenses. An independent, objective professional may have been able to protect his funds for eventual payment to the local retirement home where he would have been well cared for. Additionally, Kate was out of state and did not have knowledge of the daily schemes of Ann and Chuck. As Bertrand's daughter and his strong personality, she did not have the authority to prevent Bertrand's financial actions which eventually affected his daily care. His strong personality was intimidating as he typically countered any questions with critical verbal outbursts and gruffness that was unpleasant for her to experience.

The first step is to plan. If you don't plan, you will not achieve what you desire. The second step is to inform. You must inform all participants about the process and what you hope to accomplish. This will help create alliances for the rest of your life. Had the younger sons been included in the process, they would have understood Bertrand's intent. Their mother's legacy would have had a greater chance of being protected. The two youngest sons were not included in financial discussions and did not believe it was their business. The third step, to safeguard, means to align yourself with competent people who are honest, trustworthy, and will put the trustor and beneficiaries above their own interests. Gloriette was concerned about Chuck as she confided to her sister Faye.

Her concern, however, were not made known to other people. She was afraid of what might happen. Unfortunately, she did not protect her interests by appointing a person that would provide oversight and may have prevented Chuck from manipulating the assets. The concerns she stated to her sister were realized because the trust document hadn't been safeguarded.

Gloriette had extensive conversations with Ken Powler regarding the final distribution of their estate. They had spent almost fifty years accumulating their assets. Her intentions were detailed and specific as outlined by Mr. Powler. Mr. Powler provided this documentation to Bertrand, Chuck, and Kate, following Gloriette's death. Gloriette did not envision that Ken Powler's law firm would be removed as their estate and legal professionals, having had a twenty-year professional relationship with them. The duty to inform requirement may have prevented the hiring of Finn Nash and the firing of Bertrand and Gloriette's long-standing estate attorney.

The third step, to safeguard, is to ensure the professionals you hire have your interests first and foremost. Bertrand's accountant of over thirty years had no knowledge of the Gloriette land contracts. It became evident that his interest was primarily monetary, being paid. He did not have an allegiance to Bertrand and Gloriette's wishes. He did not know that their trust documents were changed during the last years of Bertrand's life, transferring all remaining valuable assets to Chuck. The law firm Cheetham, Steele and Morse LLP did not represent Bertrand and Gloriette's estate. They represented Chuck and themselves. They did not represent the children of Gloriette and Bertrand. They charged egregious fees and promoted the high legal expense by making undisclosed changes to the Bertrand and Gloriette's trust. Their actions may be legal in a particular state. In other states, their actions would be questioned as unethical and corrupt. Additionally, the evidence showed that this law firm was hired by Chuck. Each check paid to this firm was written and signed by Chuck using Bertrand's checking account. Additionally, loan documents were changed and executed with only Chuck's signature. Both trustee signatures should have been listed on the revised loan agreements. Safeguarding includes engaging ethical professionals. Financial advisors, law firms, accounting firms, and trustees should have a history of ethical competence. Financial professionals are closely regulated, and improper conduct is documented and sanctioned if necessary. Legal professionals should be held accountable for unethical behavior. In this case, Mr. Nash should go before a review board and answer questions as to why he changed the estate documents long after the first spouse died and the second spouse suffered serious medical issues. He should be fined and his license suspended to practice law if it is found that he acted with intent to financially harm the heirs of his estate. It was disappointing that the law firm disregarded all the children of Gloriette and Bertrand and represented one trustee and those financially aligned with him.

The fourth step of the plan is *execute*. You have planned, informed, and safeguarded; and now you must execute. This means to make sure your assets are titled correctly in the name of your trust. If an asset is not correctly titled, it is not legally part of your trust and under the direction of the trust documents. Surprisingly, many people fail to follow this important step of the estate plan.

The fifth step of the plan is *annual review*. You must annually review what you have set up and make sure your plan is operating as you have envisioned it. The annual review allows you to keep your beneficiaries informed and will serve to ensure they are aligned with your well-being and intent. This step assures that the safeguarding step is active. The annual review would have alerted all siblings to the questionable actions of Chuck and Ann the year following Gloriette's death. They were able to manipulate Bertrand to their financial benefit almost immediately following her death. This was illustrated when Ann changed her parents' life insurance policies and Chuck immediately increased his borrowing from her trust.

The five steps outlined are straightforward and easily explainable. There may be hesitation to disclose and inform confidential financial information to beneficiaries. Often, parents are reluctant to disclose their assets and wealth. The sequence of actions may be executed using competent, qualified, ethical professionals who will act first and foremost in your interest.

Gloriette may have requested that the estate administration be transferred to a well-researched and competent trust department. She probably had concerns about Bertrand's ability to manage his financial affairs. She had taken care of much of the finances after Bertrand's stroke. She did not expect Kate to be removed from her position of oversight and advice. However, anticipating Chuck's manipulation, she may have made a good case to hire a third-party independent trustee to prevent any wrongdoing on the part of one of the trustees.

The story of *Valley Egypt* illustrates the importance of using competent and ethical professionals. Chuck was able to accomplish what he did because he aligned himself with others who were self-interested and monetarily motivated. The common denominator of the professionals relied upon the last ten years of Bertrand's life were lacking in moral character and ethics.

In summary, the five integral steps to a successful estate plan are as follows: plan, inform, safeguard, execute, and conduct an annual review.

TRUST AND TRUSTS

The book *Valley Egypt* has many important parts to its story. One of the principal aspects is that of the parents' trusts. This chapter explains what a trust is and the reasoning behind titling financial and real property in trust.

Typically, a trust is a legal document clearly stating the trustee's intentions for his assets. Today, many people take advantage of establishing trusts as an estate planning tool. A trust typically will bypass the need for a will. Assets titled in the name of a trust will not be subject to the state probate process, saving time and expense. Probate, depending on the particular state, is an expensive process and makes personal information public. Currently, a small percentage of Americans are subject to estate taxes; however, estate taxes will change depending on the political power in Washington. A properly designed trust will help to minimize taxes. The estate tax laws changed dramatically in 2010. Currently, estates valued less than five million dollars are not subject to federal estate taxes. I believe this may change in the future depending on our federal government legislature and their agenda.

For the majority of individuals who own assets, a trust will help them properly designate where they want their specific assets to go at their death and the death of their spouse. It's important to use a professional, experienced estate-planning attorney. Trusts can be simple or complex, and all must understand what is involved. It is important that the attorney understands the intentions as he is instrumental in helping a person avoid all potential pitfalls along the way.

This particular story shows what can happen if trust documents are changed during the parents' last years. Chuck and Ann claim their parent was of "sound mind" and was not under "undue influence." The longtime family estate attorney was changed by the trustee's friend, Chuck's friend, and not disclosed to other family members. The attorney proceeded to draft several amendments to the parents' trust. Each new amendment was drafted with language directed against one child, the eldest daughter and the twenty-three-year financial advisor. Six children were beneficiaries, yet only one child as trustee and his wife were active participants in making all changes. The result was a lengthy and difficult legal process which was financially expensive and emotionally painful. This would not have been the case if changes had been aboveboard, transparent, and disclosed to all children named in the trust.

As an investment professional, I find this case disturbing primarily because one attorney changed the original legal documents in order to benefit one beneficiary, ignoring the other five children. There was no disclosure of the many changes prior to the death of the second parent. The parent suffered from various medical issues, including depression and dementia, yet trust amendments were signed as if the client was mentally competent. If there are changes to trust documents, they should be done after there is a reputable medical and mental competency test conducted by a medical professional. This case calls attention to potential abuse of trust documents in a number of areas. Competent geriatric mental health professionals may help in ensuring mental competency prior to major legal changes.

A first and most important decision is choosing a trustee for the trust as mentioned in the five-part plan process. The trustee is legally bound to manage the trust's assets in the best interests of the beneficiaries. A person's first impulse may be to choose a family member; however, before doing so, these questions should be asked:

1. Does he or she have the experience and knowledge
    to manage financial affairs competently?

2. When called upon to make a decision that may affect other family members, will the prospective trustee act in a fair and unbiased manner?

3. Will naming a family member as trustee create a strain within the family?

4. Does the prospective trustee have enough time to manage the trust? Does he or she want this responsibility?

5. Are there other family members who are willing to serve as trustee if the chosen trustee cannot do so?

They may consider naming a co-trustee to help with the decisions of managing the trust. They may also want to name a successor trustee who can take over if the person initially named fails or refuses to act in the capacity of trustee. If a person does not want to choose an individual, they may ask a financial institution to serve as trustee. They will benefit from objectivity and expertise with an institution; however, it will come with additional costs and requirements which may or may not make sense for the situation.

I believe one of the most important aspects of developing an estate plan and setting up a trust is to communicate the wishes and ideas to the family and anyone else who may be beneficiaries of the estate. This would have made a difference in the outcome of the Valley Egypt farm estate. The parents made their intentions known to two children; one of whom was not interested in abiding by the intent and terms of the trusts. When family members don't know what to expect, disappointment and frustration may follow.

Having all family members understand the estate plan in its entirety would have benefited the parent, the successor trustee, and each child. Bertrand's final years were affected by the bad decisions and actions of his son Chuck, who remained trustee of both trusts. Chuck exerted tremendous pressure on his father to make financial changes for his sole benefit.

"Fiduciary" is a term used when discussing trusts. The term "fiduciary" means involving trust, especially with regard to the relationship between a trustee and beneficiary(s)."[16]

I believe that the most important aspect of a legal trust is designating a proper trustee who exemplifies *trust*. Trust is the obligation or responsibility imposed on a person in whom confidence or authority is placed.[17] It is important to have a trustworthy trustee to ensure that he will do what is intended and proper and not operate for his own personal financial gain.

Congratulations for reading this book in an effort to prepare yourself and your heirs properly. I sincerely wish you success in protecting your heirs and what you intend for your financial legacy.

I am not an estate planner and cannot provide tax or legal advice. You should consult your estate-planning or qualified tax advisor regarding your particular situation.

---

16   *Oxford Dictionary:* "fiduciary."
      Wikipedia: "Typically, a fiduciary prudently takes care of money or other assets for another person."
17   *Random House Dictionary:* "trust."

ACKNOWLEDGMENTS

I acknowledge and thank the following people who supported my efforts in writing this book—Gary and Sharon Jonker, lifelong friends who are supportive of my project from its inception to the final manuscript. La Rae Dunitz encouraged my efforts and offered her editorial expertise during early manuscript revisions. I thank Brian and Judy Hibma and Kelly Sybesma for their initial editing and their recommendations to make the storyline understandable. Deborah J. Seals encouraged me to not leave anything out. Thanks to Pat and Ron Ogden for their objective opinions and Pat's editorial review of my early manuscripts. Thanks to Jayne Bittner for her honesty, thoughtfulness, and advice to ensure the accuracy of events. Sincere appreciation to Janice P. Hartzell who shared her thoughts on the original manuscript and helped provide clarity to parts of the story. I thank Dr. Rev. Cecil and Arlene Martens for their sincere and heartfelt response to my writing and their patient encouragement. Thanks to longtime friend, client, and avid reader, James Norris IV, for his editorial comments. Gratitude to Linda DeYoung for her generous comments. Thanks to Bonnie Sandbulte Hofmeyer for her enthusiastic editing and advice during the final review process.

The following financial professionals were invaluable by adding their insight and comments to the educational and professional guidance offered: David Dougherty, CFP; Deb Van Essen; Robert Hedley, CPA; Brent Greenshields; and Joanne Duncan. Each person offered professional insight and comments regarding the financial and legal aspects discussed in Part 2. Gratitude to Wendy Norris, publicist, who encouraged me to expand the story and add Part 2. I sincerely appreciate Dr. Yvonne Alles for editing the final manuscript and for her suggestions to add clarity to the storyline.

My deepest thanks and appreciation go to my dear husband, Gregory J. Hetzer, who patiently listened to each chapter and the multiple rewrites. This book would not have been written if not for two people, R. A. and B. A. They were a constant source of support and enthusiasm for the book's intended purpose—to help other families who may face similar challenges.

NOTES

Financial Elder Abuse

This book was written with the goal to help identify potential abuses being perpetrated on an aging loved one. Tragically, elderly people are vulnerable to financial scams. After studying numerous financial and medical records, the facts showed that Bertrand was a victim of elder abuse. My aunt had a financial scam perpetrated on her over the phone. Eventually, it was resolved; however, it took a toll on her financially, mentally, and physically. She hired attorneys and spent considerable time, money, and worry thinking about the loss of her savings. Her distress caused by this incident was clearly evident by those close to her.

Although Kate was an accomplished professional, she was not knowledgeable about financial elder abuse at its inception. Financial professionals should have extensive education regarding this important topic. Kate did not recognize the early warning signs because she was not knowledgeable about financial elder abuse at that time. Given Bertrand's medical history and the passing of his spouse, after forty-eight years of marriage, Kate should have insisted on independent professional oversight from either their parents' long-standing attorney or a trust department professional. Additionally, a professional within the state with trust oversight would have been advisable given the fact that Bertrand lived in Minnesota and Kate lived out of state.

The financial services industry is paying more attention to this growing problem because the baby boom generation is rapidly aging and the elderly population is growing exponentially. For these reasons, people are increasingly aware of elder abuse, and the financial industry is devoting resources to increased knowledge and awareness of the potential financial abuse.

The story *Valley Egypt* is about money and property being taken over the period of several years. Questionable signatures and significant changes to long-standing legal documents were cause for concern. Bertrand depended on Chuck for food and care, which made him very vulnerable to manipulation. Chuck coerced Bertrand to sign documents. Four years before his death, Bertrand signed the fourth amendment to his trust, relinquishing the last parcel of land owned by the trust. The transfer of this property was "buried" in a paragraph. No one, other than Chuck's wife Mildred, knew of this agreement. The property had been part of the family estate for over forty-five years. Chuck felt that he was justified and everything was rightfully his. His mantra was "I stayed; everyone else left."

Years of medical records revealed that Bertrand was kept at home years longer than was justified. Aunt Janelle said, "He has no business living in his house alone; he cannot care for himself." Ann told others that Bertrand sat alone with the lights turned off in a cold room for long periods of time. During the legal process, Kate was told that her dad was unable to light the fire in his fireplace because there had been too many close calls of him almost burning the house down. Bertrand was unable to start a fire for warmth for several years before he moved to the Maybrook assisted-living home.

Chuck had an appraisal done by Maybrook assisted-living home in 2010 to determine if assets were available to afford Bertrand transferring to an assisted-living home. This in itself was questionable because the Gloriette house was held by an irrevocable trust. None of the beneficiaries was notified of the discussions and appraisal between Chuck and this assisted-living retirement community despite their beneficial ownership of the Gloriette home. Bertrand did not enter Maybrook home until the later part of 2014. The evidence presented confirms that Chuck kept him home alone as long as possible because he was living off his money. The facts point out that Chuck did not wish to incur the increased expenditure of a nursing home for his dad.

Chuck often called Bertrand derogatory names and cursed at him. Bert, Phillip, and Diana, Bert's wife, witnessed his abusive and hurtful behavior. This fact was stated in Bert's affidavit. There was plenty of evidence that Chuck had negative feelings toward his brothers and sisters. He did not want anyone to inherit any of their parents' assets other than himself. He often told his brothers that he would be better off if they had never been born.

The financial and care decisions for Bertrand were made by Chuck and Ann during the last ten years of his life. No other siblings were consulted. Bertrand was admitted to the Maybrook nursing home during 2014. He was later removed by Ann without any consultation or discussion with other siblings. She said to others that her dad didn't like it there and he wanted to be taken out. At that time, Kate and her siblings believed that she and Chuck were operating for his best interest.

Bertrand lived most of his life in Minnesota. His two youngest sons lived close by and visited him often. Ann moved him to Arkansas without the consent of other siblings and made it impossible for the regular frequent visits of his younger sons to continue.

It is important that parents, children, and siblings each have a clear understanding of the parents' wishes as well as what to expect when their parent is no longer able to function or make decisions on their own or when they pass. This will reduce the possibility for elder abuse by select children and/or caregivers. An elderly person requiring care who is dependent on others for food and shelter is in a prime position to be abused.

Our legal system must adapt and change to better protect the elderly from financial abuse. It's difficult to prove someone is not of "sound mind." Geriatric psychiatric tests are used in court cases. Legal professionals who specialize in geriatric cases will advise regarding the use of these tests. A shut-in requires another to handle all financial transactions and is dependent on others for their meals and safety, causing them to be vulnerable. Estate plans set up when parents are of sound mind should not be allowed to be changed unless it is done with careful scrutiny and care. All beneficiaries should be informed of changes which affect the care of the parent as well as the trust assets.

There is an increasing amount of information about financial elder abuse as it is being reported more often because of our growing elderly population and their significant wealth. The following publication and research are available to better understand the subject of financial elder abuse.

The following summarizes information from the publications referenced.[18] Financial elder abuse spans a broad spectrum of conduct, including:

- Taking money or property.

- Forging an older person's signature.

- Getting an older person to sign a deed, will, or power of attorney through deception, coercion, or undue

---

18   Nerenberg, L., *Forgotten Victims of Elder Financial Crime and Abuse: A Report and Recommendations* (1999). "Produced by the Goldman Institute on Aging for the National Center on Aging (NCEA), this report summarized four roundtable discussions sponsored by NCEA, which focused on four components of the legal system: the state and criminal justice system, federal investigative and regulatory agencies, civil legal system, and victim witness assistance network. Professionals from each system described challenges they face in handling financial abuse cases and made recommendations for improving each system's response." See NCEA website.

The *Journal of Elder Abuse and Neglect* 12, no. 2 (2000) is devoted to financial elder abuse. For more information about *Journal of Elder Abuse and Neglect* and a listing of articles in the issue, see *Aging/Parents and Adult Children, Together, A/PACT.* Produced by the American Association of Retired Persons (AARP) and the United States Federal Trade Commission, this consumer education series includes ten one-to-three-page articles focusing on consumer fraud, daily money management, alternatives to guardianship, etc. Contact the AARP for more information.

influence.

- Using the older person's property or possessions without permission.
- Promising lifelong care in exchange for money or property and not following through on the promise.
- Confidence crimes ("cons") are the use of deception to gain victim's confidence.
- Scams are fraudulent or deceptive acts.
- Fraud is the use of deception, trickery, false pretense, or dishonest acts or statements for financial gain
- Telemarketing scams. Perpetrators call victims and use deception, scare tactics, or exaggerated claims to get them to send money. They may also make charges against victims' credit cards without authorization.
- The perpetrators are often family members, including sons, daughters, grandchildren, or spouses. They may:
- have substance abuse, gambling, or financial problems
- stand to inherit and feel justified in taking what they believe is "almost" or "rightfully" theirs
- fear that their older family member will get sick and use up their savings, depriving the abuser of an inheritance
- have had a negative relationship with the older person and feel a sense of "entitlement"
- have negative feelings toward siblings or other family members whom they want to prevent from acquiring or inheriting the older person's assets

Predatory individuals who seek out vulnerable seniors with the intent of exploiting them may:

- profess to love the older person ("sweetheart scams")

- seek employment as personal care attendants, counselors, etc., to gain access

- identify vulnerable persons by driving through neighborhoods (to find persons who are alone and isolated) or contact recently widowed persons they find through newspaper death announcements

- move from community to community to avoid being apprehended (transient criminals)

Unscrupulous professionals or businesspersons or persons posing as such may:

- overcharge for services or products

- use deceptive or unfair business practices

- use their positions of trust or respect to gain compliance

The following conditions or factors increase an older person's risk of being victimized:

- isolation

- loneliness

- recent losses

- physical or mental disabilities

- lack of familiarity with financial matters

- have family members who are unemployed and/or have substance abuse problems

The elderly are attractive targets because of the following reasons:

- Persons over the age of fifty control over 70 percent

of the nation's wealth.

- Many seniors do not realize the value of their assets (particularly homes that have appreciated markedly).

- The elderly is likely to have disabilities that make them dependent on others for help. These "helpers" may have access to homes and assets and may exercise significant influence over the older person.

- They may have predictable patterns (e.g., because older people are likely to receive monthly checks, abusers can predict when an older people will have money on hand or need to go to the bank).

- Severely impaired individuals are also less likely to take action against their abusers as a result of illness or embarrassment.

- Abusers may assume that frail victims will not survive long enough to follow through on legal interventions or that they will not make convincing witnesses.

- Some older people are unsophisticated about financial matters.

- Advances in technology have made managing finances more complicated.

MENTAL HEALTH

As we age, brain health research continues to advance. In the past, declining memory and cognitive functions affecting a person's ability to perform normal activities was called dementia. Today, dementia may be categorized into the following diseases: Alzheimer's disease, early onset of Alzheimer's disease, vascular dementia, Lewy body dementia, Parkinson's disease, dementia, frontotemporal dementia, Wernicke-Korsakoff syndrome, mixed dementia, and chronic traumatic encephala. These diseases have different trajectories requiring various types of care settings that are appropriate for the particular disease. The costs may be significantly different depending on the type of cognitive disease and may require difference in length of stay.[19]

stay New medical research is providing statistics that retirement without purpose and plans may increase mental decline and increase the risk of diseases, such as stroke, cancer, and heart disease.[20]

---

19   For additional information and resources, see www.BrainHealthAsYouAge.com; www. Enrichvisits.com; Mitch Anthony and Steve Sanduski, CFP, "The New Retire Mentality"; and https://www.nia.nih.gov/health/brain-health-resource.

20   See note 19 above.

REFERENCES

1 US Department of Health and Human Services, Administration for Community Living. *Administration on Aging: Aging Statistic.*

2 MetLife Mature Market Institute, National Committee for the Prevention of Elder Abuse, and the Virginia Polytechnic Institute and State University, Center for Gerontology. *Broken Trust: Elders, Family, and Finances.* March 2009.

3 The National Center on Elder Abuse. *The National Elder Abuse Incidence Study* (1998). Retrieved on August 4, 2008, from http:// www.aoa.gov/eldfam/Elder Rights/Elder Abuse/ Abuse Report Full. pdf.

See note 2 above.

4 Sklar, J. B., "Elder and Dependent Adult Fraud: A Sampler of Actual Cases to Profile the Offenders and the Crimes They Perpetrate," *Journal of Elder Abuse and Neglect* 12, no. 2 (2000): 19–32.

See note 2 above.

5 Dessin, C. L., "Financial Abuse of the Elderly," *Idaho Law Review* 36, no. 2 (2000): 203–226.

See note 2 above.

6 Quinn, M. J., "Undoing Undue Influence," *Journal of Elder Abuse and Neglect* 12, no. 2 (2000): 9–17.

See note 2 above.

7 American Association of Retired Persons. May 24, 2016. *Webster's Dictionary*. Summarized from definitions of "cognitive decline." National Adult Protective Services Resource Center. *Elder Abuse Is Common, Lethal, and Expensive.*

10 Alzheimer's Society. *What Is Dementia?* 2016.

11 Deem, D. L., "Notes from the Field; Observations in Working with Forgotten Victims of Personal Financial Crimes," *Journal of Elder Abuse and Neglect* 12, no. 23 (2000): 33–48.

See notes 2 and 10 above.

12 From the state of [redacted] in the probate court for the written petition by the law firm hired to represent the successor trustee of the mother's irrevocable trust.

13 See note 12 above.

14 Statements referencing positions and transactions:

1983, 1988, 1993, and 1997 statements

December 31, 1997 Prudential securities statement

December 2000 and December 2003 Prudential and UBS statements

December 2000 and December 2003 Prudential and UBS statements

January 2005 UBS statement and January 2007 Wachovia statement

December 1997 to December 2003 statements

January 2005 to January 2007 UBS and Prudential statements

Brokerage statement during corresponding time period securities statement

Prudential securities consolidated statements for 1998, 1999, and

2000

2005 year-end Wachovia statement

2006 year-end Wachovia statement

15 This website, https://www.mcafee.cc/Bin/sb.html, summarizes some of the common features and descriptions of the referenced psychological profile.

16 *Oxford Dictionary*: "fiduciary." *Wikipedia:* "Typically, a fiduciary prudently takes care of money or other assets for another person."

17 *Random House Dictionary*: "trust."

18 Nerenberg, L., *Forgotten Victims of Elder Financial Crime and Abuse: A Report and Recommendations* (1999). "Produced by the Goldman Institute on Aging for the National Center on Aging (NCEA), this report summarized four roundtable discussions sponsored by NCEA, which focused on four components of the legal system: the state and criminal justice system, federal investigative and regulatory agencies, civil legal system, and victim witness assistance network. Professionals from each system described challenges they face in handling financial abuse cases and made recommendations for improving each system's response." See NCEA website.

The *Journal of Elder Abuse and Neglect* 12, no. 2 (2000) is devoted to financial elder abuse. For more information about *Journal of Elder Abuse and Neglect* and a listing of articles in the issue, see *Aging/ Parents and Adult Children Together, A/PACT.* Produced by the American Association of Retired Persons (AARP) and the United State Federal Trade Commission, this consumer education series includes ten one-to-three-page articles focusing on consumer fraud, daily money management, alternatives to guardianship, etc. Contact the AARP for more information.

19 For additional information and resources, see www.

BrainHealthAsYouAge.com; www. Enrichvisits.com; Mitch Anthony and Steve Sanduski, CFP, "The New Retire Mentality"; and https://www.nia.nih.gov/health/brain-health-resource.

20 See note 19 above.

Additional Resources:

Dr. Marion Somers, PhD, *Elder Care Made Easier: Doctor Marion's 10 Steps to Help you Care for an Aging Loved One.* September 16, 2016.

http://files.consumerfinance/gov/f/201406_cfpb_guide_ protectresidents-from-financial=esploitation.pdf

http:www.americanbar.org/news/abanews/aba-news-archives/2013/10/ recognizing_and_ deal.html

http:www.aarp.org/aarp-foundation http:www.gao.gov/products/GAZ-13-14OT

https:www.preventelderabuse.org/issues/capacity.html

http:www.americanbar.org/news/abanews/aba-news-archives/2013/10/ recognizing_and_ deal.html

http:www.aarp.org/aarp-foundation

http:www.gao.gov/products/GAZ-13-14OT

https://www.nia.nih.gov/health/brain-health-resource

Bible references: KJV (Kings James Version) and NIV (New International Version)

ABOUT THE AUTHOR

Kristin Hetzer began her career in the investment business as an account executive with Merrill Lynch and Company during 1982. She is a chartered market technician, certified investment management analyst, and certified financial planner. Ms. Hetzer provides portfolio management services to a diversified group of investors. Her clients include individual investors, trusts, corporations, and qualified retirement plans.

Ms. Hetzer has worked in the financial industry for over thirty-five years. She is an active member of the Market Technician Association, past board member of the board of directors and past chair of the Los Angeles chapter. She is a member of the American Association of Professional Technical Analysts. In 2005, she formed Royal Palms Capital LLC, an independent investment advisory firm located in Rolling Hills Estates, California.